Y0-CUN-434

Why Writing Matters

Studies in Written Language and Literacy

A multi-disciplinary series presenting studies on written language, with special emphasis on its uses in different social and cultural settings. The series combines sociolinguistic and psycholinguistic accounts of the acquisition and transmission of literacy and brings together insights from linguistics, psychology, sociology, education, anthropology and philosophy.

Editor

Ludo Verhoeven
Radboud University Nijmegen

Editorial Board

David Barton
Lancaster University

Charles Bazerman
University of California, Santa Barbara

David Michael Bloome
Vanderbilt University, Nashville

Florian Coulmas
University of Duisburg

Peter Freebody
Griffith University

Eve Gregory
University of London

Nancy H. Hornberger
University of Pennsylvania

Charles Kinzer
Vanderbilt University, Nashville

David R. Olson
Ontario Institute for Studies in Education, Toronto

Mastin Prinsloo
University of Capetown

Dorit Ravid
University of Tel Aviv

David Reinking
University of Georgia

Linda S. Siegel
University of British Columbia

Brian Street
King's College, London

Daniel Wagner
University of Pennsylvania

Volume 12

Why Writing Matters. Issues of access and identity in writing research and pedagogy
Edited by Awena Carter, Theresa Lillis and Sue Parkin

Why Writing Matters

Issues of access and identity
in writing research and pedagogy

Edited by

Awena Carter
Lancaster University

Theresa Lillis
The Open University, UK

Sue Parkin
Lancaster University

John Benjamins Publishing Company
Amsterdam / Philadelphia

∞ ™ The paper used in this publication meets the minimum requirements of
American National Standard for Information Sciences – Permanence of
Paper for Printed Library Materials, ANSI Z39.48-1984.

Library of Congress Cataloging-in-Publication Data

Why writing matters. Issues of access and identity in writing research and pedagogy /
        edited by Awena Carter, Theresa Lillis, and Sue Parkin.
     p.   cm. (Studies in Written Language and Literacy, ISSN 0929-7324 ; v. 12)
Includes bibliographical references and index.
1. English language--Study and teaching--Foreign speakers. 2. English language--Study
        and teaching--Foreign speakers--Research. 3. English language--Rhetoric--
        Study and teaching. I. Carter, Awena. II. Lillis, Theresa M., 1956- III. Parkin,
        Sue, 1946
PE1128.A2W59   2009
808'.042071--dc22
                                                                                      2008051608
ISBN 978 90 272 1807 0 (HB; alk. paper)
ISBN 978 90 272 8973 5 (EB)

© 2009 – John Benjamins B.V.
No part of this book may be reproduced in any form, by print, photoprint, microfilm, or any
other means, without written permission from the publisher.

John Benjamins Publishing Co. · P.O. Box 36224 · 1020 ME Amsterdam · The Netherlands
John Benjamins North America · P.O. Box 27519 · Philadelphia PA 19118-0519 · USA

Table of contents

Preface
Roz Ivanič's writing and identity   IX
   David Barton

Introduction   XV
   Awena Carter

List of contributors   XXIII

Acknowledgements   XXIX

List of figures   XXXI

Part I. Creativity and identity

REFLECTION 1
Writing a narrative of multiple voices   3
   Courtney Cazden

CHAPTER 1
Writers and meaning making in the context of online learning   7
   Mary R. Lea

CHAPTER 2
Ivanič and the concept of "wrighting"   27
   Sue Parkin

REFLECTION 2
Identity without identification   45
   James Paul Gee

CHAPTER 3
Authoring research, plagiarising the self?   47
   Richard Edwards

CHAPTER 4
Creativity in academic writing: Escaping from the straitjacket of genre?   61
Mary Hamilton and Kathy Pitt

REFLECTION 3
Overcoming barriers   81
Min-Zhan Lu and Bruce Horner

Part II. Pedagogy

REFLECTION 4
Writing pictures, painting stories with Roz Ivanič   85
Denny Taylor

CHAPTER 5
Discourses of learning and teaching: A dyslexic child learning to write   89
Awena Carter

CHAPTER 6
Accommodation for success: Korean EFL students' writing practices in personal opinion writing   111
Younghwa Lee

REFLECTION 5
Collegiality and collaboration   127
Karin Tusting

CHAPTER 7
Advanced EFL students' revision practices throughout their writing process   129
David Camps

CHAPTER 8
Reconceptualising student writing: From conformity to heteroglossic complexity   151
Mary Scott and Joan Turner

REFLECTION 6
Roz and critical language studies at Lancaster 163
Norman Fairclough

Part III. Methodology

REFLECTION 7
Sharing writing, sharing names 167
Hilary Janks

CHAPTER 9
Bringing writers' voices to writing research: Talk around texts 169
Theresa Lillis

CHAPTER 10
Listening to children think about punctuation 189
Sue Sing and Nigel Hall

REFLECTION 8
Ivanič and the joy of writing 205
David Russell

CHAPTER 11
Recontextualising classroom experience in undergraduate writing:
An exploration using case study and linguistic analysis 209
Zsuzsanna Walkó

CHAPTER 12
Researcher identity in the writing of collaborative-action research 231
Samina Amin Qadir

REFLECTION 9
Roz Ivanič: An appreciation 245
Brian Street

Works by Roz Ivanič referred to in this book 249

Index 251

PREFACE

Roz Ivanič's writing and identity

David Barton
Lancaster University

The accolades from the contributors to this book are clear: "an inspirational teacher"; "the epitome of academic rigour and integrity… a deeply caring and generous person"; "piercingly discerning academic"; "generosity as a scholar… encouraged scholars at the margins of the academy". They mix the personal and professional and demonstrate the intertwining of Roz Ivanič's writing and identity.

For this reason it is worth providing a life history to see the strands in Roz's life which have been woven together over time (although I am aware that this account is only partial, and may not be completely accurate). Roz was brought up in a village in Sussex and went to Bristol University where she took a degree in Theatre and Classics. It may be that her attention to both the details of language and the production of language have their roots in this unusual combination of subjects. After university she had jobs in theatre in London and Worthing and she travelled in Europe. An important step in her life was when she went on an exchange programme to the then Czechoslovakia to work in theatre for children. She drove there in an old Austin van, which she had brightly painted in the style of a Yellow Submarine – much to the consternation of her parents.

It was there in 1968 that she met Milan, an art student in Prague, and they still tell funny stories of how the two of them first communicated with each other across languages. Neither spoke the other's language. Milan reports that he had just three lessons from the Essential English course – a classic course of the period. Roz, however, was learning Czech with enthusiasm and that is how they communicated for some time. On returning to Britain she went back to her theatre job in Worthing. Milan joined her soon after and they got married. They travelled round England in search of a theatre job, in Bristol, Liverpool, Manchester and London. But Roz slipped into teaching, first as a supply teacher in Sussex, and then a regular post as an English teacher in a secondary school in Devon. The link between theatre and being a teacher has never been lost on her – the public role, the sense of creating a production and, maybe, the sense of audience which is so crucial for a writer.

They lived in Devon near the sea for four years, still speaking Czech at home. A visit from a good friend whom they had met in Prague, Tim Johns, well known in the English for Academic Purposes world, convinced them that Milan would only ever learn English if they spoke English at home, and the next day they switched to English. Milan also tells the story of Roz following Open University courses in the middle of the night on a television they had bought just for this.

During this time Roz developed an interest in dyslexia and problems with reading and writing, a novelty in the early 1970s; during the summers Roz and Milan taught in summer schools for children which combined dyslexia support with art and sports. This broader interest provides a link to their move to London in 1974 where Roz got a job as director of the student support unit at the then Kingsway-Princeton College. This was at exactly the time that the adult literacy movement was taking off in England and Roz is part of the history of this period. Many people started out in the field then and many key ideas were developed at this time; the Inner London Education Authority (ILEA) was carrying out innovative work and there was a sense of possibility and excitement.

Whilst in London, she followed a Postgraduate Certificate in Education course at Garnett College which she got in 1977. She then spent a year in California at the Community College in Stockton in 1978–9 as part of a Fulbright exchange programme. Roz and Milan used all their free time to travel round the States, including visiting other colleges and making many friends they are still in contact with. They explored and developed a love of Western United States which continues today.

The time in the States probably encouraged Roz to want to move on and do an MA. She returned to Kingsway-Princeton College but in 1983 decided to do an MA in the Department of Linguistics at Lancaster; this is where I first met her. She lived on campus with a young family and they got to know and love the northwest of England, especially the Lake District and the Yorkshire Dales. Her Masters dissertation combined linguistics and pedagogy and could have stood on its own for either its theoretical contribution or its pedagogical contribution to applied linguistics. After the MA she moved back to London teaching at Kingsway-Princeton and later at Garnett College; within three years she was attracted back to a lectureship at Lancaster, where she has been ever since.

Roz and Milan bought a house halfway between the city and the university. Tim had been born in 1980 and Suzanna was born in 1985. The life one sees there is of a close family; her brother and sister visiting and, earlier, her elderly parents; there is a constant stream of visitors, work and non-work friends. The kitchen table has a convivial life hosting receptions for international visitors, student supervisions and long project meetings. There is a centrality of people and the relations between people in her life and her work. Selflessly she provides space for people to become what they will.

Firstly with her PhD, and then through research projects and supervising research students her work became key in the field of writing research and in the development of the then new field of Literacy Studies. Her work has focussed on writing with *Writing and Identity* and *The Politics of Writing* being influential books, and in the development of the field of Literacy studies with *Worlds of Literacy* and *Situated Literacies* as key. She started with students in further education and adults with difficulties in writing. The title *Writing and Identity* is central to Roz's research, to her own writing and to how she relates to colleagues and students.

Her specific research area of writing has been the basis for many studies, covering a range of areas including adult learners, academic writing, young children's writing (in a corpus study), bilingual issues, children of all ages as well as further education students, ESOL students. She has worked in different ways, collaborating with colleagues, with students, with informants in the research. She has always been motivated to do research related to the immediate contexts she has been connected to. The broader topics have included researching children, and she jokes that as her children grew up in the local school system she moved her attention from primary children, through to secondary and tertiary. Her most recent project, a major investigation bringing together universities and colleges, where she has been the overall director, the *Literacies for Learning in Further Education* project, is in many ways a culmination of these interests. The book from the project *Improving Learning in College: Rethinking Literacies across the Curriculum* combines practical concerns with theoretical frameworks.

She has put her stamp on the Literacy Research Centre at Lancaster, always emphasising the focus on research and practice, drawing attention to processes and ways of working. The links to practice, the enthusiasm and understanding of the field were essential when we were setting up the Research and Practice in Adult Literacy network (Rapal) in the early 1980s and she always had practical ways of linking research and practice. I have memories of how events were always fun and full of laughter, as well as being quite ground breaking at the time. Taking over the sober Senate House of the university for workshops with adult educators and students was memorable; and when we generated too many posters, it was Roz's idea that we should display them across all the windows, and that we needed to walk around on the tables to organise things.

An important aspect of Roz's special contribution to academic life is the bringing together of research and teaching in ways that each inspires the other. The idea of linking research and teaching is commonplace, but with Roz it is fundamental; and it is creative and productive. And it comes from a strong sense of herself, of knowing where she is coming from. Her exemplary teaching was recognised by one of the university's first teaching awards and many people were touched by her teaching. And it was not just students. I remember a course of lectures she and Norman Fairclough gave and which I attended along with other colleagues. She is always inspirational to listen to, and for me the clarity comes from the deep way she understands the topic she is talking about.

As Professor of Linguistics in Education, her professorial title is key to the contribution she has made to the discipline, linking linguistics and education and showing the value of linguistic knowledge for addressing educational questions. As Chair of the national organisation CLIE (the Committee for Linguistics in Education) for many years, she had close links with examiners and practitioners as well as the linguists behind developments in curriculum. She is recognised internationally and has received invitations to teach and lecture across continents in Europe, Australia, Tanzania, United States, Hong Kong and elsewhere.

Roz has always been inspirational to research students, as the comments in this book attest. Many will remember the characteristic green pen all over a student's draft. Discussions get quickly to what the student is trying to do, enthusiasm about what the student has written and always finding something good, and supporting ways to move it forward. Green ticks in the margin and the word "YES!" in capitals with an exclamation. Whole phrases circled and arrows indicating how to rearrange the paragraph to make things clearer. Questions: Why this? Why that? This approach is open and giving, and at the same time demanding that students take responsibility for their ideas and clarify them. A generation of students thank Roz for the way she supports them as writers. (And the same green pens still write supportive, helpful and demanding comments over colleagues' work.)

Twenty eight research students have worked with her, covering all areas of language and education but particularly writing and identity. A summary of some of the topics they have written about provides a kaleidoscope of key topics in the field. It is a long list but it is an overview of a whole field of research: *Entering a disciplinary community; Evaluation of student academic writing; History in secondary education in Greece; Introducing study skills at intermediate level in Pakistan; Writing professional science: genre, recontextualisation in learning professional and scientific writing; The classroom as a heteroglossic space: dialogic talk in small group interaction; Moral repertoires and gendered voices in argumentation; Identity in narratives of self; Adapting and recreating writing practices for their academic purposes; A critical ethnographic case study of teacher beliefs and practices in a classroom; Factors influencing perception of intended arguments in persuasive-expository discourse; Theme in argumentative texts; Alignments and detachments in EFL writing pedagogy; Critical thinking pedagogy in university education; How dyslexic children develop literacy; The linguistic characteristics of personal investigations for*

A level; Language ideologies in trilingual primary education; Contribution of classroom interaction in EFL writing development; Academic Literacy; Teaching of writing in Adult Basic Education; The discoursal construction of teacher identity; Literacy practices of EFL teachers engaging in professional writing; Academic literacy practices involved in writing literature reviews; Student writing in higher education; Writer identity and reader-writer relationships. This range of topics provides a fitting record of the breadth of Roz's vision and inspiration.

References

Barton, D., Hamilton, M. and Ivanič, R. (eds.). 2000. *Situated Literacies: Reading and writing in context.* London: Routledge.
Clark, R. and Ivanič, R. 1997. *The Politics of Writing.* London: Routledge.
Hamilton, M., Barton, D. and Ivanič, R. (eds.). 1994. *Worlds of Literacy.* Clevedon: Multilingual Matters.
Ivanič, R, 1998. *Writing and Identity.* Amsterdam: John Benjamins.
Ivanič, R., Edwards, R., Barton, D., Fowler, Z., Hughes, B., Mannion, G., Martin-Jones, M., Miller, K., Satchwell, C., and Smith, J. 2008. *Improving Learning in College: Rethinking literacies across the curriculum.* London: Routledge.

INTRODUCTION

A Plan

A festschrift to honour Roz Ivanič! When David Barton first suggested this to me in an e-mail entitled "A Plan" I was thrilled at the whole exciting concept. "The idea would be to do it without Roz knowing," he wrote, and it has been a closely guarded secret – amongst some thirty people across four continents – for eighteen months. My fellow editors, Theresa Lillis and Sue Parkin, decided that I should write the first draft of the introduction. And now, as I sit down at my computer screen I am scared. As Mary Hamilton and Kathy Pitt point out in this volume, writing is hard and lonely work – and I for one find it scary. Here are some of my first efforts:

> Given the considerable impact of Roz Ivanič on the New Literacy Studies and on the field of writing research in particular over the past twenty years, this book is a timely opportunity to illustrate the extent of her influence on current research and pedagogy…

> The book brings together key strands of Ivanič's research, theory and pedagogy, as well as indicating a number of future directions. The contributors draw on her theoretical insights, on her empirical and pedagogical approaches, and on her social concerns with issues such as diversity, access and inclusion…

> The underlying theme is the role played by identity: both the conflicting identities of the writer, and the ways in which writing offers new possibilities for identity…

> The authors use the lens of a social practices understanding of literacy to view the sweep of writing and learning to write in formal educational settings from primary school to post doctoral research. It thus brings to educationalists and to researchers the experiences of writers at every stage of their academic careers in their engagement with the demands of a dominant literacy…

> We believe the book is unique in this respect: just as its scope is explicitly comprehensive so it aims to meet a broad target audience of scholars and practitioners working around the world…

Most of these sentences are cut, pasted and edited from the book proposal we wrote for John Benjamins and, in the spirit of Richard Edwards' chapter in this book, I cannot now remember how many of the words are mine. (Pace, Bakhtin).

In any case they do not seem right for the introduction to a book in which more than one chapter subverts the dominant discourse of the academy. And no doubt, as I continue to write, I will continue to slip in and out of more than one genre, as I have done in this paragraph. Mary Scott and Joan Turner's chapter in which they unravel the heteroglossic strands of students' writing is salient here.

Social practice perspectives are instantiated in different ways

In what is often framed in the West as a post modern environment, it is often assumed that there is considerable freedom about how we can/should move between genres to challenge the hegemony of the dominant discourse of the academy. Yet such freedom can be severely constrained, by ourselves very often, and in some disciplines more than others, in our Western academic practices. Mary Hamilton and Kathy Pitt, after exploring ways of bringing creativity into academic discourse, comment at the end of their chapter in this volume on the "attractive and practical aspects of... high status writing" drawing attention to the "[s]tability, recognition, authority and professional identity" which are a part of writing in the traditional powerful genres of the academy.

A social practices perspective underpins all the chapters in this book but how "social practice" plays out or is taken up differs according to the very specific cultural, linguistic and material conditions under which people live and work. One of the themes of many of the chapters is the way people tussle with dominant discourses. Mary Scott and Joan Turner, in their chapter, point to the way in which Roz Ivanič has always been "on the side of students in their struggle to achieve authorship (i.e. to write with authority) in the midst of 'jostling voices'". However they also point out that this does not mean that they, as university teachers, neglect to enlarge students' "understandings of academic writing in its concrete situatedness and of its possibilities and constraints." In my own chapter I point to the ways in which I aimed to help my pupils to be at ease not only in the vernacular discourses of their peers but also in the dominant discourse of the classroom. In their chapters, David Camps and Younghwa Lee, point out different ways in which the dominant discourse of text books and what tends to be called "standard English" is tied in with the qualifications EFL students aim for; David Camps brings out the importance, to students and academics alike, of the status of graduates' professional employment. In this domain the students, and perhaps even their teachers, are not free to choose a discourse that will gain low marks or result in the lowered reputation of the Institution.

What this book aims to do

This book has more than one purpose. First of all it celebrates Roz Ivanič: her seminal work on the discoursal construction of identity; her overturning of perceived ways of writing in the academy; the radical energy she has brought to teaching; the discernment she has brought to research; her innovative contribution to methodological stances. Secondly it tracks the way Ivanič has been a catalyst who has engaged others in her ways of theorising, teaching and researching. Thirdly, it develops issues of writing and identity in showing some of the exciting ways in which people who have been influenced by Ivanič have built on and extended her work.

The contributors to this volume have all been enriched by Roz Ivanič. The book has been centrally written by some of her former research students, now academics in their own right: their chapters are among the fruits of her outstanding ability as a PhD supervisor. Other chapters have been written by people in the field whose work she has influenced in both personal and scholarly ways. And this personal and scholarly influence is seen very clearly in the reflections, from distinguished scholars, which weave between chapters. These short contributions from people who are themselves hugely influential show the way Roz has touched and influenced their lives as scholar, colleague and friend.

The structure of this book

The critical framing of this book developed as Theresa, Sue and I worked across all its contributions. However in this part of the introduction we are each going to write about the sections in which our own chapters appear. Sue Parkin will write about the chapters which explore the themes of identity and creativity, I will write about the chapters that appear in the section about pedagogical concerns and Theresa Lillis will write about the chapters which explore methodological stances in researching writing.

Identity and creativity – Sue Parkin writes

The issues of creativity and writer identity are key concerns running through Ivanič's research and thinking and the four chapters in this section reflect this.

The section begins with Mary Lea's chapter in which she writes about student contributions to on-line fora in a British Higher Educational setting. Her interest in their choices of visual affordances is echoed in her choice, as a writer, in adding her own comments in the form of a "comment tool" running literally alongside pages in her chapter. Within the constraints of the type setting, the publishers have replicated these comments in as near a form as possible to the word processed text. These comments are an integral part of this chapter and they remind us that in changing times, genres also change because of new resources available to writers. Self reflections are an integral part of the process of writing, albeit usually hidden from the reader, but here they are available for all to read. All of this reflects Ivanic's commitment to new technologies whilst never losing sight of the fact that it is writers' voices and writers' identities that are important.

In this section's second chapter, I hint at my own loss of identity on being rejected by the art community at an early age and how I identified myself as someone who could not understand art. However, my PhD, supervised by Roz Ivanič, focuses on the very language of art and in my contribution here I show the ways in which an art student I have called "Dylan" wrote his art project. It is multimodal and I build on Ivanič's concept of the "wrighter" of a text, bringing together words and images in the same way that a wheelwright brings together diverse materials to "wright" a wheel. I examine in detail the grammatical choices made by Dylan and in this way my work deals with both creativity and identity. I recall Roz's commitment and engagement at every supervision session because each one began with Roz saying "Isn't this exciting?"

Richard Edward's concern in the third chapter of this section is on the influence of computers on the life of texts and on the life of writers. Texts acquire multiple ownerships and writers acquire multiple identities. Creativity for him includes the possibility of plagiarism of the self and he considers this to be no bad thing. He discusses the concept of the "hyper-real" and embraces and celebrates, as does Ivanič, the creative possibilities of new technologies for writers and writings.

Mary Hamilton and Kathy Pitt conclude this section on creativity and identity by arguing that writing genres can act as constraints – we need to be careful not to put on such a "straitjacket". Writing is a lonely occupation and they discuss this here in a dialogue. Their contribution highlights the collaborative nature of their work and it goes on to explain the various ways they have been able to honour not only the question of individual creativity but also that of multiple identities that lie at the heart of Ivanič's work.

Pedagogy – Awena Carter writes

Roz's own doctoral research, for which David Barton was her supervisor, was into the ways eight mature students struggled to engage with the demands of the dominant discourse in which they were expected to write. This theme – students' struggles with dominant discourses – underlies the chapters in this section. The students, and the teachers who write about them, come from three different continents so that the theme is instantiated in very different ways.

The section opens with my chapter which to some extent acts as bridge between the issues of identity explored in the previous section, and the pedagogical focus of this one. My concern is with the struggles of a dyslexic child, not only with the dominant discourse of education, but with the very act of writing itself. I use Ivanič's (2004) framework of the discourses of writing and learning to write as a heuristic with which to examine my pupil's writing and my own journey from practitioner to researcher. This involved me in constructions and reconstructions of conflicting identities, and I build on Ivanič's framework of the socially available possibilities for self hood (Ivanič 1998; Clark and Ivanič 1997) in order to explain how this is possible.

The second chapter, by Younghwa Lee, working in a university in Korea with EFL students, examines their personal opinion writing. Drawing on Ivanič's framework of the discourses of writing and learning to write and her own theoretical construct of claim/opinion/reason in argumentative writing, she examines three students' texts. Lee concludes that the students in her study have taken on the rhetorical conventions of the text book in order to achieve a good mark. She argues that the Korean educational culture of equating learning with memorising facts should be widened to develop students' critical thinking.

In the third chapter, David Camps looks at the revision practices of EFL students in a private university in Mexico and finds that, far from being confined to the last stages of composition, revision takes place recursively throughout the writing process, from the pre-writing discussion to the production of the final draft. Using four elements from Clark and Ivanič's (1997) social practices view of writing, he explores the students' own perceptions of their literacy practices and uncovers the particular ways in which they approach writing in English. He concludes by adding to Clark and Ivanič's four elements with new findings of his own.

Mary Scott and Joan Turner close the section with their examination of the enactment of heteroglossia in L2 students' texts, as I have already mentioned. They show how they mediate between what the students bring to the texts they write, and the demands of the academy. This "mediation of academic literacy" not only draws on Ivanič's view of language as a range of resources for meaning making, but on her stance of understanding and respect towards students. It leads them to look critically, neither at the text alone, nor at the student alone, but at the often conflicting voices students bring to the texts they have written.

Methodology – Theresa Lillis writes

The section on Methodology illustrates the powerful influence Ivanič's work has had on opening up what count as meaningful ways of researching academic writing. At the heart of Roz's work is her deep respect for writers and a commitment to exploring what is important to them (us). At the same time, her love of linguistics, a discipline that offers and provides intellectual space for the development of tools for researching writing, is evident in much of her explicit theorising of methodology. Each of the four chapters in this section on methodology reflects, with different emphases, these two dimensions to Roz's research methodology.

I open this section by focusing on a specific methodology developed by Ivanič which has made a significant impact on the field of writing research; "talk around texts". I offer a brief overview of the values underpinning both Roz's pedagogy and her academic-theorising, which are enacted in this methodology, and argue that it "constitutes a fundamental contribution to writing research in three ways; firstly by disrupting conventional researcher-researched positioning; secondly by keeping writers centre stage even whilst using text-linguistics; and thirdly by opening up opportunities for re-examining textual practices, by questioning what should (and could) be valued in formal institutions of learning". I discuss how I have tried to use talk around texts in my own research and the challenges and opportunities it throws up.

The second chapter in this section, by Sue Sing and Nigel Hall, also illustrates the value of "talk around texts" and focuses in particular on the value of such a methodology for researching punctuation practices. Their chapter illustrates how they responded to the challenge of seeking out children's perspectives on punctuation – by developing activities which would promote discussion. Children's discussions – drawn from a study with 96 UK primary school children – are analysed in the chapter for the meanings and understandings they attach to punctuation. The chapter clearly demonstrates how a methodology used by Ivanič in exploring punctuation practices with adults, "was so effective for unpacking children's theories of how punctuation works".

The following chapter by Zsuzsa Walkó, which also draws on talk and texts in an exploration of two under-graduate thesis writers' practices in Hungary, is a powerful reminder of the centrality of the linguistic dimension in Roz's work. Following Roz's interest in "voice types", Walkó shows how van Leeuwen's (1995, 1996) specific framework of recontextualisation can be used to track instances of the complex relationship between text and context. Using this framework Walkó "shows how the writers foreground and background different elements of the contexts in their texts and what kind of weighting they give to each context" – the contexts in this instance being "classroom practice", "research" and "thesis writing". Walkó illustrates the value of combining case study data and careful linguistic analysis of specific aspects of texts; together they advance our understanding of choices and voices in academic writing research.

In the final chapter in this section Samina Qadir directs our attention to the research process, and in particular to challenges relating to the writing (up) of collaborative or collaboratively framed research. She outlines two projects where teachers working with secondary school students (aged 13–16) in Pakistan wanted to introduce specific pedagogic innovations, relating to language learning, into a tightly prescribed curriculum. The chapter shows that researcher and teachers collaborated effectively in trialling such innovations – the use of specific reading strategies and grammar practice tools. However, whilst the collaborative and action dimensions to the research process had clearly been successful, the teacher-researchers were reluctant to be involved in the writing (up) of research. Qadir reflects on the reasons for such reluctance, central ones being the teachers' sense of identity as researchers and their perception of the purpose of research: "they felt no social or academic responsibility for documenting the process and findings of their research" – situating the research process and the teacher participants' interests. Qadir raises important questions about what doing research means to different participants and situates perspectives about the writing (up) of research within debates about access to, and participation in, writing and literacy in Pakistan more widely.

Conclusion

Now, as I write the concluding paragraphs, as in so many times in the last eighteen months, I wish I could ask your advice Roz. I would welcome your characteristic green penned comments – "supportive, helpful and demanding" – as David Barton describes them in the Preface. He seems to have bagged all the best things to be said, including the felicitous phrase "the intertwining of Roz Ivanič's writing and identity". In this volume we have encouraged people to use *Roz* for personal reminiscences and *Ivanič* in drawing on your work. But this is an artificial separation. As I write, in my mind's eye, I see you at a Lancaster Literacy Research and Discussion Group seminar speaking with your characteristic emphasis and with warm friendliness towards the speaker, whilst asking a devastatingly searching question that gets right to the heart of the matter. For the contributors to this book it is hard to separate "Roz" from "Ivanič" (sorry about the scare quotes….) nor would we want to.

And so I have finished the introduction, the use of the first person shamefully masking the text's collaborative development. So, for "I" read "we". We hand it to you, Roz, with our love and thanks.

Awena Carter, July 2008

References

Clark, R. & Ivanič, R. 1997. *The Politics of Writing.* London: Routledge.
Ivanič, R. 1998. *Writing and Identity.* Amsterdam: John Benjamins.
Ivanič, R. 2004. Discourses of writing and learning to write. *Language and Education,* 18(3): 220–245.
van Leeuwen, T. 1995. Representing social action. *Discourse and Society,* 6: 81–106.
van Leeuwen, T. 1996. The representation of social actors. In *Texts and Practices: Readings in Critical Discourse Analysis,* C. R. Caldas-Coulthard & M. Coulthard (eds.), 32–69. London: Routledge.

List of contributors

David Barton is Professor of Language and Literacy in the Department of Linguistics at Lancaster University and Director of the Literacy Research Centre. His current interests include: the changing nature of literacy in contemporary society; reading and writing on the internet; literacy and social justice; research methodologies. His work with Roz Ivanič has included *Situated Literacies*, (Routledge); *Literacy, Lives and Learning*, (Routledge); *Worlds of literacy* (Multilingual Matters) and *Writing in the Community* (Sage).

David Camps is a full time professor in the Language Department at the Tecnológico de Monterrey, Mexico. He holds a PhD in Linguistics from Lancaster University. His supervisor Roz Ivanič's views about writing influence his teaching: he passes on her words "make writing your friend" to his own students. Dr Camps has shared the findings of his research, into writing as a social practice, at symposia in Mexico, Brazil and the United States and has published in journals in the field of language teaching.

Awena Carter is an Honorary Fellow in the Literacy Research Centre at Lancaster University. Her research interest is into how dyslexic children can be enabled to develop literacy in the same ways as their non-dyslexic peers, and in the ways this development can be traced in discoursal constructions and reconstructions of dyslexic children's identities. She formally worked as a dyslexia specialist in Primary schools and now gives tutorial support to dyslexic university students.

Courtney Cazden is the Charles William Eliot Professor of Education (emerita) at Harvard University. Her research and teaching have focused on the development and uses of oral and written language in and out of the classroom. She continues to be active in writing and consulting – most recently in Singapore and Australia.

Richard Edwards is Professor of Education at the University of Stirling, Scotland. He was Co-director with Roz Ivanič of the Literacies for Learning in Further Education research project from 2003 until 2007. His research is informed by poststructural and postmodern framings and is mostly in the areas of adult education and lifelong learning. He has written extensively in the field. His most recent book is R. Edwards and R. Usher (2008) *Globalisation and Pedagogy: Space, Place and Pedagogy*, London: Routledge. He is still working with Roz on writing up the outcomes of the Literacies project. The book from the project should appear in 2009.

Norman Fairclough was Professor of Language in Social Life at Lancaster University until his retirement in 2004. He is now Emeritus Professor, and Emeritus Research Fellow in the Institute for Advanced Studies at Lancaster. His research focuses on developing critical discourse analysis within transdisciplinary social research. Recent books: *New Labour, New Language*? (2000), *Analysing Discourse: Textual Analysis for Social Research* (2003), *Language and Globalisation* (2006).

James Paul Gee, a linguist by training, has worked over the last several decades on sociocultural approaches to literacy and learning. He is the Mary Lou Fulton Presidential Professor of Literacy Studies and a member of the National Academy of Education. He is the author of *Sociolinguistics and Literacies* (1990, Third Ed. 2007), *An Introduction to Discourse Analysis* (1999, Second Ed. 2005); *What Video Games Have to Teach Us About Learning and Literacy* (2004, Second Edition 2007); and *Situated Language and Learning* (2004), among others.

Nigel Hall is Professor of Literacy Education at Manchester Metropolitan University. He has a long-standing interest in how children develop understanding of punctuation, having initiated the Punctuation Project in 1996. His also has interests in literacy as a social practice, and in children as language brokers. He has now developed a specialism in the history of writing, in particular the history of the materiality of writing, and is currently completing a book on the social, material and educational history of the writing slate. He has written or edited over twenty books on aspects of literacy and was a founding editor of the Journal of Childhood Literacy.

Mary Hamilton is Professor of Adult Learning and Literacy based in the Department of Educational Research at Lancaster University, England, and Associate Director of the Lancaster Literacy Research Centre. She is co-author of a number of books including *Local Literacies* (with David Barton); *Powerful Literacies* (with Jim Crowther and Lynn Tett) and *Changing Faces of Adult Literacy, Language and Numeracy: A Critical History* (with Yvonne Hillier).

Bruce Horner is Endowed Chair in Rhetoric and Composition at the University of Louisville, where he teaches composition, composition pedagogy and theory, and literacy studies. His books include *Terms of Work for Composition: A Materialist Critique*, winner of the 2001 Winterowd Award for Most Outstanding Book in Composition Theory, *Key Terms in Popular Music and Culture*, co-edited with

Thomas Swiss, and, with Min-Zhan Lu, *Representing the "Other": Basic Writers and the Teaching of Basic Writing* and, most recently, *Writing Conventions*.

Hilary Janks met Roz Ivanič when she was a doctoral student at Lancaster University in the 1980s and they have remained friends and colleagues ever since. She is currently a Professor in the School of Education at the University of the Witwatersrand, Johannesburg, South Africa and an adjunct Professor at the University of South Australia. Her teaching and research are in the areas of language education in multilingual classrooms, language policy and critical literacy. Her work is committed to a search for equity and social justice in contexts of poverty.

Mary R. Lea is a Senior Lecturer in the Institute of Educational Technology at the Open University, UK. She has researched and published widely in the field of academic literacies and student writing, drawing on data from a wide range of university contexts. Her present research is broadly within two areas, 'literacies and digital technologies' and 'academics as writers', within the changing landscape of higher education.

Younghwa Lee is a Full-time Lecturer in the Division of English at Sun Moon University, Republic of Korea. Her research interests lie in the teaching of writing in an EFL university context, and focuses on the theory of social practices and classroom language teaching and learning from socio-cultural perspectives. Dr Lee is currently working on outside practices of EFL writing with the support of a Korea Research Foundation Grant funded by the Korean Government.

Theresa Lillis is a Senior Lecturer in Language and Communication in the Centre for Language and Communications at the Open University, UK. She has authored and co-authored books on academic literacies including *Student writing: Access, regulation, and desire*, (Routledge, 2001) and *Teaching academic writing: A toolkit for higher education* (Routledge, 2003) as well as articles on academic writing for publication in a global context, including those published in: Language and Education, Written Communication and TESOL Quarterly.

Min-Zhan Lu is University Scholar and Professor of English at the University of Louisville, where she teaches composition, composition pedagogy and theory, life writing, critical and cultural theory, and theories of languages and literacies. Her books include *Shanghai Quartet: the Crossings of Four Women of China; Comp Tales*, co-edited with Richard Haswell, and, with Bruce Horner, *Representing the "Other": Basic Writers and the Teaching of Basic Writing* and *Writing Conventions*. Her essays are winners of the Braddock and Shaughnessy awards.

Sue Parkin is an Honorary Research Fellow at the Literacy Research Centre at Lancaster University. She has spent her life teaching and her research interest is in her work with art students at a local Tertiary College. She now teaches an English Language Foundation Year course in the International Study Centre at Lancaster, and EAP and study skills Summer Courses to prospective post-graduates. Whenever possible, Sue visits a project she has set up in Kenya to enable street children to go to school to acquire basic literacy skills.

Kathy Pitt is a critical discourse analyst and research fellow at the Literacy Research Centre. She is the author of *Sourcing the Self: Debating the relations between language and consciousness.* (Peter Lang) and *Debates in ESOL Teaching and Learning: Cultures, communities and classrooms.*(Routledge)

Samina Amin Qadir holds a PhD in Linguistics from Lancaster University, UK where her supervisor was Roz Ivanič, and a MEd in TEFL from University of Wales, Cardiff, UK. Dr Qadir is Dean of the Faculty of Social Sciences and Liberal Arts, at Fatima Jinnah Women University, Rawalpindi where she teaches literature, language, study skills and linguistics. She has also introduced and developed courses in Comparative Literature and Written English, including Pakistani Literature in English. Her interests include: Women in Higher Education Management, Pragmatics and Mentoring.

David R. Russell is professor of English in the Professional Communication area at Iowa State University. He has published widely on writing across the curriculum (WAC), international writing instruction, and computer-supported collaborative learning in the disciplines. His book, *Writing in the Academic Disciplines: A Curricular History,* examines the history of American writing instruction since 1870. He co-edited *Writing and Learning in Cross-National Perspective: Transitions from Secondary to Higher Education* and two collections on genre and activity theory.

Mary Scott is the Founding Director of the Centre for Academic and Professional Literacy Studies at the Institute of Education, University of London. Her fields of interest include: teachers' readings of students' writing in higher education; the hidden complexities of cross-national comparisons of student writing; the teaching of literature in English. She presents at national and international conferences and publishes in peer-viewed journals. She is the leader of the Interuniversity Academic Literacies Research Group which has an international membership (http://ioewebserver.ioe.ac.uk)

Sue Sing is a Research Fellow in the Faculty of Education and Language Studies at the Open University UK. Having completed a Masters degree in Linguistics at Lancaster University, she completed a Ph.D at Manchester Metropolitan University. For this she studied young children's developing understanding of the apostrophe. She then worked as a researcher at Manchester Metropolitan University before moving to the Open University where she is researching the nature and quality of the provision of foreign language learning in primary schools, and assessing its impact on pupils' learning in languages and across the curriculum.

Brian Street is Professor of Language in Education at King's College, London University and Visiting Professor of Education in the University of Pennsylvania. He has a commitment to linking ethnographic-style research on the cultural dimension of language and literacy with contemporary practice in education and development. Over the past 25 years he has undertaken anthropological field research and been consultant to projects in these fields in countries of both the North and South (e.g. Nepal, S. Africa, India, USA, UK). Books include *Literacy in Theory and Practice* (C.U.P. 1984), edited *Cross-Cultural Approaches to Literacy,* (CUP 1993), and one on academic literacies that complements Roz's work (co-ed *Student Writing in the University: Cultural and Epistemological Issues* Benjamins 2000).

Denny Taylor is Professor and Doctoral Director of Literacy Studies at Hofstra University New York. She has been engaged in ethnographic literacy research since 1977 and for the past six years her focus has been on the impact of catastrophic events on the lives of children and the social response of the educational community to mass trauma. She is the author of nine books including *Family Literacy* (Heinemann 1983), *Toxic Literacies: Exposing the Injustice of Bureaucratic Texts* (Heinemann 1996) and *Many Families, Many Literacies: An International Declaration of Principles* (Heinemann 1997).

Joan Turner is a Senior Lecturer and Head of the Language Studies Centre at Goldsmiths, University of London. Her research interests are in language in higher education. She has published on academic literacy, EAP, and intercultural communication. Academic literacy is seen as both a cultural construct with deeply embedded values and rhetorical conventions, and a site of contemporary struggle for many students, both home and international. She is currently collaborating with Mary Scott on a British Academy project entitled: *Perspectives on Proofreading*.

Karin Tusting is RCUK Research Fellow in 'Changing Literacies in Work, Education and Everyday Life' at the Literacy Research Centre Lancaster University, UK. Her research interests are in the detailed study of social practices using qualitative methods, including ethnography and discourse analysis, with a focus on the role of language in learning in communities. She worked with Roz Ivanič on the Adult Learners' Lives project, an ethnographic study of the relationship between learning and other aspects of people's lives, funded by the National Research and

Development Centre for Adult Literacy and Numeracy. She has published on extending the concept of communities of practice, models of adult learning, creativity in everyday literacy practices, community-based local literacies research, time and the new literacy studies, the legitimation of cultural generalisations through appeal to personal experience, and French text analysis.

Zsuzsanna Walkó obtained an M.A. in English and Italian and a PhD in Language Pedagogy at ELTE University, Budapest. She has taught academic writing, discourse analysis, linguistics foundation courses, language development and ELT Methodology at the Centre for English Teacher Training of ELTE University and at the College of Nyíregyháza, Hungary. In her PhD thesis she compares novice and professional writers' representations of classroom-based research. Her main field of interest is in combining linguistic and context-based approaches to the analysis of texts.

Acknowledgements

The editors are grateful to all the people who have helped them with the genesis and development of this book. We particularly thank: David Barton, whose suggestion it first was, for being an unfailing source of help and advice; Kees Vaes of John Benjamins Publishing Company for supporting us by patiently answering our many questions; and the members of our families, always in the background cheering us on and often coming to the foreground with hot meals and reviving drinks.

We are grateful to all the contributors and give extra thanks to those who also reviewed chapters. The external reviewers, who generously gave their time to this project, deserve especial thanks and here we take the unusual step of listing them because we want Roz Ivanič to know how pleased they all were to be asked to be a part of her festschrift. They are: Pat Currie; Mary Jane Curry; Zoe Fowler; Carolyn McKinney; Sara Michael-Luna; Uta Papen; David Pollack; Candice Satchwell; Lucia Thesen; Karin Tusting; Dimitra Vladimirou; and Anita Wilson.

A unique contribution to Roz Ivanič's festschrift is the cover illustration by her husband, Milan Ivanič. We are most grateful to him for this visual contribution to the book.

List of figures

Figures appearing in chapters:

Figure 1.1:   Aspects of writer identity
Figure 2.1:   Dylan's page 22
Figure 2.2:   Dylan's page 24
Figure 2.3:   Dylan's page 9
Figure 2.4:   Dylan's page 11
Figure 5.1:   Discourses of writing and learning to write (adapted from Ivanič 2004)
Figure 5.2:   A multi-layered view of language (Ivanič 2004: 223)
Figure 5.3:   Writing as a tidy linear process
Figure 5.4:   Brainstorming ideas for the story
Figure 5.5:   The first lines of 'Detective Sam'
Figure 5.6:   Page 3 of the first draft of Detective Sam
Figure 5.7:   The text in the published book
Figure 5.8:   Changes showing recursiveness in practice
Figure 5.9:   Reading, writing, and speaking in a creativity discourse of writing and learning to write
Figure 5.10: The skills discourse implanted in the process discourse of writing and learning to write
Figure 5.11: Subject positions mapped on to discourses
Figure 6.1:   Optional stages in 'Claim/Opinion-Reason' pattern
Figure 6.2:   Textual structures of the nine samples of writing
Figure 7.1:   EFL advanced students' revision practices
Figure 7.2:   List of ideas and outline of Group 1
Figure 7.3:   Sample of the first draft of Group 1
Figure 7.4:   The outline and first draft of Group 2
Figure 7.5:   The first page of the final version of Group 2
Figure 7.6:   The two main points of discussion of Group 3
Figure 7.7:   The first page of the final draft of Group 3
Figure 7.8:   The first draft of Group 4
Figure 7.9a: Practice mapped onto theory, Groups 1 and 2
Figure 7.9b: Practice mapped onto theory, Groups 3 and 4
Figure 8.1:   Ideologies of knowledge-making (Ivanic 1998: 304)
Figure 9.1:   Three aspects of talk around academic texts
Figure 9.2:   Extract from Ivanič's analysis and interpretation
Figure 9.3:   Extract from a journal article alongside the reviewer's comments
Figure 9.4:   Extract from an essay alongside Ivanič's summary
Figure 11.1: The representation of social action
Figure 11.2: The representation of social actors

PART I

Creativity and identity

REFLECTION 1

Writing a narrative of multiple voices[*]

Courtney Cazden
Harvard University

A decade ago, Roz Ivanič was a visiting lecturer in a writing course I was giving at the Oxford University venue of the (US) Breadloaf School of English. I have treasured her handouts for that visit, especially "Issues of identity in literacies for learning" (July 1998) – a concentrated version of her book published that same year. For my students, those two full days with Roz were a summer highlight. And I continue to benefit from thinking of my own academic writing in her framework (Figure 1.1) of the socially available possibilities for self hood, especially in "writing for speaking."

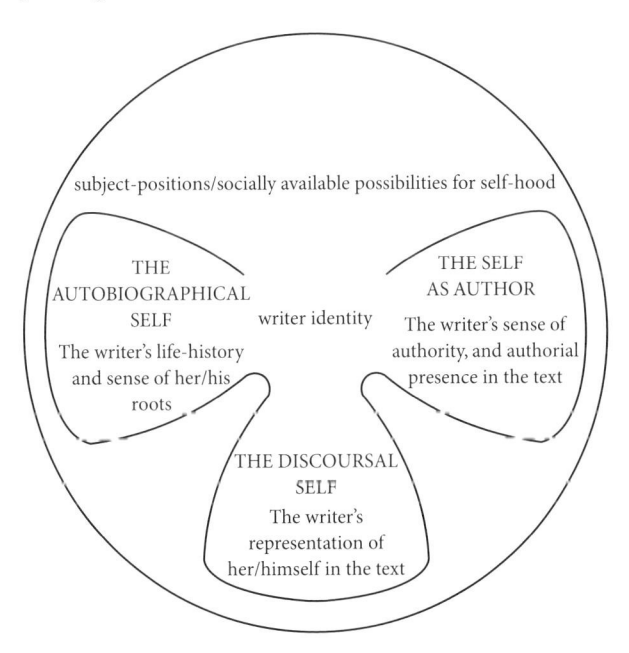

Figure 1.1 Aspects of writer identity

---

[*] The editors are grateful to Routledge Publishers for permission to reproduce Figure 1.1.

Earlier this year, I wrote an unusual talk for an audience at the University of Illinois. Now known as a retired academic, I was to give a personal narrative of my years at that same university, 1950–1953, as a faculty wife, graduate student, and "housewife." My purpose was to return to that community a piece of its history. 1950–1953 was the time in the US we now call "McCarthyism", and I participated in all my three roles in an inspiring, and ultimately successful, state-wide fight against an Illinois state version of anti-subversive legislation well documented at the federal level. But, while the community fight was won, my husband was denied tenure in the music department and didn't have another academic job for sixteen years. So the talk had to include both legacies of those three years a half-century ago: social victory and personal loss.

I have long been aware of crossing many categorical boundaries in my eight decades – of social class, religion, political ideology, for three – and aware of too-frequent uncomfortable self-consciousness about how I am "performing" myself in academic (and even everyday) life. This self-consciousness was acute in writing this Illinois talk as a personal narrative to an academic audience. Roz's notion of the aspects of writer identity gave me a way to organise, and thereby clarify, retrospectively, that otherwise diffuse self-consciousness.

Using just her diagrammatic overview of "socially available possibilities for self-hood" (Figure 1.1), I can understand that the questions I had about what autobiographical facts to include or omit hung on which subject positions I wanted to display. Should I mention, for example, that the governor of the state of Illinois until 1952, when he decided to run as the Democratic candidate for the US presidency (which he lost in both 1952 and 1956 to World War II General Eisenhower) was my brother-in-law, Adlai Stevenson – a fact that I never disclosed to anyone at that time? Should I admit that my husband and I had been in the Communist Party in 1953 and probably formally still were? The answer is yes to these aspects of what Roz calls the "autobiographical self." In co-drafting and co-signing two influential "Letters to the Editor" that I read excerpts from, as authentic 1953 voices describing the threat to civil liberties and then the campaign, why did I and four other women faculty wives identify ourselves in print as "housewives" ("self as-author")? Was my subjective freedom to speak in these and other multiple voices strengthened by the title power-point slide on the screen as the audience assembled that identified me securely, in advance, as now "Professor Emerita of Education, Harvard University" ("discoursal self")?

As Roz's handout says so straight-forwardly, "Each of us brings many voices to writing." After this very preliminary analysis of this one talk, I realise that speaking deliberately openly, in public, in some of my multiple voices felt very good indeed.

References

Ivanič R. 1998. *Writing and Identity: The discoursal construction of identity in academic writing.* Amsterdam: John Benjamins.
Clark, R. & Ivanič, R. 1997. *The Politics of Writing.* London: Routledge.

CHAPTER 1

Writers and meaning making in the context of online learning

Mary R. Lea
Open University, UK

In this chapter I use the 'comments tool' to provide reflective comments on a recently published paper, *Emerging literacies in online learning* (Lea 2007), and to draw out the seminal contribution of Ivanič's work to my own thinking. A short extract of the original paper appears below.

> I argue that we should approach online textual interactions by students as sites of academic writing and I provide evidence of 'intertextuality', 'metadiscourse' and 'epistemic modality' I conclude that student messages are institutionally significant spaces for the negotiation of ownership and authority in the meaning making process of these emerging literacies.

Introduction[1]

In this chapter I provide some comments on a recently published paper of mine, as a vehicle for drawing out both the seminal contribution that Ivanič's work has made to my own thinking and the ways in which our work has come together and overlapped for more than a decade in a shared conceptual understanding of texts and practices – writers and contexts. Although we have worked closely in different ways over the years, the only formal recognition of this relationship has been a jointly authored publication which considers the implications of developments in the teaching of writing in the UK through a historical lens (Ivanič and Lea 2006).

In writing into my own published text – in order to foreground the implicit influences of and relationship to Ivanič's work – I am attempting to turn the spotlight on a literacies approach in practice. Rather than write about my article and Ivanič's implicit contribution to it, I am using the 'comments tool' to keep my own voice as

---

1. I use the word 'tutor' in this paper in the UK sense. That is, tutor refers to any academic member of staff in relationship to their students, thus a "professor", "lecturer", "graduate teaching assistant" all take on the role of "tutor" in their teaching role with students.

reflective commentator separate from my original text. As Street (1996) illustrates, academic writing convention requires academic authors to refer to the contributions of others in their writing through the use of agreed citation practices. This also has the effect of hiding the actual words of the original author and subsuming their voice within the text of the author who is publishing the particular work in question. In subverting the genre features of the academic article, Street kept the voices of the other authors he was drawing on public. Rather than paraphrasing their contributions and using citations to indicate this, he integrated the actual and original texts of those who had contributed to his article on academic literacies, keeping all the voices visible. He argued that in so doing he was able to foreground the practices around academic writing that we take for granted. In challenging academic convention, he also raised questions about the nature and validity of academic argument and whether this would be as clear and accessible to the reader when the voices stood for themselves in their own words, rather than being drawn seamlessly into a text written entirely by him. He argues that:

> by keeping the responses separate, in a sense of reproducing them in terms of their own conditions of production – letter heads, full text, signatures and address conventions – I believe that I have made more apparent the nature of their different writing styles and conventions, and the subtleties of their argument.
> (Street 1996: 128)

It goes without saying that such opportunities to subvert academic conventions are normally only available to established academic writers with a publication record in their field. This is a far cry from the experience of Rachel Dean, a mature social work student in Ivanič's study of writing and identity (Ivanič 1998). Although both Rachel and Brian Street were taking account of reader identity, whereas Street was able to rely on his academic authority in addressing the reader of his hybrid text, Rachel had to consider what shared knowledge she could assume on the part of her reader:

> part of the mainly (but not entirely) subconscious process of constructing an impression of herself..... as sharing the required stock of academic knowledge and understanding.
> (Ivanič 1998: 165)

All established academic writers have completed such a journey but its traces are easily forgotten. In common with that of others (Lillis 2001), Ivanič's work illustrates with cogency how issues of power and authority are always central to meaning making and identity in writing and learning in higher education. In choosing to reflect upon and write explicitly into my own text, in order to foreground the relationship to Ivanič's work I, too, am making assumptions about control over knowledge and who has the right to write in particular ways in academic contexts – notions which are central to any exploration of literacy as social practice. This can also be interpreted as an intertextual journey, as I attempt to make explicit connections between my present work and the underlying and implicit influences on it of Ivanič's seminal publication on writing and identity. What this does is to enable me to draw comparisons between issues of meaning making in online message postings and in conventional undergraduate student essay writing, which further contributes to the argument I am making in the article itself.

On first sight, the paper I am considering here, with its focus on post-graduate student writers in an online environment, may seem a far cry from Ivanič's work with students who are on the margins of, or outside, Higher Education (Ivanič 1998; Ivanič et al. 2007). However, I believe that the reason I have continued to benefit from the insights that her work offers is precisely because it has been so successful in bringing the relevance of theories from applied and critical linguistics to the day-to-day work of practitioners working with student writers, in whatever context and at whatever level. The field of academic literacies research – and I situate Ivanič's work firmly within this broad conceptual and theoretical frame – pays attention to issues of meaning making and identity within the wider institutional context of the academy. As the field develops further to encompass explorations of a range of academic writing practices (see Lea 2004; Lillis and Curry 2006; Goodfellow and Lea 2007), it continues to foreground the value of this framing, which centrally incorporates Ivanič's work, for exploring power and authority, access and gate keeping in the texts and practices of the academy more broadly.

(The article from which this extract is taken, 'Emerging Literacies in Online Learning' was first published in the Journal of Applied Linguistics 2007, 4(1): 79–100.)

Background

This paper explores the nature of literacies in online learning and throws light on the question concerning how research in language and literacies can contribute to our understanding of texts produced in this context. It takes as its starting point the position that language is central to any learning experience and adds a dimension which is still largely absent in the field of online learning. Focusing on the texts of online discussion as significant sites of academic writing produced in the institutional context of tertiary education – in particular that of assessment – it provides evidence that we can usefully take a similar lens to online writing to that used in explorations of other writing in the academy. In aligning itself with previous research in the field of academic literacies, the paper focuses on issues of ownership and authority in the meaning making process evident in students' online message postings. Attention to these issues in the process of student meaning making has been particularly important to academic literacies research to date. In exploring literacies emerging in the online communicative landscape, the emphasis in this paper is to build on what we know about other more conventional student writing contexts and to develop similar methodological principles in applying them to this new domain. In so doing it raises questions concerning how online messages are implicated in students' knowledge construction, challenging the boundaries of what counts as academic writing. It draws specifically on theories of 'intertextuality' (Fairclough 2003; Bazerman 2004) the use of 'metadiscourse' (Hyland 2005) and 'epistemic modality' (Coates 1987), in order to examine the ways in which authorial positions are rehearsed online. It suggests that in foregrounding these textual features it is possible to unpack the nature of the writing and emerging literacies in this particular context of online learning, and concludes that student messages are institutionally significant spaces for the negotiation of ownership and authority in the meaning making process.

> **Comment: Method and methodology**
> Although this approach shares much in common with Roz's research, in this instance our methods diverge since I rely on observation of the online environment, rather than privileging interview data and reflections on writing, as is more common in research on writing as social practice. My focus here is on the entirety of the online learning experience, or at least what is made visible in the textual communication that goes on between students in course-based discussion fora.
> The claims I make around writer authority are based on message postings and considering these in relation to the broader institutional context of online learning. In common with much of Roz's work, I use a case study approach to access issues of meaning making in student writing. The context of this research is one in which students never meet each other face to face. Since all their communication is written online, I am interested in taking a similar perspective in research terms, reading off authorial positions without the additional paralinguistic resources and interview data, that would be available in other more conventional research contexts of higher education.

> **Comment: Meaning making**
> In her work on student writing and identity (Ivanič 1997), Roz introduces the notion of multiple possibilities for self-hood in the academic community, arguing that, far from being monolithic, academic discourse is always a site of struggle over meaning and knowledge. I develop a similar perspective in this paper in considering how students use online discussion in order to position themselves in relation not to academic tutors but to their peers – other students on the course – and to jostle for authority in their writing.

A case study of online writing

The paper draws on data collected as part of an ongoing research project being carried out in the context of my own teaching at the Open University in the UK. It is a textual investigation, which foregrounds language as contextualised social practice in exploring the nature of the writing being enacted in online learning encounters. The focus has been specifically upon the observation, collection and analysis of the texts that constitute the visible part of students' online experience. I draw on methods which have become established in academic literacies research, namely the analysis of data from a range of textual sources, including students' assessed texts, tutor feedback on those texts and institutional texts around writing. Previous publications have focused on the relationship between online messages and students' assessed work (Lea 2001; Goodfellow et al. 2004) and the concomitant shift in traditional relationships of authority and attribution in student writing. However, in this article the lens is focused only upon the written texts of online messages.

The context from which the data are drawn is a postgraduate course for practitioners in online and distance learning. As co-chair I share responsibility – with a colleague – for the overall academic organisation of the course, including providing support and training to the tutors who teach in the electronic tutor groups. The students are situated in diverse, global tertiary education contexts and never meet each other or their tutor face-to-face during their study. It is important to emphasise the power of the online tutor group in determining how meanings are negotiated. Logging on to a course which is delivered entirely online can be regarded as equivalent to entering the physical classroom or seminar group, in more conventional contexts of higher education. What distinguishes online learning – on this course – is that all communication takes place in written discussion, either within the tutor group or in one to one email communication. One of the main drivers for the research has been to examine the nature of writing in online interaction and communication and what this can tell us about the process of knowledge construction in this context. This is of particular significance because the course design privileges the written texts created during online communication and the permanent nature of these texts – continually visible throughout the life of the course – leads to their being regarded as authoritative by both students and tutors. Students on this course are explicitly introduced to the idea that their interactions with others in the online fora will enable them to critically explore issues and arguments which are generated by both readings and web resources and, further, that these will provide opportunities for refining and building upon their own knowledge and understanding. The idea of knowledge construction in dialogue with others is therefore both built into the course design and made explicit to the students in the guidance they receive. In addition, students are frequently asked to make explicit links between online discussion and their written assignments (see Goodfellow et al. 2004; Lea 2001, for detailed discussion of this) and gain marks of up to ten per cent for their participation in online debate in the weeks preceding the submission of a particular assignment. Arguably, there is some tension here between the requirement to engage in collaborative work with other students online and the awarding of credit – albeit

> Comment: The institutional context and selfhood
> In this article I argue that the data I present are aligned with the norms and values of higher education, and that we should pay attention to this despite the fact that these particular texts are produced in a virtual rather than physical environment. As Roz indicates, "in any institutional context there will be several socially available possibilities for self hood: several ways of doing the same thing". (Ivanič 1997:27)

very small – for online participation. Due to the limitations of space, this is not explored in the discussions which follow around issues of ownership and authority in student message postings but the connection with assessment is part of the context for this particular online writing, as it is with other more conventional forms of student writing. What distinguishes this context, however, is that on one hand students are being asked to work collaboratively in written dialogue with their peers online but at the same time to engage in individually marked conventional assessment procedures, a practice that is extremely common in online learning.

Twenty-seven students, divided between two electronic tutor groups, were registered on the course. The data are drawn from the postings made by 22 of this cohort to a designated computer conference. During a three-month period students were asked to post comments to the conference in response to a number of activities (see Appendix for details of these). As a result students posted 189 messages from which the data presented in the discussions below are drawn as illustrative exemplars. The names of students referred to in this paper have been anonymised and in line with ethical clearance, signed permissions were given by them for their online contributions to be used for research purposes.

Incorporating others' words: Intertextual moves in message postings

> **Comment: Intertextuality**
> Roz draws substantially upon the concept of intertextuality in her work, paying particular attention to this in relation to writer identity. That is, writer identity is constructed in large part through the way in which a student writer is able to incorporate and use the words of others. It is about drawing together and utilising a range of resources. Methodologically, I think there are similarities between our work but slightly different positions in our approach to exploring intertextuality. My concern here is with the interplay between literacies and technologies; what students are able do with texts and message postings in the online context and the implications that this has for meaning making. Roz's interest is in exploring students' interpretations of their own writing. I think this contrast raises interesting methodological questions around academic literacies research, which, in order to explore the relationship between texts and practices, usually draws upon participants interpretations of their own practices. Her interview data enables Roz to show the ways in which writers establish their identity through using the words of others in a variety of ways. In order to explore similar themes, I have focused on the totality of the online environment, with the focus on what students read and write when they log on to the course, that is their various message postings.

In online learning students have a set of choices to make about different elements of their message postings. These choices make a significant difference to the way in which their posting is read for the first time by others in the tutor group and also to the long term visibility of the message. There are a number of explicit uses of intertextuality which are evident in the data from messages A-Q, presented and discussed below. These include: the use of hyperlinks in 75 messages; the use of the 'reply with quote' facility in 89 messages; the use of attachments in 32 messages; the use of Harvard referencing conventions in 96 messages.

Students make extensive use of hyperlinks to websites and documents which are relevant to the subject under discussion, for example in Message B, below. This takes the reader out of the message and away from the original words of the message author. In contrast, the 'reply quote' option explicitly integrates text from another message, indicating the author of the message from which the text is drawn. It is used to explicitly incorporate the words of others from previous messages, and its use ensures that these continue to be associated with the original author. However, the choice of whether to choose this option or whether to merely refer to, or paraphrase, the original message lies with the new, rather than the original message author (see Message C below). In addition, the threading facility privileges ownership of messages by associating a particular message with a particular name. Threading keeps a running header in the subject line of the message thus giving authority to the first posting in the thread. These particular features, 'threading' and 'reply with quote', privilege the ownership of ideas by particular students – in their message postings – and are integrally related to manifestations of authority in online writing.

An additional feature which distinguishes message postings is the choice students have concerning the use of attachments. They are able to attach relevant documents to their postings, providing a different dimension from the immediately visible message. If students choose to use an attachment, their complete contribution is less immediately visible to the reader. Consequently, a student who posts an attachment, rather than putting her text into the body of the message may, unsuspectingly, be leaving her words out of the developing conversation, see for example Message A, a complete message posting relating to Activity 6 (see Appendix).

Message A

> I enclose an attachment with a summary of possible problems for education policy, plus an overview of advantages and problems associated with use of computer technology.
>
> Gillian

An attachment has to be opened and stored in a separate virtual space away from the main conference area, and may become disconnected from the original message, which in turn loses its significance without the attachment. Text in the main body of the message is visible immediately the message is opened and easily accessible to form the basis of a 'reply with quote' in subsequent messages by others developing related ideas. Although some students do integrate text from attachments – posted by other students – into their own messages, the name of the author of the original words becomes hidden because it is not automatically emboldened, as is the case with the 'reply with quote' facility (as shown in Message C).

A further explicit form of intertextuality evident in the message data is the use of Harvard referencing. For example, Message B uses referencing both in the body of the message and in a References section at the end of her message, thus invoking the authority provided by more conventional academic writing practices.

Message B

> **Comment: Referencing and selfhood**
> We only have to look at students' message postings, for example, the way in which they do or do not use dominant referencing conventions, to see how possibilities for self-hood are mediated by the dominant institutional context. The use of the first person and anecdotal experience is frequently juxtaposed with more conventional attention to referencing. My data show how constraints and possibilities for writing are closely related to issues of authorial identity and presence in the online context. This resonates closely with Roz's argument concerning the use of the first person pronoun in student writing that "those writers who choose to make their role in knowledge-making explicit are taking a different ideological stance from those who don't". (Ivanič 1997: 308)

I used the ICDL database to search for information about the history and practice of open and distance education in the United Kingdom. Not surprisingly there are many articles on this subject, although none are online.

For example, Freeman (1988) discusses the history of open learning in the United Kingdom in relation to the Open University, the National Extension College, the Open Tech Programme, and the Open College.

Tinsley (1988) discusses the development and achievements of the Open Tech Programme as part of the history of the involvement of the Manpower Services Commission (MSC) in promoting open learning in the United Kingdom. Tait (1991) describes the Open University, the Open Tech, the Open College, and the Open Polytechnic.

Sargant (1992) describes the impact, successes and failures of open and distance learning in the context of the Open University, Open Tech Initiative, The Open College, the Open Polytechnic, the National Extension College, the Open College of the Arts and the Open School in the United Kingdom.

An interesting approach is taken by Bell and Tight (1993), who argue that there is a long and varied tradition of educational development in the United Kingdom. They cite the external degree system at the University of London, the Royal University of Ireland before the First World War; and the work of St Andrews University in offering an external degree-level qualification for women between 1877 and 1931, as well as the correspondence colleges and the university extension movement.

References

Bell, R. and Tight, M. (1993) Open universities: A British tradition? Society for Research into Higher Education and the Open University Press.

Freeman, R. (1988) The National Extension College: Open learning in the making, Open learning, Vol.3, no.1, February 1988, pp. 42–44.

Sargant, N (1992) 'Open and distance learning: A brief outline', Adults learning, vol.4, no.1, September 1992, pp.17–19.

Tinsley, D. (1988) 'Facing the future: The role of the Training Commission in support of open learning'. In N. Paine (ed.) Open learning in transition: An agenda for action, Cambridge, National Extension College.

Tait, A. (1991) 'Distance education in th e United Kingdom today: Current trends', The American journal of distance education, vol.5, no.2, pp.42–46.
Relevant web sites include:
The National Extension College
http://www.nec.ac.uk/
The Open College of the Arts (OCA)
http://www.oca-uk.com/intro.html

These, then, provide examples of some of the more visible instances of intertextuality which occur as a result of the interplay between literacy practices and particular technologies. Emerging literacies in this context are mediated by the particular affordances of the software design, enabling students to do particular things with their own and other students' messages and documents, with concomitant implications for issues of authority and ownership in their online writing. There has of course always been a complex interplay between technologies and the production of written texts, but with older technologies, for example, the pen or pencil, the technologies have become hidden, what (Morgan et al. 2002) refers to as black-boxed. In online courses the affordances provided by the technology are still fairly new; consequently the complex interplay between the technology and texts, and the associated practices developed as they rub up against one another, is more evident than those associated with established technologies.

Having considered some of the features of explicit intertextuality, I turn to some more nuanced and implicit intertextual features in order to explore the nature of emerging literacies in online learning. All can be found in more conventional forms of academic writing but the context results in these features being brought together and enacted by students in particularly significant ways. They are powerful markers of writer authority and central to the processes of meaning making. I argue that it is only by approaching these messages as we would any other written texts in the academy that we can really begin to understand how meaning is negotiated in online learning contexts.

Message C

Rebecca P. Glazer writes:

The real key to success I feel is more collaborative projects on an equal footing between different institutions (north and south), better global investment in education, health and standards of living (with investment pouring from the north to south) and a recognition of the added values and benefits that can be learned from each other.

I agree – and I think it is possible to have more collaborative projects on equal footing. I have actually tried that myself with five professors at the Makerere In university in Uganda. Together, we have developed social constructivist courses at MSc level. We all felt that the process was on absolutely equal terms, and we were all very happy with the process and the result.

Alas – more money from the north to the south, the OECD countries have not managed to come close. Unfortunately, the money flow is the other way, from the south to the north.

Cheers

Norman

Message C, a change in font indicates a shift from the original words (from Rebecca) to the words of the author of this message (Norman). Although students frequently keep the different fonts and colours in messages to indicate either 'reply with quote', or text copied and pasted from the study guide or the web, some students unify the font, its size and colour, so that it becomes very difficult to see where the words came from in the first place. The focus on the visual aspect of the posting is an important one in terms of the multimodal nature of a primarily written environment. Multimodality is played out through the use of embolded or italicised typeface, font design, colour and size, which may appear insignificant to an outsider but are of particular relevance to both the author and reader of the message in terms of the ownership and authority of the ideas being rehearsed. Choices such as these enable the writer to weave together the words of others and make them her own, with attribution being more or less evident. Where a student retains the original font she is attributing the source of these ideas to someone other than her. The authority for them remains with the original contributor rather than the poster of the later message as, for example, in Message C. This reflects a practice more usually adopted in student essay writing in relation to published works, where attribution is academic convention. Indeed, a student who fails to attribute the words of others in such a context can be accused of plagiarism. No such admonishment would be meted out on a student who incorporated other students' words into his or her own message posting without attribution but, nevertheless, the complex interplay of students' implicit knowledge of the institutional context, the affordances of the technology and the emerging literacy practices of the online class can result in the explicit marking and maintenance of the ownership of messages.

> **Comment: Multimodality**
> Roz has paid attention to multimodality and issues of writer identity in her later work, particularly the research project she has led around literacies in further education (Ivanič et al., 2007). The findings have highlighted the contrasts between the extensive use of multimodality, mediated through a range of technology assisted media in student's everyday lives, and those of the more conventional college-based literacy practices that students are required to engage in during their studies. Although a markedly different context, there are synergies with the argument I am presenting here about writer choices, presentation of self and issues of ownership and authority in technologically mediated multi-modal textual environments.

We see a contrasting practice illustrated by Message D, in which the poster uses neither the "reply with quote facility" nor different fonts to indicate message contribution, but instead refers explicitly to other students' contributions, using a summary of these as the basis of the message.

Message D

> As Clare, Simon and Shelley have already said, the main problems highlighted by Perraton in relation to moving towards computer technology in terms of educational policy are:
>
> ☐ access and availability (and maintenance – education by this method becomes limited to those who can afford it and have ready access to the channels of information delivery)
>
> ☐ costs (initial and continuing running costs to the institute and individual for the hardware, software, connection charges, maintenance etc.)
>
> ☐ provision of reliable and sufficient local student support (at the academic and pastoral levels and as opposed to online support)

Message E, posted by Sarah, adopts a related strategy adding her points to a thread started by Rebecca – whose authorship is acknowledged – indicating first that her contribution is both new, " my points are complementary but don't duplicate", and also that it is authoritative, calling into the arena a recognised published authority – Perraton – in the field.

Message E

> I'm adding this to Rebecca's thread as I think my points are complementary, but don't duplicate. I have put my notes from Perraton at the end of this message (on the assumption that most people will have already done this reading).
>
> Sarah

Using personal experience in order to build knowledge in the field is a dominant practice in the message postings, reflecting the professional development focus of the course, which privileges reflection on experience in the construction of academic knowledge. Personal experience or anecdote is used frequently, even to respond to a more academically worded enquiry, as in Message F.

18 Mary R. Lea

> Comment: Autobiographical self. The sense of identity which people bring with them to this course, including their background and experience, where they are coming from, is particularly apparent for students who are bringing their professional identity into a post-graduate course where they are institutionally positioned as novice students. Being an experienced professional is a dominant strand running throughout students' message postings. As Roz says about the co-participants in her research, their writing is a way of representing experiences, and their developing life history, rather than representing some kind of essential self. In revisiting Roz's work, the question this raises for me now is how the autobiographical self might be said to shape my students' writing in an online learning context.

Message F

Hi Simon,

Thanks for the reply. You asked

"To what extent, however worthily intended, does that put pressure on developing countries to take a particular position, even if the infrastructure of the country does not support the technology"

Recently the British Council attempted to set up a new model for its teaching centres in Tanzania. The problem we have in certain countries is that we cannot afford to offer an English language teaching service in the traditional face to face manner. The costs of providing a teacher cannot be met by the amount of money the students can afford to pay us – and I should add – that I'm not talking about the less well off students here. This is not an exercise in trying to improve access to all. We have a very carefully defined target audience and the people we are trying to "get to"(!) are people that are likely to have an influence on their society in their professional lives at some point now or in the future (future politicians, teachers, top businessmen etc). The new model in Tanzania was to be a mix of self study (using computer based and online materials) with face to face support from a teacher. I've been trying to get more information on how successful the project has been but as far as I know it hasn't worked very well to date. When you mention infrastructure, Tanzania has one of the lowest levels of connectivity in the world (Castells 210:2001) and I don't think this has helped. However, in this situation for us to provide a service we just can not use the standard "old-fashioned" model. It simply does not work unless you are prepared to lose money doing it.

Cheers

Andrew

References

Castels, M. *The Internet Galaxy*. 2001. OUP.

Despite using personal experience as the main claim to authority, the message writer, Andrew, also utilises academic referencing conventions in his posting. The visual framing of the posting is of particular significance. The message begins with a simple greeting and then the reference to Simon's question is set out on the page in a similar format to an assignment question. This is followed by a professional response to the question posed, and the message closes with a reference to Castells. In one message then the author draws, intertextually, on different conceptions of authority: another message posting; personal/ professional experience; anecdote; published work. In addition, in responding to the question set out at the beginning of the message given by Simon's previous message, Andrew reflects upon his personal experience through invoking the professional voice of the "British Council, English language teacher" and uses "we" to draw the reader into this particular view of the world, "The problem we have in certain countries is that we cannot afford to offer and English language teaching service…. However in this situation for us to provide a service we just can not use the standard "old" fashioned model". The repeated use of an intertextual "we" associates this text and the arguments being rehearsed with a specific domain outside of this particular course but from which much of the authority of the writer appears to be drawn.

In contrast in Message G in the same discussion thread, whilst also drawing on experience, Belinda constructs her position primarily through a personal voice, foregrounding the use of "I". She relies on the authority of her personal experience alone in order to present her perspective. Her questions at the end of the message invite the reader to provide additional or contradictory evidence for her position, which, arguably, could result in her authority being challenged in future messages.

Message G

> I spent 8–9 months in Latin America a couple of years ago (happy days!) – in Ecuador, Peru, Chile and the tip of Argentina. I've also spent a few weeks in Bolivia. My experience of Ecuador, Peru and Bolivia – all poor countries – is that you can hardly walk down a street, even in a remote town in the Andes – without finding an internet cafe (sometimes a room with only a couple of PCs). Of course, this may be driven by tourism as much as anything else, although I didn't notice a substantial difference in Ecuador and Bolivia, whose tourist numbers are (I believe, still lower than in Peru). Chile and Argentina were different. With the exception of San Pedro de Atacama in northern Chile (the entire population seemed to be either tourists or orientated around tourists), I found finding an internet cafe much harder; they existed, just less "in yer face". And similarly in Argentina (this was only a few weeks after the banking crisis, so still the structures of a booming economy.
>
> This experience – combined with experience in the UK and Germany, where I find internet cafes less than "two a penny" – led me to formulate the tentative thesis that there's an inverse relationship between a country's economy and the number of internet cafes – poorer the country, the more the cafes – on the basis

that there's no fixed cost expenditure of PC and power lines, just more controllable variable use costs (from the user's perspective).

How does this chime with your experiences of Africa? Or, indeed, your or anyone else's experience elsewhere?

Belinda o:)

Addressing the reader: Use of metadiscourse

The message data also illustrate how students regularly make use of metadiscourse; a strategy used by writers to signal to the reader what kind of text to expect. This provides support for both readers and writers in decoding the text as it passes from writer to writer. Many of the online messages use metadiscourse in the provision of directions as to how to read a particular posting. This not only informs message readers but it also establishes the writer as having authority over his or her posting. For example in Message H, the author, Clare, lays claim to the ownership of her observations at the beginning of the message. The observations *(not shown)* then follow, and the message concludes by inviting the reader to disagree with the ideas she puts forward.

Message H

> I would like to make several observations if I may. *(opening message)* ....
> ....
> I would like to hear your and other's comments on these observations. Feel free to disagree. I am just articulating my thoughts. *(closing message)*

Another student, Richard, Message J, also uses metadiscourse, "I have taken the same approach", in order both to align himself with Meg and also distance himself and present his own authority, evidenced in his closing sentence of the message, "I have come to a different conclusion". Arguably, this can be seen as taking control and moving debate further in the direction of his argument.

Message J

> I have taken the same approach, Meg, but have come to a different conclusion *(opening sentence of message)*
> ....
> All of which supports the view that flexible learning is not just another name for open learning, but may be seen as open learning subject to limitations. *(closing sentence of message)*

Rebecca, in posting K, opens a long message with the text below, explaining to the reader how she set about the activity, although there is no requirement in the activity itself, Activity 12, to provide such reflection (see Appendix). She uses metadiscourse to foreground the fact that this is her own work, not influenced by postings of other students, thus claiming authority for the opinions being expressed.

Message K

> I set about this activity by initially comparing the reference lists for the two chapters before reflecting on how I perceived Terry Evans and Mary Thorpe used the literature to back up their understanding of learners and learning. Once I'd reflected on my first impressions of the two authors, I then read their personal synopses in the *Contributors* section of the book and reflected on how this compared with my first impressions and personal perception.
>
> I've also posted my thoughts and reflections before reading everyone elses – I wanted to get my thoughts clear before comparing. So now I have, I'll go see what you've all said!

Comment: Discoursal self
The impression of self these students present, through their own messages, is often evident through their explicit use of metadiscourse. Roz's work foregrounds the interaction which takes place around text production, which implicitly leads students to position themselves in particular ways in their writing. In contrast, metadiscourse is concerned with the more explicit ways in which writers engage readers, rather than with the broader issues of power and authority which are often implicitly embedded in any such acts of writer engagement.

Ownership and authority: Commitment to propositions

Another way in which issues of ownership and authority in terms of meaning making are operationalised in the text is through the choice of specific linguistic devices which foreground the writer's relationship to particular propositional knowledge. Coates' work (1987) provides us with some tools to make more sense of the way in which students are able to indicate their level of commitment to a particular proposition, which is central to meaning making in academic writing. In particular I concentrate in the data upon: forms of address; interrogatives; categorical and hedged assertions.

Students use a range of openings and forms of address, which position them authorially in relation to the propositions being rehearsed in their own and others' contributions. For example, Message B provides a general opening statement, with no reference to other messages. Other messages start with a "reply with quote" reference to another student's message, for example in C, where Norman frames his message by beginning with a quote from Rebecca.

Another choice is to make a direct reply to one or more students, as illustrated in Message D. In Message F, Andrew addresses his reply to Simon although the placing of the message in this particular conference indicates that the message is intended for everyone in the group. Some messages also begin with an indication of the tentative, less authoritative nature of the posting, as in Message L.

Message L

> Correct me if I am wrong..

Interrogatives are commonly used as knowledge building devices and are taken up as the basis of other students' messages indicating the writer's stance on the proposition being rehearsed in message threads. This is illustrated in the relationship between the following linked messages: M, N and P. The original student's posting was in the form of an attachment; this document is referred to at the beginning of Message M, "Here is my offering for activity 9".

Message M

> *Michael Grange 5 writes:*
>
> *Here is my offering for activity 9*
>
> I have been struggling to find *much* in the way of evidence that Nunan cites in support of his argument that "from the perspective of those dealing with information and communications technology, education is already changing to a new "flexible" paradigm" (p. 57, Reading 5).
>
> Evidence to me means facts – data – bodies of supporting statements, examples, etc. All he cites – as you indicate, Michael, – is "a number of government commissioned reports" – McCann et al. 1998, Yetton and Associates 1997, Tinkler et al. 1994, 1996, which he claims identify the role of these technologies in creating this new "flexible" paradigm for HE.

In posting a response to Message M, the student posting Message N uses questions as a knowledge building device, both authoritatively responding to the previous posting but also hedging somewhat in inviting responses from others, and as a result being less categorical and conceding some authority.

Message N

> But firstly, as you say, these are all to do with university education in Australia. (And which universities show these changes? how many? in what respects?). What about in other "developed" countries? How "general" is this new "flexible" paradigm to which we are changing? Does it apply in the developing world? (Should it? Are the contexts appropriate?) Can he back up his statement more broadly?
>
> Secondly, all the reports are commissioned by government – might one be too cynical in wondering whether that leads to any "sponsor-bias" in the list of char-

acteristics this new paradigm is supposed to show? "Lifelong learning" in particular has a ring of governmental rhetoric.

Looking at the characteristics that Nunan says the new paradigm displays it strikes me that there is a mix of characteristics that are "drivers of change", others that are "features in response" – and some, depending on perspective, are both. It would have been interesting – and perhaps more powerful? – if Nunan had cited specific examples to illustrate these characteristics. Or am I missing the obvious?

The third student, in Message P, responds to the questioning tone of Message N, providing a more categorical perspective, "I think", "We will be required", "what is evident is that this model is underpinned by technology", "I believe". In contrast to the questioning tone of Message N, the writer of Message P, then, presents as more authoritative and more knowing.

Message P

> Hi
>
> I think the new the "flexible paradigm" reflects the realities of current day employment where the majority of people in the developed world will change roles or jobs, as well as a continual change of the role itself due to economic and social pressure. We will be required to be lifelong learners, even if we do not realise that is what we are doing. To help with this is a flexible model, filled with "ambiguities and contradictions" [Jakupec and Garrick p 55], that do not help us understand it, but what is evident is that this model is underpinned by technology. The level in which the deliverers of education, or more importantly deliverers of "employment based learning" engage with this technology will result in how that organisation will need to reorganise. If technology is "critical to and critically underpins" [Jakupec and Garrick p 56] the strategy then the result will a drastic change to the Learning and Development structure of the organisation. But more importantly I believe there will need to be a complete culture change within and organisation and the attitude to workplace learners.

However, Message Q appears more tentative, using hedges such as, "I am not sure", "It seems to me", appearing less authoritative and, in Coates' (1987) terms, less committed to the proposition.

Comment: Modality and knowledge making
Coates's work on epistemic modality is closely allied to Roz's identification in her students' texts of the use of particular forms of modality, which position her writers as students, rather than more authoritative contributors to knowledge. The analytic lens may be similar but the different contexts of student writing lead to nuances in the articulation of issues of writer identity in our two different contexts. In this instance, although positioned as students, the sense of authority as experienced professionals comes through in my data and indicates an explicit tension between the different writer identities which are available to them, in terms of the contribution that they can make to knowledge creation, in the context of this particular course.

Message Q

> I would say it is true that open learning and flexible learning have been inextricably linked to popular perception, what I am not sure about is if it is in reality. It seems to me that flexible learning if the post-Fordism analogy is appropriate at all, then flexible learning is less fixed and more prone to outside forces than open learning is.

In conjunction with the opportunities offered by the use of both explicit and implicit intertextual strategies and the use of metadiscourse to direct the reader, the use of specific linguistic devices also provide the possibilities for message writers to situate themselves more or less authoritatively in the ongoing written debate, foregrounding their own perspectives to different degrees in juxtaposition to those of their peers.

Afterword: The unfinished text

A text is never finished. There is always more that can be written, more voices to be incorporated. I am powerfully reminded of this having reflected upon Ivanič's work, and in the way I have chosen to do this, in this chapter. In her own words:

> In my view the guiding questions I was asking are worth pursuing with different groups: what versions of self are these writers constructing for themselves discoursally, which do they own and disown and why? (Ivanič 1998: 333)

This will continue to be an ongoing challenge to all of us who are concerned with issues of writing in the academy in changing times and asking searching questions about whose voices are privileged and whose remain hidden.

Appendix: Study guide activities

Activity 4

Find ICDL on the H805 web site. Now use the ICDL database to search for information about the history and practice of open and distance education in your own country.

Activity 6

As you follow Reading 3, make some notes on what you think Perraton sees as possible problems with the move towards computer technology in terms of educational policy.

Also, look at the African Virtual University web site. What evidence do you think there is that its provision is technologically driven in the way that Perraton suggests?

Discuss this with your colleagues on-line.

Activity 8

Look back at the brief list, in Section 2.3, of possible limitations on open learning that may make it less than "totally "open"." Now, keeping in mind what you have just read in Reading 4, particularly the challenges mentioned (p. 3) and the responses to them, how reasonable is it to see flexible learning as just open learning by another name? Does flexible learning operate under any of the limitations in Section 2.3?

Activity 9

Nunan suggests that "… from the perspective of those dealing with information and communications technology, education is already changing to a new "flexible" paradigm …" (p. 57).

What do you think Nunan means by this?

What evidence does he use to support his argument, as reflected in the above quote?

Discuss your findings on-line with others in your tutor group.

Activity 12

What do you see as the differences between the literature Evans draws on to support his argument and that used by Thorpe?

In what ways do you think Evans differs from Thorpe in his approach to learning and the learner?

References

Bazerman, C. 2004. Intertextuality: How texts rely on other texts. In *What Writing Does and How it Does it: An introduction to analyzing texts and textual practices*, C. Bazerman & P. Prior (eds), 83–96. Mahwah NJ: Lawrence Erlbaum Associates.
Coates, J. 1987. Epistemic modality and spoken discourse. *Transactions of the Philological Society*, 110–131.
Fairclough, N. 2003. *Analysing Discourse: Textual analysis for social research*. London: Routledge.
Goodfellow, R. & Lea, M. R. 2007. *Challenging e-Learning in the University: A literacies perspective*. Maidenhead: Open University Press/Society for Research into Higher Education.
Goodfellow, R., Morgan, M., Lea M, R. & Pettit, J. 2004. Students' writing in the virtual university: An investigation into the relation between online discussion and writing for assessment on two masters courses. In *Doing Literacy Online: Teaching, learning and playing in an electronic world*, I. Snyder & C. Beavis (eds), 25–44. Hampton: Hampton Press.
Hyland, K. 2005. *Metadiscourse*. London: Continuum.
Ivanič, R. 1998. *Writing and Identity: The discoursal construction of identity in academic writing*. Amsterdam: John Benjamins.
Ivanič, R., Edwards, R., Satchwell, C. & Smith, J. 2007. Possibilities for pedagogy in further education: Harnessing the abundance of literacy. *British Educational Research Journal* 33(5): 703–721.

Ivanič, R. & Lea, M. R. 2006. New contexts, new challenges: The teaching of writing in UK higher education. In *Teaching Academic Writing in UK Higher Education*, L. Ganobcsik-Williams (ed.). Hampshire: Palgrave MacMillan.

Lea, M. R. 2001. Computer conferencing and assessment: New ways of writing in higher education. *Studies in Higher Education* 26(2): 163–182.

Lea, M. R. 2004. Academic literacies: A pedagogy for course design. *Studies in Higher Education* 29(6): 739–756.

Lillis, T. 2001. *Student Writing: Access, Regulation, Desire*. London: Routledge.

Lillis, T. & Curry, M. J. 2006. Professional academic writing by multilingual scholars: Interactions with literacy brokers in the production of English-medium texts. *Written Communication* 23(1): 3–35.

Morgan, W., Russell, A. L. & Ryan, M. 2002. Informed opportunism: Teaching for learning in uncertain contexts of distributed learning. In *Distributed Learning: Social and cultural approaches to practice*, M. R. Lea & K. Nicoll (eds), 38–55. London: Routledge Falmer/Open University.

Street, B. 1996. Academic literacies. In *Challenging Ways of Knowing: In English maths and science*, D. Baker, J. Clay & C. Fox (eds), 101–134. London: Falmer Press.

CHAPTER 2

Ivanič and the concept of "wrighting"

Sue Parkin
Lancaster University

How writers create an identity has been a major focus for Ivanic's work (1998) and in this chapter I demonstrate how her concept of the "wrighter" of a text (2004) helped me to understand how art student Dylan's choices of visual and verbal resources created not only a multimodal text (Kress and van Leeuwen 2001) for the examiner but also an identity for himself. Dylan is able to identify himself as a knowledgeable art practitioner-guide "wrighter", sharing with us his skills, abilities, insights and achievements in a text which has a beauty and integrity of its own. All of these are things that excite Roz Ivanic because she believes they are important.

Introduction

In this chapter I will show how Ivanič's work guided and shaped my own thinking about students' writing. I will explain how I came to understand the precise linguistic mechanisms used by sixth form college art students as they weaved together images and words to create their art projects, and much of the chapter analyses ways in which this linking is achieved. In this analysis I am able to show precisely how a writer becomes a "wrighter", to use Ivanič's term. This is when a writer puts together different modes in the same way that a wheelwright wrights a wheel. Both call on resources beyond the primary one. A wheelwright uses wood but adds metal and an art student uses words but adds images

Background

Ivanič's work has established that "literacy" involves more than a simplistic, skills-based view of reading and writing. The concept of "literacy practices" (Ivanič 1998) enables the researcher and the teacher to not only take a holistic view of what people actually do as they read and write but also to analyse closely their actual produced texts. One of her concerns in this is the ways in which writers set about creating an identity for themselves (ibid).

Contemporary texts tend to be multimodal (Kress and van Leeuwen 2001) in that they rely upon visual as well as verbal modes – images and words work together to create meaning. Ivanič argues that all texts are multimodal and the analysis in this chapter is adapted from my doctoral thesis, for which Ivanič was the supervisor. I have based much of it on my findings about "Dylan". He was a sixth form art student at the college where I taught English. He created a Personal Study for his art course about two paintings, *India House* by Adolphe Valette and *The Lake* by L.S. Lowry. A Personal Study in art has a number of genre requirements that appear in various assessment documents issued by the relevant examination board. One such requirement is that the student should create an argument and another is that the whole text should incorporate images – in other words it needs to have a stance and to be multimodal.

The ways in which images and words can be woven together saw Dylan as a novice wrighter and me as a novice grammarian. I relied on Hallidayan Functional Grammar (1994) and here I am able to demonstrate the linguistic resources available to Dylan for attaching words and images together.

I allied my own discovery of attachment mechanisms which I called "close", "loose" and "open" to Barthes' (1977) three functions of anchorage, relay and illustration. It is on this last function that I have chosen to concentrate this chapter because it is here that arguments can be created that are multimodal. Claims can be made in words, but evidence can be presented in images. The debate between Andrews and Prior (2005) calls for exactly this creative way of arguing.

Dylan identifies himself by what he does in the literacy practices he adopts and I argue that he is a knowledgeable art practitioner-guide, sharing with us his skills, abilities, insights and achievements in a text which has a beauty and integrity of its own. All of these attributes are things of which Ivanič, as pedagogue, practitioner and theorist, has never lost sight.

My background

At the age of 14 I was ejected from the art community. At school it was decided that I would not be allowed to study art any more and the reason given was that I could not draw "properly". I still cannot draw, so it is something of a surprise to me that my PhD thesis is about the language of art.

Roz Ivanič was my supervisor and her commitment to the research shines through every chapter of my thesis. Having read the latest instalment, she would start every supervisory session by saying "Isn't this EXCITING!" Ever the teacher, she actually meant it and her confidence in my work helped to mitigate the undermining of my identity at the point of rejection from the art community.

Specifically, my work is concerned with the genre of art coursework of 17 & 18 year olds in a Sixth Form College in North West England and how the minute linguistic detail of twenty nine students' writings weaves together coursework that is written and visual. Their work is not only beautiful and multimodal, but it also conforms to examiners' and teachers' expectations.

My research question was

> What are some of the salient features of the genre of coursework in art…in the early years of Curriculum 2000 (see below), and what influenced them?

This chapter is about two of those salient features: argumentation and multimodality. Contemporary texts tend to be multimodal (Kress & van Leeuwen 2001) in that they rely upon visual as well as verbal modes – images and words working together to create meaning. Ivanič's claim that all texts are multimodal means that even a densely written page such as this reflects my choice of font, size, colour and layout to create significance for you, my reader.

Curriculum 2000 involved a shift in post 16 academic work in England and Wales, from the traditional two year, linear A levels to something more fragmented. From 2000 there was a modular approach with purportedly more "choice" for students. As a member of the English department and the Student Support department at my Sixth Form College, I was asked to help Joe, a gifted Chinese student who was studying "A" level art. He seemed to be unable to start his art coursework, his "Personal Study" of Monet, part of the first module in art. I, knowing nothing about art, did at least know how to do coursework, having supported a number of students in a number of other academic subjects over a number of years. Thus it was that I agreed to support Joe and, unknowingly, to start my doctoral thesis (see Parkin 2006).

My past students had always understood what was expected of them in any type of project because they had all attended mainstream, British schools. I could always rely on them to explain to me what was needed and I could then support them, even if the subject was beyond my expertise. Thus I was able to collaborate with students of physics, geography, graphic design, mathematics and a number of other subjects that were new to me. Joe, by contrast, was a good artist but, coming from Macau, had had no experience of what was expected of projects in the British education system. He knew about art but not about how to write and to compile art projects. It was at this point that I needed to admit to myself that I knew nothing about art itself, nor indeed about how to start an art project.

For the first time in my career as a teacher I was unable to help a student and the shock of that started a quest that in 2002 took me knocking on the door of

Roz Ivanič in the Linguistics Department at Lancaster University to talk about the literacy practices of another of my art students, Dylan.

Ivanič's work on literacy and writer/wrighter identity

The concept of "literacy practices" (Ivanič 1998) enables both the researcher and the teacher to take not only a holistic view of what people actually do as they read and write but also, at the same time, to furnish them with the tools closely to analyse the actual texts produced. One of Ivanič's concerns in all of this is the ways in which writers set about creating an identity for themselves (ibid.).

Heath's concept of "literacy events" (1982) had been a useful starting point for Ivanič's own thinking. Heath defines them thus:

> Occasions in which written language is integral to the nature of the participants' interactions and their interpretive processes and strategies…In such literacy events, participants follow socially established rules for verbalising what they know from and about the written material. Each community has rules for socially interacting and sharing knowledge in literacy events.
> (Language in Society vol. 11: 50)

Ivanič's view of literacy events stems from her 1998 work where she notes several other considerations about the social elements involved. For her, writing may be central or peripheral to the event itself; there may be more than one text involved; writing, speech and visual features may be intertwined and she identifies within a given literacy event, several "sub-events". In addition, texts themselves can participate in more than one single literacy event and in any case, they bring with them a whole past history and a whole store of future possibilities. The paper Roz Ivanič and Fiona Ormerod published in 2000 cites the work of Edward, one of the children they were studying. He was doing a project on tigers and it is clear that he saw this literacy event as having a very long time scale of sustained endeavour:

> Whenever he or his parents read a newspaper they note any articles about tigers and he cuts them out and slips them in [to his file]. He says, "I'm always going to be updating this".
> (Ormerod and Ivanič 2000: 102)

His identity as a writer thus continues for a long time but of course, he is not isolated. He belongs to several communities, one of which can be called the discourse community. Barton, Hamilton and Ivanič (2000: 11) say that these communities

> …are groups of people held together by their characteristic ways of talking, valuing, interpreting and using written language.

They also establish that these communities are fluid – people move between them – and there is much overlap, so Ivanič has reservations about the concept of a literacy event being able to explain adequately all that goes on when people read and write. Texts may be at the centre of the event, but surrounding it are the associated social and discoursal conventions and practices, which in turn are framed by the broader cultural systems of beliefs, values, purposes and power relationships. All of this is shown graphically in Figure 3.2 in "Writing and Identity" (Ivanič 1998: 64): the text itself cannot be separated from social practices and in any case, the concept allows her to argue that literacy is more than mere skills. Skills acquisition does not allow writers to understand and utilise the generic and discoursal conventions necessary to succeed because those conventions themselves are neither static nor universal. For Ivanič, the key to entry lies in how writers see themselves and how others in power see them. Identity is something for us to acquire and for others to interpret:

> …students' writing [is] the product of their developing sense of what it means to be a member of a specific academic community, of who they are and how they want to appear to be. (Ivanič 1998: 343)

This is relevant to me in two ways: personally, it explains how I was able to be accepted as a writer about art even though I had no real background in art and as far as my student, Dylan, was concerned, it explains how he was able to portray himself through his emerging identity.

This developing identity is an important step on the way to acquiring the literacy practices of an institution and it needs much insider knowledge, not only about genre, but also about the "context- and content-specific details" (ibid: p. 344) of, in Ivanič's case, the writing of academic essays and in mine, the constructing of a multimodal piece of art coursework. Institutions have a role to play in all of this and for my student, Dylan, those include, on the one hand the art galleries he visited, with their own imposed choices of what is to be viewed and where and how, and on the other, the College and examination board constraints about what will and will not gain a good grade. What we have here are structures of power which Foucault explains (1980) via his concept of "engraining". Ivanič's concept of literacy practices seems to provide one way of understanding how this engraining takes place. For Foucault power is diffused through society to such an extent that it enters "into the very grain of individuals, touches their bodies and inserts itself into their actions and attitudes, their discourse, learning processes and everyday lives" (ibid: p. 39).

Systems other than writing are involved in this engraining and Ormerod and Ivanič (2000) demonstrate that the "materiality" of texts carries important messages. They decode, for example, children's texts that include material things to touch and move as well as things to taste and things to smell. Dylan's work, in my research, included 2D visuals to see and also samples of jute, to touch. Other students had clay figures, metal and leather boxes, plastic bags, tins, embroidered fabrics and flowers and leaves as integral parts of their projects.

Kress and van Leeuwen (1990, 1996, 2001) explore the incorporation of modes other than writing, which they call "multimodality". Verbal and visual modes for them realise meanings in ways that can, but do not have to, share commonalities:

> The meanings that can be realised in language and visual communication overlap in part, that is, some things can be expressed both visually and verbally; and in part they diverge – some things can be "said" only visually, others only verbally.
> (Kress and van Leeuwen 1996: 2)

The different modes have different ways of "saying". Language-based messages use words and semantic structures and visual-based messages use colour, salience and composition. Dylan uses both modes in his art project; I am able to demonstrate the mechanisms available for combining the two modes and I conclude that Dylan emerges with an identity not only as a writer of his text, but as a "wrighter" of it as well (Ivanič 2004).

Dylan was one of the first of the new Curriculum 2000 students and he gave me permission to analyse in detail his second art project, his Personal Study. He chose two painting: *The Lake* by L. S. Lowry and *India House* by Adolphe Valette. Both hang together in Manchester City Art Gallery.

My work builds on that of Ivanič

By 2004 Ivanič had created her concept of the "wrighter" of a text that helped me to answer my question, "How does Dylan incorporate words and images?" I believe that the concept of the "wrighter" of the text crosses the boundary between the pedagogical and the theoretical fields of Ivanič's life's work. Here I try to build on her work by demonstrating HOW Dylan wrights his text. What follows, then, is a close analysis of some of Dylan's work to explicate the precise linguistic mechanisms he chooses to link the two modes he employs in his art project.

He does it by linking certain linguistic resources to certain images. It is by examining Dylan's grammatical choices (Halliday 1994) that I am able to discover some of the ways in which multimodality works. As Kress and van Leeuwen established, words can fulfil some functions better than images can and images can fulfil some functions better than words can. A multimodal texts allows words and images to fulfil their own functions at the same time as allowing them to combine into one clear message.

Images are incorporated into a Personal Study by what I have called "attachment mechanisms" which allow varying degrees of distance between the picture and the writing. In my thesis (with its sample of 29 student texts) I show that "close", "loose", and "open" attachments can be mapped respectively on to Barthes' (1977) three functions of anchorage, relay and illustration, thus:

Barthes (1977)	Parkin (2006)
Anchorage can realise connotation	*Close* attachments are short and can refer explicitly to the image
Relay is where words & images work together	*Loose* attachments are less explicit but relate to specific things in the image as in an annotated art book
Illustration is where image clarifies writing	*Open* attachments have a variety of functions and can provide visual evidence within a verbal argument

It is this last function of illustration that I write about here as it is the one whereby Dylan can present in his arguments his equivalence claims, such as

> dark colour = distance in the painting.

He uses his own images as evidence as called for in the Andrews/Prior argumentation debate of 2005, where they argue that images can have a role to play in the creation of an argument. They cite cartoons as one possibility and in my thesis I show that drawings and paintings in academic texts can do the same.

All of these details go unacknowledged in the official documents issued by the examination board but learning how to merge images into the text by linguistic mechanisms is precisely what allows students to move from being apprentice writers to becoming members of the discourse community of art. Ivanič's work allowed me to trace Dylan's journey and, crucially, enabled me to identify exactly what linguistic choices he made in order for his project to convey a multimodal message.

Dylan identifies himself by the end of his project as a knowledgeable art practitioner and guide, sharing with us his skills, abilities, insights and achievements in a text which has a beauty and integrity of its own. All of these are values of which Ivanič has never lost sight: she continues to hold them dear to her heart as writer and teacher.

Dylan used all three of my attachment mechanisms but the "open" ones are of most interest as they allow him to create arguments, part of which are based in the visual mode. I called them "open" because I see them as lace, fragile and of differing patterns. "Close" attachments are like felt, physically pummelled together and "loose" are like jute or sacking, with an open weave but still sturdy. "Open" ones, on the other hand, are more fragile and can be misinterpreted. All three mechanisms can be called upon by a writer to create a multimodal text, where words and images work together to create a coherent message and an identity as a "wrighter".

What then does Dylan do to create an argument that relies, at least in part, on the non-verbal mode? I created a taxonomy of Dylan's visual resources and when I showed him this he was both surprised and pleased. He had no real idea that he had such variety in what is, after all, a short text with a word limit of 3,000 words. These visual resources included 24 of his own pictures – either pencil drawings, with or without coloured outlines on paper; watercolours or oil paintings on canvas or work on jute. The rest of his visuals included 23 images that he had found or produced mechanically. These included pictures cut from actual books; photocopies; postcards and images generated by a computer. For the project to be truly multimodal, these visual resources need to be integrated with words and it is the close, open and loose attachments that allow this to happen.

What follows is about argument, claims and evidence, and I state that Dylan presents his *claim* in the verbal text but his *evidence* in the visual. I am aware that I am asking you, my readers to accept judgements about the function of images to which you only have mediated access. It is only by having first-hand access to galleries that students can make the fine judgements needed for their art coursework and the same is true here: only the original Personal Study in its actual emplacement, materiality and physical presence carries the fine meanings intended. Even with Dylan's original work in front of me now as I write, everything I conclude here is, of necessity, mediated and subjective.

Much of what I write here hinges on what I have called "equivalence claims". By this I mean simply that one thing is equivalent to another in the writing: very often painting technique equals effect. For example, use of colour equals depth in the painting. This is usually formulated as

> technique = effect.

By "open attachments" I mean that the writing and the image are linked but not in any way that fits into my categories of close or loose so that it is impossible to create a line between words and a part of an image, as we find in certain art analysis books. These open attachments fulfil the function of illustration. "Illustration" is when the image clarifies the writing and in Dylan's work it does that by evidencing in visual mode a claim made in the verbal. In Dylan's work, the images are ones he has painted himself.

Bourne and Jewitt (2003:65) include in their transcripts of a discussion in an English Literature lesson not only the speech, but also the gaze, gesture and posture of teacher and students alike and they demonstrate that these are equally important multimodal signs in the co-creation of meaning. The meanings of these multimodal signs, like the meanings of speech, are located in the social origin, motivation, effect and result of the sign that is made.

Open attachments allow Dylan to gesture to an image as he would if he were orchestrating a slide show in an art classroom. His motivation is to clarify in some way via the visual mode the claim that he makes in the written and the intended effect or result is that we, the readers, gaze upon the image and receive its message: there is an equivalence claim set up in the verbal text, realised by three lexico-grammatical mechanisms of material processes; the -ing form of the verb and circumstance clauses of reason. However, the *evidence* for the claim is to be found elsewhere, in the visual text, whose message is "Look ! This is what is meant. This is the evidence."

How exactly does Dylan create open attachments and equivalence claims, thereby weaving or "wrighting" his text?

As mentioned above, he has three ways:

1. by *material process type*
2. by *-ing construction of the verb*
2. by *circumstance clauses of reason.*

All three are found in the rheme part of the clause and in each case the written claim is made first and is followed logically by the visual evidence. The rheme part of a clause in Hallidayan Functional Grammar is the part that follows the verb.

Material process type

A process in Halliday's work is typically realised by the verbal group (1994:109) and a material process is one of "doing" and has typically an Actor (who or what "does" the doing) plus a Goal (who or what "receives" the doing). These processes usually happen in the physical world, as opposed to the worlds of relationships and consciousness. Dylan has one main material processes in his equivalence claims which is *"gives"*:

> This [dull colours and thickly-applied paint] **gives** the sky a greater depth.
> (Dylan's p. 22)

Colour (dull) + technique (thick) = depth.

> All of this [use of deep blue and purple] *gives* the smoke more depth and shape. (p. 24)

Colours = depth and shape.

> Lowry left all the brushstrokes in the paint rather than trying for a smooth finish, which *gives* the final result a raw look. (p. 25)

Technique = raw look.

Figure 2.1 Dylan's p. 22 (To see the colour version of Figures 2.1, 2.2, 2.3 and 2.4 please go to http://dx.doi.org/10.1075/swll.12.figures)

Effects are in the Rheme and function as Goal and, crucially, in each case, effects are illustrated in Dylan's own image and presented as visual evidence. It seems to me that in a 2-D representation of a 3-D world, these are acceptable claims within the discourse community of art. Each claim has its own-image standing alone, reproducing the colours/ technique *and* the effect. Evidence is in the image, but as we are not prompted to look at it, we may not find it and herein lies the danger of such a fragile attachment.

-ing Constructions of the verb

Dylan's second structure is the -ing form of the verb. He has two:

> *"creating"* and *"making"*

Ivanič and the concept of "wrighting" 37

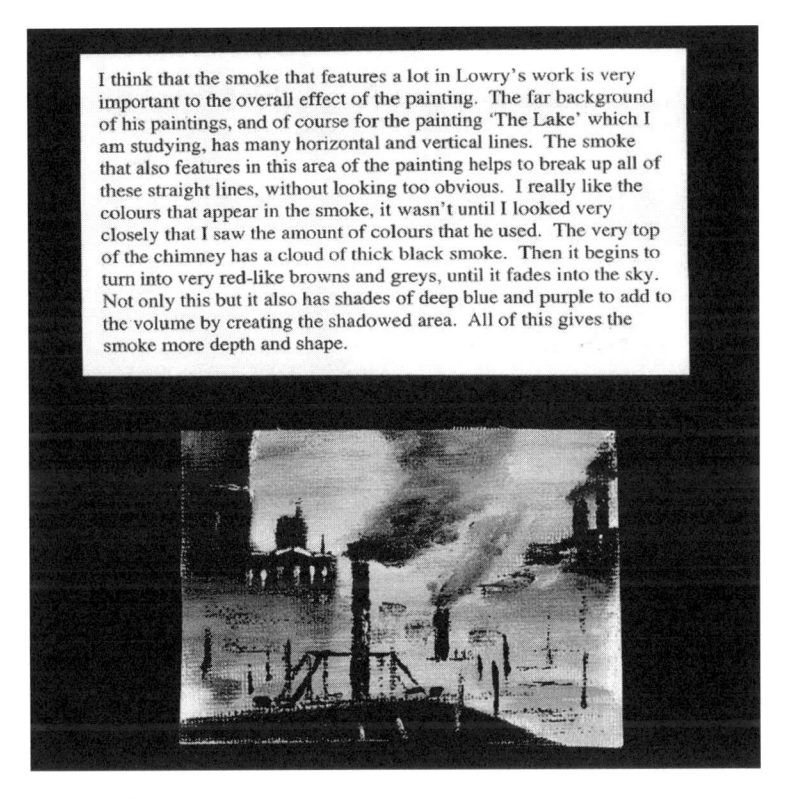

> I think that the smoke that features a lot in Lowry's work is very important to the overall effect of the painting. The far background of his paintings, and of course for the painting 'The Lake' which I am studying, has many horizontal and vertical lines. The smoke that also features in this area of the painting helps to break up all of these straight lines, without looking too obvious. I really like the colours that appear in the smoke, it wasn't until I looked very closely that I saw the amount of colours that he used. The very top of the chimney has a cloud of thick black smoke. Then it begins to turn into very red-like browns and greys, until it fades into the sky. Not only this but it also has shades of deep blue and purple to add to the volume by creating the shadowed area. All of this gives the smoke more depth and shape.

Figure 2.2 Dylan's p. 24

His equivalence claims are about volume and about the difficulty of dividing water from sky visually:

> ...it also has shades of deep blue and purple to add to the volume by ***creating*** the shadowed area. (Dylan's p. 24)

> The colours used are very similar to the rest of the painting, ***making*** it very difficult to divide the two. (Dylan's p. 20)

Equivalences are:

> shadowed area = volume
> similar colours = difficulty in dividing.

In cases where the eye needs to be guided to several specific parts of the image, the use of colour is a significant mode in the openly-attached image, like a red laser dot used in lectures based on slide-shows. This need not be confined to v-ing clauses, but can be found there for example, on his pages 9 and 11 which have red wavy lines, and on page 13 where he uses areas of green (see Figures 2.3 and 2.4).

38   Sue Parkin

> In the painting 'India house' the layout varies a lot from the layout of Lowry's typical urban landscape, in this case, 'The Lake'.
>
> Lowry uses foreground, middle, and background very distinctively in the landscape paintings. This painting demonstrates this very well. The long, sweeping horizontal lines of the many hills split the painting into different sections, giving the painting more distance.

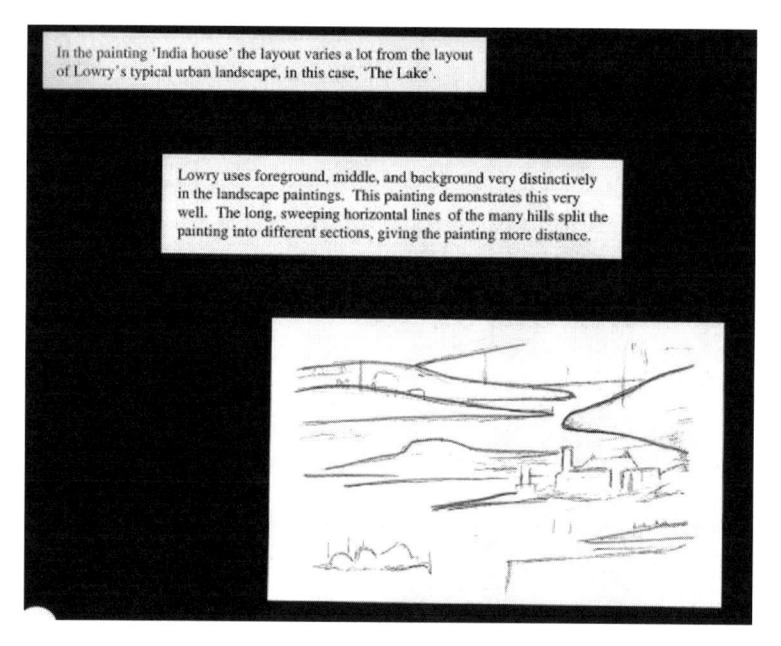

Figure 2.3 Dylan's p. 9

> The long, sweeping horizontal lines of the many hills split the painting into different sections, *giving* the painting more distance. (Dylan's p. 9)
>
> the darkly coloured hills that sweep across the painting and disappear into the water *creating* a border for the lake. (Dylan's p. 11)

"Giving" and "creating" set up the equivalences:

> sections = distance
> hills = border.

On page 13 Dylan uses green crayon to show us where to look:

> Each of the hills that sweep across the painting overlaps the next, *giving* this section of the painting several layers.
>
> Each of these [layers] gets slightly lighter in colour as they [sic] move into the distance, therefore *giving* the painting yet more depth.

In two consecutive sentences, two related claims are made:

> overlaps = layers
> light colour in the layers = more depth.

Ivanič and the concept of "wrighting" 39

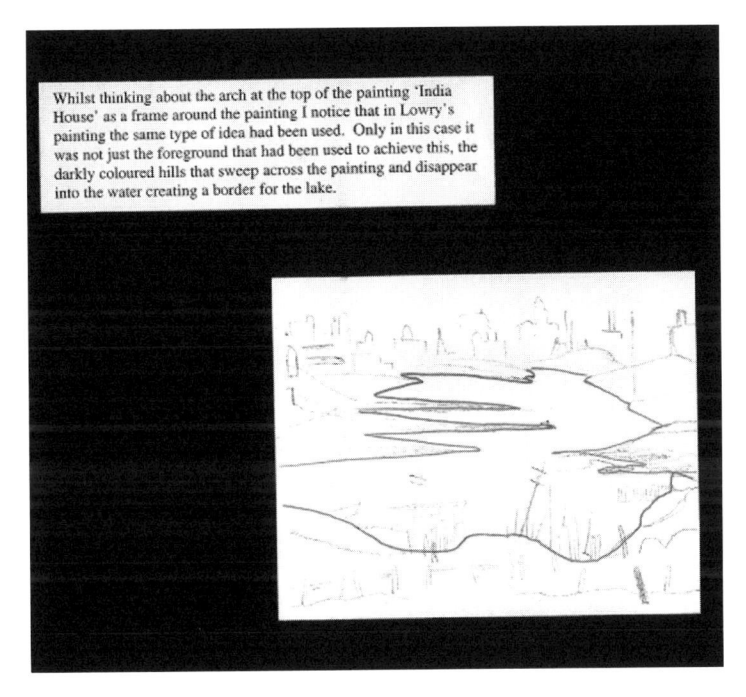

> Whilst thinking about the arch at the top of the painting 'India House' as a frame around the painting I notice that in Lowry's painting the same type of idea had been used. Only in this case it was not just the foreground that had been used to achieve this, the darkly coloured hills that sweep across the painting and disappear into the water creating a border for the lake.

Figure 2.4 Dylan's p. 11

The image shows two lots of evidence, again diffuse. Overlapping hills are coloured green and do look like layers, but also the green gets lighter and seems further away. Again, these are reasonable 2-D claims and in each case, evidence is made salient by colour.

Circumstances of reason

There are two structures here,

> *"because" + verb clause*
> *"because of" or "due to" + noun clause.*

The syntax is slightly different, but the function in both is the creation of claims. Halliday (1994:155) says that clauses of reason answer "why" and "how" question. These are, according to interviews held with an examiner, are the very questions that a student needs to ask to gain the precious available marks for analysis. Writing a circumstance clause of reason is a way of attempting to improve one's grade in the project:

> This [painting of reflections by Valette] differs to [sic] what Lowry has done *because* he [Lowry] painted the water and didn't [sic] include the reflections.
>
> (Dylan's p. 20)

The equivalences here include a negative:

> Valette's reflections = not Lowry's technique = lack of reflections

Two further circumstances of reason are spread over two consecutive pages:
> On first glance to [sic] the painting, the lake seems to resemble snow rather than water, this was [sic] ***because of*** the cool blue colours that he used.
>
> (Dylan's p. 18)

> It is still easy to tell that it is water. This is mainly ***due to*** the positioning of the water (ie it's all on one level) and *[due to]* the objects that appear from beneath.
>
> (Dylan's p. 19)

Equivalences are:

> Blue = cool = snow
> Level = water
> positions of objects = level = water.

Because of the syntactical force of "because of" and "due to", the effects here are mentioned first, but in all cases, images provide evidence, as long as we accept that blue is a cool colour (as in Varley 1980), and that water in a lake is level and may contain half-visible objects.

In an interview with Dylan, in August 2004, I asked him about his page 19 and his reply gives details of the way he sees the verbal and the visual working together:

me: Which bit of that [written] text is the image supporting? Is it a word, a sentence or the whole thing?
Dylan: I think it's the reflections…and the objects that appear out of the water and mainly the boat with no reflection.

Visually he has reduced the danger of a misreading by only copying a section of the Lowry and his verbal response has a listing of three features that he thinks the image provides as evidence.

However, there are limits to the evidence that can be invoked in the visual mode and Dylan's page 23 offers a useful contrasting example of mechanism failure. There are two images – a found colour one, cut from a book depicting the top right-hand section of the core painting "The Lake" and an own-image which, at first glance seems to be a painted version of that same section. However, the verbal claim hinges on Lowry's use of hills: although the shades of colour [in sky and water] are very similar they never actually touch each other, they are split up by the hills that come in from each side of the painting.

The equivalence claim is

> Hills = division between sky and water.

One such hill is included in the imported image, but with the own-image there is a mismatch because there is no hill. A second mismatch concerns the use of colour:

> This light colour contrasts more and more as it moves towards the foreground, because the shades of green [of the hills] become darker and almost turn to black.

The equivalence here is

> dark hills = contrast.

The imported image shows the start of this contrast but the own-image uses colour in a contradictory way because Dylan's greens are darker at the top and lighter towards the foreground. It is this undermining of the verbal claim by an inappropriate piece of visual evidence that is disconcerting and it this very breakdown that confirms the success of all the others.

I have shown in this section the various mechanisms used to join words and images to created a "wrighted" or multimodal text of argumentation.

Conclusion

Writing and image are integrated in such a way that readers need to look beyond the word to understand the argument. At the same time, a credible identity is established for the "wrighter". Loose attachments allow us, indeed direct us, to look elsewhere as Dylan becomes the knowledgeable art guide and practitioner, taking us round his own gallery of images and explaining effects, all within an original text valid in its own right and thus I hope to have shown that what Dylan does in his art project corresponds exactly with Ivanič's concept of the wrighting of a text. He calls upon resources beyond the mere word and he takes us on a journey of discovery in the two modes of visual and verbal. He analyses the work of two different artists less as a "compare and contrast" exercise and more as a way of exploring his own artistic capabilities. When asked he maintained that he was better at drawing than writing and that the images were there to "help" the reader understand what he had written:

> *Dylan*: I tried to use a picture on every page to describe exactly what I'm saying in the picture with it being art as well, and not just writing, I thought the pictures

> made it look more interesting and helped to describe it as well.Instead of having to write it down I found a way of drawing it or explaining it in a picture. I tried to help it along with the pictures…some of the time I did the writing and then found the pictures to go with it, but with the drawings, I did them at the same time, to go alongside it.

He clearly differentiates here between not only "pictures" that he found and "drawings" that he did himself but also the time-frames in which he worked for both. Rather than Edward's " I'm always going to be working on this", Dylan talks about the way he organised the time within the project itself, which, of course, had a deadline imposed by the powerful institutions, "engrained" in Dylan's practices.

All of this seems to be a long way from the beginning of my own journey into art and art projects. I had stared at Joe's Monet project, totally bemused as to how to help him start it. Of course I could not draw. I was not required to. The fact that I had no idea how to help was a shock to us both. Joe, if you are reading this by any chance, I am sorry. I know you did get a good grade for your art at college and you have gone on to do other good things. At the same time, I thank you because without your lack of understanding of what we needed to do, my research and hence this chapter would never have existed. Dylan, I thank you too, for obvious reasons. You said to me, "Here's my art project, Miss. You can keep it as long as you like." It is now safely back with you and I know you will treasure it. Roz, without you I would still be the puzzled teacher that I was. I am glad we worked together and I honour here, in this chapter, not only your contribution to pedagogy, to theory and to practice, but also to my own learning and to my own personal and professional development.

References

Andrews, R. 2005a. Models of argumentation in educational discourse. *Text* 25(1): 107–127.

Andrews, R. 2005b. Response to Paul Prior. *Text* 25(1): 145–147.

Barthes, R. 1977. *Image, Music, Text*. Essays selected and translated by S. Heath. Glasgow: Fontana/Collins.

Barton, D., Hamilton, M. & Ivanic, R. (eds). 2000. *Situated Literacies. Reading and writing in context*. London: Routledge.

Bourne, J. & Jewitt, C. 2003. Orchestrating debate: A multimodal approach to the study of the teaching of a higher order of skills. *Reading, literacy and language* July: 64–72

Foucault, M. 1980. *Power/Knowledge. Selected interviews and other writings. 1972–1977*, C. Gordon (ed.), C. Gordon, L. Marshall, J. Mepham & K. Soper (trans.). Brighton: The Harvester Press.

Halliday, M. A. K. 1994. *An Introduction to Functional Grammar,* 2nd edn. London: Arnold.

Heath, S. B. 1982. What no bedtime story means: Narrative skills at home and school. *Language in Society* 11: 49–76.
Ivanič, R. 1998. *Writing and Identity. The discoursal construction of identity in academic writing*. Amsterdam: John Benjamins.
Ivanič, R. 2004. Intertextual practices in the construction of multimodal texts in inquiry-based learning. In *Uses of Intertextuality in Classroom and Educational Research*, N. Shuart-Faris & D. Bloome (eds). Charlotte NC: Information Age Publishing.
Kress, G. & van Leeuwen, T. 1990. *Reading Images*. Geelong, Australia: Deakin University Press.
Kress, G. & van Leeuwen, T. 1996. *Reading Images. The grammar of visual design*. Geelong, Australia: Deakin University Press.
Kress, G. & van Leeuwen, T. 2001. *Multimodal Discourse. The modes and media of contemporary communication*. London: Arnold.
Ormerod, F. & Ivanič, R. 2000. Texts in practices: Interpreting the physical characteristics of children's project work. In *Situated Literacies: Reading and writing in context*, D. Barton, M. Hamilton & R. Ivanič (eds), 91–107. London: Routledge.
Parkin, S. M. 2006. Could you teach him a few adjectives? An investigation into genre expectations for A level coursework in art & into influences that shape them. PhD dissertation, Lancaster University.
Prior, P. 2005. Towards the ethnography of argumentation: A response to Richard Andrews' 'Models of argumentation in educational discourse'. *Text* 25(1): 129–144.
Varley, H. 1980. *Colour*. London: Mitchell Beasley.
Manchester City Art Gallery http://www.manchestergalleries.org

REFLECTION 2

Identity without identification

James Paul Gee
Arizona State University

In our work, Roz Ivanič and I have struggled with many of the same issues (Gee 2007). One of her pieces that I like best is the paper "Rachel Dean: A Case Study of Writing and Identity" in her 1998 book *Writing and Identity: The Discoursal Construction of Identity in Academic Writing* (pp. 125–80). Here Roz deals lucidly and movingly with a core issue in literacy studies: society often asks people to take on identities with which they don't identify. Rachel, an older student returning to university for a degree in social work, was a working-class, lesbian feminist who needed to learn to talk and write like a social worker "even though she felt extremely ambivalent about her identity as an apprentice social worker" (156).

Identity without identification: that is an interesting concept and an interesting phenomenon. It is a phenomenon that many of us have felt. Indeed, for me, it is the real-life basis of why and how I have written about identity and Discourses. It seems a contradiction in theory – identity without identification – and it feels like a contradiction in practice when people live it as an embodied experience. Nonetheless, it is real. Let me give an example: being an academic (of a certain sort) is very much one of my identities – that is the right word for it – it is a "way of being" not just a way of doing. But when I see academics, myself included out of the side of my eye, I still feel a lack of intimacy; I don't fully identify; it is like looking at someone's else hand, you can immediately tell it's not your own, even when it is your identical twin (and I have one of those). But, alas, and nonetheless, I am now through and through an academic.

If we can have identity without identification, then who is this "self" that refuses to identify with an identity, but pushes on in that identity nonetheless? Is it some sort of essential "real" self? No, as Roz points out, there is no such thing. Rather, there is only for each of us our own unique historical trajectory through the spaces of Discourses and the contestations, negotiations, and tensions among and across and within their ever porous, shifting, momentarily solidifying boundaries.

There is wisdom in the hesitations that our historical trajectories give us – wisdom from our embodied lives amidst the Discourse wars and peaces of our lives, our societies, and our times – wisdom to be wary of claims of power, naturalness, rightness, appropriateness, and stability. This wisdom can lead to resistance and disavowal; it can lead to compromise; and it can lead to change, creativity, and innovation. Those of us who have the most checkered Discourse histories – like Rachel – have the most insight into the reasons not to trust "Discourses of power". That is why creating and learning and keeping trust is the central skill of a good teacher. Such trust requires telling the truth about Discourses even as one opens the door.

References

Gee, J. P. 2007. *Sociolinguistics and Literacies: Ideology and Discourses.* (3rd edn). London: Taylor and Francis.

Ivanič, R. 1998. *Writing and Identity: The discoursal construction of identity in academic writing.* Amsterdam: John Benjamins.

CHAPTER 3

Authoring research, plagiarising the self?[*]

Richard Edwards
The Stirling Institute of Education, University of Stirling

Following Roz Ivanič's influential work on writing and identity, this chapter explores the effects of information technology in the writing of research and on the identity of the researcher. In particular, it suggests that the facility to copy, cut and paste is undermining the notion of research texts making original contributions to knowledge. By contrast, this capacity to copy, cut and paste is providing opportunities for the plagiarising of the self, bringing forth different possibilities for research and the identities of researchers. Here simulation rather than representation becomes crucial to understanding research practices.

Introduction

Traditionally plagiarism is treated as a problem in education. It refers to the unattributed referencing of the work of others. This is an issue which has been of increasing concern with the rise of digital media and the growth of the Internet. However, in this chapter I wish to explore a different notion of plagiarism, which enables "copy", "cut" and "paste" to be positioned as part of the practices associated with the authoring of research texts, and also in the construction of the identity of the researcher. Here, rather than research texts representing an authentic and original contribution to knowledge and the writer an authentic researcher, representation is replaced by simulation and writer identity is manifested in the various embodiments of subjectivity *in* the text and subjectivity *as* a text. The chapter will therefore follow Roz Ivanič's (1998, 2006) influential work on writing and identity, and explore the substance of research and researcher identity in the context in which the practices of writing and representation are being reordered by the use of technologies in the authoring of research. It also draws upon experience of working with Roz on a three year research project (see www.lancs.ac.uk/lflfe),

---

[*] This is a revised and updated/plagiarised version of a chapter in Evans, T., Jakupec, V. and Thompson, D. (eds). 1997. *Research in Distance Education 4*. Deakin: Deakin University Press.

within which issues of literacy and identification have been a key focus for discussion. Here we have worked with Hall's (2000) notion of identification as a process rather than identity as a thing. We have also been exploring the digital literacy practices of lecturers and students within this project. These dialogues have entailed discourse across subject boundaries – between applied linguistics and education – which have enriched the discussions. In this chapter, only a small aspect of Roz's work and the work we have jointly done with others is drawn upon. The key focus is on issues of writing and identity in the context of the use of information and communications technologies in the authoring of research texts.

Over the years there has been much written on issues of identity formation in educational practices and the impact of emerging technologies for teaching, learning and pedagogy. The notion of persons as cyborgs has become an influential metaphor through which to examine the changing human-technology relationship/interface. In distance education and e-learning, there has been the discussion of pedagogy as "choreography" and the exploration of the "absence-presence" and "tech(no)body" of the lecturer and student (Evans and Green 1995; McWilliam and Palmer 1995). The changing identities of adults as learners rather than students has been posited and the assumptions and consequences of this explored (Edwards 2002). Thus, questions of identity, pedagogy and the role of technology have become part of the discussions in and about education (Kress 2003; Jewitt 2005).

However, less has been written about the relationship between the researcher and technology in education and the effects of this upon the identity of the researcher and research texts. Indeed, while the discussion of pedagogy has done much to expand debate beyond the instrumental "needs meeting" approach of much of the traditional discourses of teaching and learning, this has not been incorporated significantly into the discourses of research in education. In many ways then, this chapter opens a space (or file) within which to examine certain issues surrounding the identity of researchers and the status of research texts, one which has been, and no doubt will be, returned to (re-opened) on many occasions for review, amendment and development (editing and saving).

The chapter is in three parts. First, I outline the role of research as a set of social practices which are productive of certain "regimes of truth" (Foucault 1980). This counters much of the almost common sense assumptions that research is a reflection of reality and research texts simply a reported representation of a reality found "out there" through the practices of research. This introduces the notion of research as text which is addressed more explicitly in the second section of the chapter. Here, in part drawing upon Baudrillard's (1996) notion of the simulacra, I explore the possibilities for the engendering of a condition of hyperreality through the use of information and communications technology in the practices of research. In particular, I focus on the use of information technology in the production of research texts. Third, I shall explore the implications of these processes for the identities of researchers. Here I shall focus on whether the possibilities for "copying, cutting and pasting" in the construction of research texts can be said to result in a plagiarising of the self – a perspective which assumes an authenticity in the identity of the researcher – or a self which is itself in a pleasurable and constant process of simulation, for whom authenticity is not a characteristic. Very crudely, these positions would signify a modern conception of the researcher and research to which some notions of authenticity and originality are central, and a postmodern conception in which the processes which are held to be at work – in particular, intertextuality – are reflexively manifested in our understandings of research and the researcher.

A discussion such as this does not lead to ready conclusions – a form of closure (saving and quitting) – and none will be attempted here (as suggested, the file can be re-opened and edited). Others may feel there is no opening to be pursued or it is one that can or should be readily closed. It is in the process of intertextual dialogue that such positions can be established.

Research reflecting reality?

The relationship of research to its object and what legitimately constitutes knowledge is a profound and probably irresolvable question, one which has occupied philosophers, sociologists of knowledge and others for as long as here has been a question, what is knowledge? To review the many attempts to answer that question would take longer than a lifetime and would itself be subject to continuous reinterpretation. Here I wish to make only a few observations upon what oversimplistically I will position as a modernist position. Here for research to be knowledge, it must in some sense provide a true, that is, methodologically validated reflection or representation of reality. In this view, reality is out there to be examined. What that reality is, how it works and why it works in the ways it does is the rightful terrain of research. It is through the practices of research that reality gives up its truths. Although discipline-based, positivist and quantitative approaches to research in education have tended to a large extent in certain contexts to be displaced by practice based, action-oriented, interpretative and qualitative approaches, the modernist assumptions of and about research largely underpin both sets of practices.

However, a number of problems arise in relation to the notion of reflection – ones which, it could be argued, are equally problematic for reflection in notions of professional development and certain other reflective approaches to teaching and learning. First, research is not a transcendental activity. It is itself a set of social practices, ones that are knowledge-claiming and truth-producing and located in certain research communities (Usher 1993). To say that research reflects reality is to imply that research is a transcendental process, both capable of and providing a god-like view on that which it investigates. This ignores the issue that, as social practices, research acts on, interacts with, or constructs what it researches, which, in effect, masks the ways in which "data", "knowledge" and "truth" are generated in the very practices of research (Atkinson 1996; Atkinson and Housley 2003). Even if research is undertaken to establish what those effects might be, these are themselves a practice interacting with what is researched, a process which potentially results in an infinite process of regression in the search for the real that is really there by uncovering the factors which cause it to be other than it really is.

While there are important epistemological issues to be addressed in relation to research, it can be argued that what is viewed as legitimate knowledge in a particular arena is established through the practices of the different research communities and their maintenance of certain boundaries, inclusions and exclusions. In this context, we might ask in what ways education may be considered a research community, what organisations, institutions and journals choreograph that community, and what forms of openness and closure, inclusion and exclusion, are made possible and constrained through these practices. In other words, while objects of research are "an effect of stable arrays or networks of relations" (Law 2002: 91), they are usually treated as naturalistic objects, pre-existing in the social world. I am therefore following Pels et al. (2002: 11) in the view that "objects need symbolic framings, storylines and human spokespersons in order to acquire social lives; social relationships and practices in turn need to be materially grounded in order to gain spatial and temporal endurance". In other words, they need ordering and mobilising, part of which is provided through the circulation of discourses: "different modes of ordering produce certain forms of organisation. They produce certain material arrangements. They produce certain subject positions. And they produce certain forms of knowledge" (Law 2001: 3).

The simple referential and representative relationship between the objective independent world and knowledge of it through research posited in the notion of reflection as a measure of legitimation is therefore problematic. Accurate representation of a discovered world is posited as the goal of research. However, there are fundamental questions about the nature of representation and how truthful representation is achieved within particular research practices (Edwards et al. 2004). The transcendental possibility of discovering truth is assumed, displacing the examination of the ways in which different truths are produced and realised, including those of research. Here reflexivity is a problem to be overcome rather than a resource with which one can work.

Further, to see research as reflection in many ways is to work with an impoverished and limited conception of research. In essence, research becomes necessarily and narrowly empirical in nature, a linear staged process without effect, the only form of research through which reality can be known. This displaces from consideration the complexity of research as a set of practices mediated by artefacts, language, discourse and power (Latour 1999). This includes the power of the research community and its conventions of speech, writing and embodiment, as illustrated in the acceptable forms of journal writing and the giving of conference papers. Research becomes absorbed into a technical rationality, a set of instrumental processes aimed at uncovering the truth of reality. "Research is both disembedded – an essentially ahistorical, apolitical and technical process, a transcendental, contextless set of procedures and disembodied in the sense of being carried out by isolated, asocial, genderless individuals without a history or culture" (Usher 1993: 105). In this sense, conventional forms of research produce the transcendentalism they assume – transcendental truth is a realisation of certain research practices and communities. For, as Foucault (1980: 131) argues: "truth is a thing of this world: it is produced by multiple forms of constraint".

These critiques are of a certain view of research. They are intensified in many ways through the use of information and communications technologies in the conduct of research. Within the conception of research as reflection, these technologies may be thought of as simply additional tools or instruments to be used in the conduct of research – data collection, data analysis, reporting on research. Even here, there are issues, such as the researching of the disembodied learner, or "no-body", through the use of electronic mail, or the shifting possibilities for identity among the researched through the mediation of different technologies. This raises questions about how technologies provide particular possibilities for the "who" who may be the subject of research.

However, the notion of research as a set of knowledge-producing practices traversed by artefacts, language and power suggests that, rather than being considered simply instruments, the use of these technologies needs to be reflexively situated within understandings of their effects. In other words, the emerging technologies are not simply better or more appropriate tools to be used in the research process, but in many ways start to make the knowledge-producing effects of research ever more apparent. In particular, the increased use of information and communications technologies for research, that is the increased communication and media-tion of research, raises questions about its textuality – the fact that reality comes always and already interpreted, as a text (Usher and Edwards 1994, 2007).

Texts, textuality and simulacra

The textuality of research challenges the scientific and social scientific notions of the "fiction that research is reported not written" (Barthes 1986: 70). Rather than there being an end to research which is reported in what is assumed to be a transparent language, its very nature as written and therefore constitutive of meaning and capable of multiple interpretations is brought to the fore. Here there are issues of the sorts of writing and texts which are accepted as legitimate by a research community and the practices and criteria through which they are constructed and legitimised.

Usher (1993: 110) argues that "through the textual strategy of realism [academic texts] direct attention away from themselves as texts to that which they purport to be about". Realist texts assume and construct a particular relationship between the world and text. Insofar as certain texts are given legitimacy by a research community, they support a particular set of epistemological and narrative assumptions about what constitutes research, knowledge and truth. To produce a different form of text, such as if I had written this chapter in rhyming couplets, is to invite rejection for breaking the narrative rules of a certain research community. Similarly, to suggest that a teaching/learning text may also be a research text can be to push against the boundaries of accepted and acceptable norms. Occasionally such texts may be seen as ground-breaking, but this is the exception rather than the rule.

We might then ask, what constitutes a research text and a text as research in education? An implicit answer to these questions lies in the books, academic journals, and doctoral theses in this arena – those texts which are accepted by the specific research community as legitimate. Indeed, it is often a precursor to having a paper accepted for publication that one reads, learns and adheres to the narrative forms of the journals within the arena of research. Decisions most often lie with peers and, even then, only certain peers, who advise publishers, sit on editorial boards, review papers and examine theses. Here, although all research may be said to be invented and therefore in a sense fictional, only certain texts have legitimacy within the research practices and among research practitioners in education. What is written and what can be written is therefore policed. "Communities decide rules of exclusion, set boundaries and impose closures. Consequently, this narrows what can be done and what will count as legitimate research and valid knowledge outcomes" (Usher 1993: 101). Such parameters are, of course, neither entirely homogeneous nor stable, but they remain powerful.

To bring to the fore the textuality of research is to bring into focus the reflexive question of the practices through which meaning is constructed in research, issues which are displaced from consideration by strategies which constitute research as representative and language as transparent. In previous work (Usher and Edwards 1994), it was suggested that this requires researchers to themselves become reflexive, subjecting their practices to critical self scrutiny in order that they become critical readers as well as writers of research, capable of examining the textual strategies and intertextuality at work in research texts. This involves an examination of the con-text, pre-text and sub-text of research. The con-text is that which is "with the text" – the situated and located self of the writer/reader, embodied and embedded, marked by, for example, gender, class, race, age, geography. These affect the forms, outcomes and consequences of research and the particular readings or interpretations of texts. The pre-text is that which is "before the text". Here there are the effects of, for instance, language as a signifying system, the adoption of certain writing and textual strategies through which meanings are organised, and certain cultural and interpretative traditions. The sub-text is that which is "beneath the text", such as, the professional and research paradigms and power-knowledge formations which make certain research powerful and capable of being a regulatory part of the governmentality of modern socialities, even as the neutrality or emancipatory potential of the research is often proclaimed. The textuality of research therefore raises questions of reflexivity which require the examining of research as intertextual, tracing that which makes its very existence as a text possible.

However, this very notion itself becomes radicalised and problematised with the proliferation and diversification of research texts made possible by the development of different information and communications technologies. There has been an expansion of traditional paper-based academic and professional journals – the costs of the production and distribution of which has been cut due to the technologies of globalisation. Similarly the number and range of academic books have expanded greatly. Research is also made available through websites, terrestrial and satellite television, etc. There is the proliferation and globalisation of research texts and research conferences made possible by cheaper international travel. And, with the World Wide Web, there is an explosion of developments in making available research in a range of formats, for instance, through restricted bulletin boards, podcasts, conferences, or in formats which follow the lines of traditional academic journals. Academics and researchers have themselves started to develop their own home pages on the web, from which interested surfers can download copies of articles and papers, which themselves may be subject to continued updating and amendment.

The increased importance given to the relevance and usefulness of research (Lyotard 1984) and "socially distributed knowledge" (Gibbons et al. 1994), and the popularising of research have brought to the fore and made possible, at least to a certain extent, the greater possibilities for the communication of research in diverse formats to diverse audiences. Traditional conceptions of the dissemination of research to a waiting audience at the end of the research process have been questioned as to their adequacy and efficacy. Engagement with users throughout the research process has been put forward as the future direction for research. Given the greater prevalence of research and proliferation of research texts, what I wish to explore here is how or whether this not only contributes to the foregrounding of the textuality of research, but also starts to contribute to what, drawing on Baudrillard (1996), might be called a hyper-real world of research. Here the very availability of such texts brings into question what counts as a legitimate research text and the possibilities for policing its boundaries by the research community. This can be seen as both the outstripping of the policing mechanisms by the possibilities raised through the use of information and communications technology and as part of the crisis of disciplines and the rise of multi-disciplinary research and trans-disciplinary competences (Gibbons et al. 1994). What counts as research and what is worthwhile reading as research would appear to be coming less obvious even as research activities overall grow.

Baudrillard's work has been very influential in the formulation of the postmodern and also extremely controversial in his, at times, apparent fatalism in the face of a revitalised consumer capitalism with all its associated pleasures and oppressions (Plant 1992; Poster 1996). He is often accused of hyperbole rather than analysis and there is something in that criticism, although it fails to acknowledge that he is writing in ways which, at least in part, seek to disrupt established common sense approaches to reading and writing. While such issues are beyond the scope of this chapter, it is the suggestive nature of some of Baudrillard's ideas which will be drawn upon here, rather than a simple adoption of the particular position he espouses.

For Baudrillard, the proliferation of information and communications technologies makes representation and meaning increasingly problematic. There is an accelerated production of the real which means that meaning slips away amidst a "confusion of signs, images, simulations and appearances" (Plant 1992:194). Thus, even as representations have a power to invest themselves as something behind which lies the real, the true, the authentic, the meaningful, their very proliferation results in a production of the hyper-real in which "ubiquitous images, simulations, and reproductions no longer distort or conceal the real; reality has slipped away into the free-floating chaos of the hyper-real" (Plant 1992:155). In this situation, representations and the real are not separable and, for Baudrillard; representations become more real than the real. They become simulacra, part of the production of the hyper-real in which everything becomes undecidable.

> Everywhere the same "genesis of simulacra:" the interchangeability of the beautiful and the ugly in fashion; of the right and the left in politics; of the true and false in every media message ... All the great humanist criteria of value, all the values of a civilisation of moral, aesthetic, and practical judgement, vanish in our system of images and signs.   (Baudrillard 1996: 128)

Thus, for Baudrillard the possibilities for the production and reproduction of representations through technological mediations result in a situation in which it becomes no longer possible to determine what is authentic or original. "The real becomes not only that which can be reproduced, but that which is always already reproduced: the hyper-real" (Baudrillard 1996: 145–6). In other words, the real is always media-ted and therefore always already interpreted. It is on this basis that he identifies four phases of the image: the reflection of a basic reality; a masking of a perversion of a basic reality; masking the absence of a basic reality; and, bearing no relation to any reality, it becomes its own pure simulacrum. Here while "representation tries to absorb simulation by interpreting it as false representation, simulation envelops the whole edifice of representation as itself a simulacrum" (Baudrillard 1996: 170). There is no real behind representation, merely the practices of simulation and the production of the hyper-real.

Within this context, it might be argued that the proliferation of research texts is itself part of the process of simulation, of the production of the hyper-real in which it may be criteria other than their representativeness or originality that are paramount. The notion of research as an original contribution to knowledge is undermined as its absorption in the processes of simulation and production of the hyper-real are foregrounded. There is no original contribution to make, merely simulation and the traces of intertextuality to be examined.

Rather than the search for truth or deep meaning, there is a pleasurable pursuit of a range of truths and truth-telling practices. This resonates with Barthes' (1986) view of research as texts of at times "disturbing pleasure". And, as Game (1993: 18) argues, "this is perhaps to suggest that the central issue in the evaluation of a text – theoretical or otherwise – is its capacity to provoke disturbing pleasure: not a refusal of knowledge, but a reformulation of what the desire for knowledge might be about". Such reformulations may include truth as revelation (religious knowledge), or truth as advocacy (feminist or post-colonial knowledge), as well as truth as correspondence (scientific knowledge). It is disturbing pleasure in many truth-tellings and the multiple possibilities for identity which underpins the desire for knowledge – an openness – rather than the desire to assert the truth – a closure – raising questions about the aesthetics and eroticism of research texts. This is something already pursued in relation to pedagogy by McWilliam (1996).

Research, texts and identity

The suggestion, then, is that the introduction of new information and communication technologies into research practices brings to the fore and radicalises the textuality of research texts, resulting in the production of the hyper-real through simulation. What then of the identity of the researcher? What are the possible implications for researcher identity of participating in research practices subject to these processes?

At the heart of research as representation in the search for truth is the rational and humanistic researcher – governed by reason and humane values – making original contributions to knowledge. While this narrative of researchers can be countered by their contribution to, for example, warfare, famine and ecological degradation, it nonetheless provides a powerful prescription of how the researcher should be governed and should govern themselves. Modernist metanarratives legitimise the social practices of research communities who, even as they police research texts, also and at the same time, establish boundaries for the identity of the researcher, boundaries which are often grounded in the discipline of the particular community. Yet this governing of identity is not explicit in the narratives of research and researchers. Rather, there is a mirroring of the real external world in the real internal world of the researcher. In other words, in the view of research as representation – as finding out the truth of the real world "out there" – there is an implicit view of the identity of the researcher – of the real world "in there", of an authentic self governed by reason and humane values. The real world out there is posited upon and posits a real internal world. Researcher identity is centred, unified and authentic.

It is within this set of assumptions and the practices they produce that the plagiarising of research texts is constructed as a problem. Here I am using the notion of plagiarising in an unfamiliar way. Traditionally plagiarising has been used to refer to drawing upon the work of others without due reference. However, what I want to suggest is that the possibilities of simulation in the production of research texts raised by information and communication technologies result in the potential for a plagiarising of the self of the researcher. If authenticity is a primary characteristic marking the researcher, then the texts of research they produce also have to be evaluated by the criteria of authenticity and originality. If the researcher produces multiple research texts, then we have to judge which the original is and whether it is original. In an earlier period, when there was more limited production and circulation of research texts, this would have been fairly straightforward. We could have simply worked through the dates when research became available and examined the texts for references and examples of plagiarising. However, with the proliferation of research texts, their differential production schedules and with the possibility for them to be continually reworked (as, for example, with a personal home page on the Web), authenticity, origins and originality become far more problematic. Research texts may appear in a variety of forms and formats, in response to which we can continue to search for the original text or, recognising textuality and the processes of simulation, we can take disturbed pleasure in particular texts and examine their intertextual traces and graftings, placing to one side questions of authenticity and originality. On this basis, research texts can no longer claim originality, but rather are examined and enjoyed for their intertextuality and sampling. This involves a reformulation of research practices which it can be argued is actually taking place as the use of information and communications technologies problematises the policing of boundaries. However, this should not discount the modernist self-understandings that still continue to be powerful within certain research communities.

If we hold to the search for authentic texts, then there is also the constant policing of the identity of the researcher to ensure their authentic self. The multiple productions of research texts are evaluated in terms of how the researcher might be plagiarising themselves (and others) in the multiple use of certain aspects of the text. Authenticity, like meaning therefore, becomes something which is achieved through social practices, rather than something which exists to be dis/un-covered through research practices and counselling/psychotherapy.

However, if we consider the processes of simulation made possible by the proliferation of information and communications technologies, then the questions of originality and authenticity and, with that, the importance given to the notion of plagiarising fall to one side – at least in relation the self of the researcher. Here the identities of the researchers may be argued to be more open-ended, decentred, multiple, capable of generating a range of narratives about their research and themselves as researchers, traversed as they are by the many ambiguous and contradictory discourses of identity. Here, the use of "copy, cut and paste" in the construction of research texts may be considered a metaphor for the identity of the researcher, taking pleasure in the various embodiments of the self in texts and self as text rather than being concerned with questions of originality and (in)authenticity.

Troubled pleasure?

Roz Ivanič has demonstrated a consistent interest in issues of writing and identity over the years and the importance of identification to the meaningful engagement of people in literacy practices. This chapter has attempted to explore similar terrain from a different angle, focussing on the writing of research and researcher identity in the context of the use of information and communications technologies as artefacts. Whether a research community, with its concerns for boundaries, inclusions and exclusions, can live with the open-endedness of simulation is open to question. Perhaps, more importantly, given the availability of information and communications technologies, it is able to police their boundaries effectively in the face of increased challenge from various quarters is open to question and struggle. However, there can be little doubt that part of the introduction of new technologies into research practices necessitates a questioning of the assumptions underpinning those practices. For example, in this text it is possible for me to identify earlier manifestations of parts of the text which have been "copied, cut and pasted" from elsewhere. There are intertextual traces to be discerned. The trace of my ongoing collaboration with Robin Usher can also be found. The chapter itself (a file on a computer) has been subject to much "opening" and "editing" – it is no longer original. Indeed, as author, I can no longer remember what the first version of this discussion looked like.

Taking troubled pleasure in the research texts of education and making no claims to authenticity in my identity as the author of this text or its originality may appear to be unlikely conclusions (at the point of saving and quitting – for the moment). However, they are not intended as conclusions, but as textual possibilities, open to re-reading and re-writing-and even maybe further plagiarising. The use of new technologies begins to raise important issues about writing and identity in research wherein simulation and plagiarism may take on an unexpected significance. Whether Roz Ivanič would approve of this proposition is open to question. I suspect there may be some troubled pleasure and a little mirth.

References

Atkinson, P. 1996. *Sociological Readings and Re-readings*. Aldershot: Ashgate.
Atkinson, P. & Housley, W. 2003. *Interactionism*. London: Sage.
Barthes, R. 1986. *The Rustle of Language*. Oxford: Blackwell.
Baudrillard, J. 1983. *Simulations*. New York: Semiotext.
Baudrillard, J. 1996. *Selected Writings*. Cambridge: Polity Press.
Edwards, R. 2002. Mobilising lifelong learning: Governmentality and educational practices. *Journal of Education Policy* 17(3): 353–365.
Edwards, R., Nicoll, K., Solomon, N. & Usher, R. 2004. *Rhetoric and Educational Discourse*. London: Routledge.
Evans, T. and Green, B. 1995. *Dancing at a distance? Postgraduate studies, 'supervision' and distance education*. Paper presented at the Annual conference of the AARE, 26–30 November, Hobart.
Foucault, M. 1980. *Power/Knowledge*. Brighton: Harvester Press.
Game, A. 1993. *Undoing the Social*. Buckingham: Open University Press.

Gibbons, M., Limoges, C., Nowotny, H., Schwartzman, S., Scot, P. & Trow, M. 1994. *The New Production of Knowledge*. London: Sage.

Hall, S. 2000. Who needs 'identity'? In *Identity: A Reader*, P. du Gay, J. Evans & P. Redman (eds), 15–30. London: Sage.

Ivanič, R. 1998. *Writing and Identity: The Discoursal Construction of Identity in Academic Writing*. Amsterdam: John Benjamins.

Ivanič, R. 2006. Language, learning and identification. In *Language, Culture and Identity in Applied Linguistics*, R. Kiely, P. Rea-Dickens, H. Woodfield & G. Clibbon (eds), 7–29. London: Equinox.

Jewitt, C. 2005. *Technology, Literacy, Learning*. London: Routledge.

Kress, G. 2003. *Literacy in the New Media Age*. London: Routledge.

Latour, B. 1999. *Pandora's Hope: Essays on the Reality of Science Studies*. Cambridge, Mass.: Harvard University Press.

Law, J. 2001. *Ordering and obduracy*. Published by the Centre for Science Studies and the Department of Sociology, Lancaster University at http://www.comp.lancs.ac.uk/sociology/soc068jl.html (accessed 27 March 2003).

Law, J. 2002. Objects and spaces. *Theory, Culture & Society* 19(5/6): 91–105.

Lyotard, J.-F. 1984. *The Postmodern Condition*. Manchester: Manchester University Press.

McWilliam, E. 1996. Touchy subjects: A risky inquiry into pedagogic pleasure. *British Educational Research Journal* 22(3): 305–317.

McWilliam, E. & Palmer, P. 1995. Teaching tech(no)bodies: Open learning and postgraduate pedagogy. *Australian Universities Review* 38(2): 32–4.

Pels, D., Hetherington, K. & Vandenberghe, F. 2002. The status of the object: Performances, mediations, and techniques. *Theory, Culture and Society* 19(5/6): 1–21.

Plant, S. 1992. *The Most Radical Gesture*. London: Routledge.

Poster, M. (ed.). 1996. Introduction. In *J. Baudrillard: Selected Writings*, Cambridge: Polity Press.

Usher, R. 1993. From process to practice: Research, reflexivity and writing in adult education. *Studies in Continuing Education* 15(2): 98–116.

Usher, R. & Edwards, R. 1994. *Postmodernism and Education*. London: Routledge.

Usher, R. & Edwards, R. 2007. *Lifelong Learning – Signs, Discourses, Practices*. Dordrecht: Springer.

CHAPTER 4

Creativity in academic writing
Escaping from the straitjacket of genre?

Mary Hamilton and Kathy Pitt
Lancaster University

This chapter addresses issues of creativity and identity in academic writing. It links with some key themes in Roz Ivanič's work including notions of audience, purpose and the struggles with identity experienced by both new and established academic writers. We begin by outlining some of the features of academic writing processes. We then move on to discuss barriers to and possibilities for genre change in response to forces both inside and outside the academy.

Introduction

The roots of this chapter are two fold. The first (in line with the main aim of this Festschrift collection) is our experience of working within the Literacy Research Centre at Lancaster University, in the same intellectual environment as Roz Ivanič. Because of this shared experience we want to respond to her contributions to the study of writing, especially her interest in the boundaries and possibilities of academic writing. The second root is a shared interest the two of us have in issues of creativity and identity, and how these are expressed through writing and other modes of representation. We define "creativity" in relation to academic writing as the imaginative use of communicative resources, by combining these in novel ways and/or experimenting with conventions, to produce ideas that are both original and productive to the academic endeavour

We have written this chapter alongside running a series of workshops on creative academic writing for faculty colleagues at Lancaster. In the workshops we have been looking at new ways to approach our writing that depart from the dominant expectations of the academy. We offer here a reflection on some of the multiple dimensions of academic writing in the UK, and on the possibilities and processes of genre change.

One starting point, for the workshops and for this chapter is that, as Jonathan Wolff says, "reading academic writing is so often a chore and so rarely a joy" (Wolff 2007) and often perceived by readers to be boring and difficult to read. Many academic writers pay little attention to the form and style in which they present all-important findings and arguments, or to the problems that their readers might face. Others find the process difficult and constraining as they struggle to find an authoritative voice that meets the expectations of their profession. Getting work published presents further hurdles that may involve negative or contradictory comments from reviewers, extensive revision, and demands from publishers that do not fit well with the professional vision that academics bring to their work. Ivanič's work on the development of writing has, we think, been centrally concerned with these issues. She has insisted that becoming an academic writer is not a matter of study skills, but involves re-working a writing identity with all the personal struggles and rewards that attend such processes of change (see Clarke and Ivanič 1997: 94–98). In her work, Ivanič has focussed mainly on new and apprentice academic writers though she acknowledges that issues of identity are relevant to all:

> I have often had the experience myself of not being able to find the right words for what I want to write, and then realising that it is not so much a problem of the meaning I want to convey as a problem of what impression of myself I want to convey. I have come to see every act of academic writing as, among other things, the writer's struggle to create a discoursal self which resolves the tension between their autobiographical self and the possibilities for self-hood available in the academic community. (Ivanič 1998: 336)

In this chapter we extend her work, arguing, as she does above, that these issues don't fall away once individuals become fully fledged academics. The writing process itself can be a challenge, even for prolific writers, as each new piece of writing entails giving voice to new ideas or perspectives.

Despite the growing research literature on academic writing, there seems to be very little day-to-day discussion or support within the academy for the development of the professional academic as a writer, or to consideration of the reader. We have found only one or two other universities in the UK where workshops similar to our own are being run. Recruiting for our workshops was problematic as colleagues assumed they were aimed at students and thus had a remedial function despite our carefully worded publicity. In this chapter we aim to explore some of these, at times contradictory, aspects of professional academic writing, and in this way to continue Ivanič's work on writing.

In our discussions of academic writing here we, like Ivanič, theorise writing, and indeed all language use, as embedded within situated, social practices (see, for example Barton, Hamilton and Ivanič 2000; Fairclough 2003). Within this broad theory we draw on the concept of genre to explore writing as a social action that locates individual writers within specific social relations and practices. We use Fairclough's understanding of genre as the discursive dimension of conventionalised "ways of acting and interacting in the course of social events" (2003:65). Writing as a professional academic entails using written language in specific ways that are recognised and acceptable to the established networks of colleagues, superiors, publishers and editors that populate academic writing practices in the Anglo-American universities we work and write in. These recognised ways of using language are maintained or changed over time through the networks of practices they are part of. We discuss some aspects of these social dynamics in this chapter.

In the first part we explore some of the multi-faceted dimensions of current academic written genres that may inhibit creativity and present a challenge to the individual writer in Anglo-American universities. We describe how power, identity and convention can bind the writer into particular straitjackets. In the second part, conversely, we discuss some of the ways these bindings have already been broken, or stretched into new shapes.

Part 1: Writing within the strait jacket of genre

In the first section of this part we present a reflective dialogue, about our different experiences of the writing process, which emerged at an early stage of writing this chapter. Here we separate our voices for you, the reader, to reflect on shared characteristics of the writing process, and individual experiences of it. In the rest of the chapter we weave our voices together, as in most Anglo-American academic, collaborative writing.

Writing is hard work

One of the reasons that much academic writing is accused of being boring may well be because the act of writing itself is a difficult one.

Kathy: I have recently been talking with five visual artists about their creative processes, as part of a study exploring the roles of discourse in understandings of "self" and the sources of agency (Pitt 2008). In analysing their accounts I explore their frustrations and the length of time and commitment needed to produce a new piece of art work. Writing for me is a similar creative process. Producing any kind of long, coherent argument can feel like a lonely struggle, involving hours of seeming inactivity in front of a blank screen or pad of paper, searching for the right words. The professional fiction writer, Ian McEwan, voices the frustrations of this part of the process, which I also share. He says:

> I would sit without a pen in my hand, framing a sentence in my mind, often losing the beginning as I reached the end, and only when the thing was secure and complete would I set it down. I would stare at it suspiciously. Did it really say what I meant? Did it contain an error or ambiguity that I could not see? Was it making a fool of me? Hours of effort produced very little, and very little satisfaction.
> (McEwan, cited in Lillis 2006: 431)

McEwan's description here evokes in me an instant recognition of the effort involved in translating thoughts into words. From this perspective, the writing process feels like a lonely pursuit. Where is there space for creativity when it feels so hard to give voice to your thoughts and ideas through connected sets of words?

Mary: I also recognise in this the hard work involved in writing. However, this is not the whole story. My own experience is of a slow absorption into the process of writing and the world I am creating, where time is forgotten. It is the writer's side of "being lost in a book". It is dogged work, rather than painful, and it can be very lonely. I wonder whether much of the difficulty felt by professional academic writers is the lack of dedicated time to write, the constant interruptions from other tasks that makes it hard to maintain a level of creative absorption. The repeated editing to arrive at the final version is also very hard for me to cope with. I have to do it and I know when I have reached what I am aiming for but it is such a long process with little to show for it. When I was writing the *Changing Faces* book (Hamilton and Hillier 2006) I was really comforted by a Matisse painting called "The Dream" that I saw in an exhibition. It looks very simple, as if it was drawn quickly with a few deft and well-chosen strokes of the brush. You can view it on-line at a number of locations, including **www.matisse-picasso.com/artists/matimages.lasso** [Accessed 5/08]. When I read that Matisse had painted *forty-four* versions of this picture over a whole year before he was satisfied, I understood that the simplicity had been hard won. I would like to understand more about this process of simplification, of paring the meaning down to the bone.

Kathy: I, too, know the quiet sense of "rightness" that comes from the absorption of a period of writing, however halting it has been. In a poem I described this as *"replete with the temporary fullness of writing, written in a room full of morning."*

Mary: Writing *is* hard work but fiction writers (and other artists) also talk about the compulsion to write, the drive and satisfaction that keeps them involved in the task. Some talk about transcendent moments where the meaning flows, where writing is a release, is joyful. It would seem that some writers do find it generally easy to produce words, and they do it quickly and prolifically. Although writing is seen as integral to being an "academic" producer of knowledge, each individual has a unique relationship with the words that are their medium of expression.

Kathy: Yes – the visual artists I interviewed all talked about experiencing a "need" to paint or draw, and the pleasures that are part of the eventual outcomes of this process. Although I started this discussion with a gloomy picture of struggle and frustration, the other "face" of achievement and the satisfaction of creation is equally important in this process. Without these would any writer continue to produce more work in whatever genre?

In this section we have been considering academic writing as a creative process, comparing it to other creative processes. This has helped us understand and appreciate some of the difficulties that individual professional writers continue to face. Yet, once past the apprenticeship of the doctoral thesis, this fundamental part of being an academic is given little support in the academy.

Academic writing is dialogic

The discussion above presents the writer as struggling alone with the text. However, from a different perspective the writing process can be seen as one of intense interaction with others, even though the writer may be physically alone at their desk. Filling the blank space with words is only one part of the writing process, as Ivanič has analysed in detail in her work with student writers (Ivanič 1994, 1998; Ivanič, Aitchison and Weldon 1996). All the words that both novice and professional writers may use have already been used by other writers (or speakers if the writer is trying to bring in new voices or styles). The essential "resource" of all writers is language, which, as Bakhtin has explained so well, is inherently dialogic (Bakhtin 1986; Maybin 2001):

> All words have the "taste" of a profession, a genre, a tendency, a party, a particular work, a particular person, a generation, an age group, the day and hour. Each word tastes of the context and contexts in which it has lived its socially charged life. (Bakhtin 1981 cited in Maybin 2001: 68)

To produce our own written voice we all have to use words that, as Bakhtin said, have been in the mouths of others before us. Bakhtin's theories have informed much academic writing on different kinds of language use. Theresa Lillis, for example, draws on them to explore ways to help student writers work towards bringing their own diverse voices into the academic context (Lillis 2003).

Any individual who sets out to write in a particular genre has to come to terms with the dominant discourses[1] and the successful writers in their particular field. The individual writer finds her words are actually part of a collective conversation. Joining in this conversation can be daunting, even for the academic who has passed through the apprenticeship of the doctoral programme. Ian McEwan voices similar fears about the field of prose writing. In the same interview quoted in the previous section he goes on to say that his insecurity about his own words was due partly to his awareness of joining *"the great conversation of literature"*. Whilst struggling to create his own voice *"the voices of giants were rumbling over my head as I piped up to begin"* (McEwan, cited in Lillis 2006: 431). The creation of one's own "voice", we argue, is an on-going process for all writers.

In many genres, this dialogue with the voices of others is merely implicit. Academic writing such as journal articles and books, however, is usually "manifestly" dialogic, or "intertextual", because writers are expected to name and quote or summarise the words of others (see Fairclough 1992; Ivanič 1998: 47), as in this chapter and book, where the voices of other writers, such as Ivanič, are often starting points for our own. Academic writers have to synthesise these powerful voices with their own, and our writing frequently abounds with their actual words. Close reading is therefore an essential dimension of writing in academic genres. Roz Ivanič, with Romy Clark, has analysed and explained the difficulties student writers often find with this dialogue (Clark and Ivanič 1997). Having to start from what are often very powerful, already published voices, can again feel very restrictive and disempowering. Ivanič expresses the inhibiting effects of this on new academic writers:

> ...the one thing that characterises most of the writers I worked with was a sense of inferiority, a lack of confidence in themselves, a sense of powerlessness, a view of themselves as people without knowledge and hence with out authority. For some this was the legacy of a working-class background. For others, it was associated with age or gender, for all it was associated with previous failure in the education system and uncertainty as to whether they had the right to be a member of the academic community at all. (Ivanič 1998: 88)

Adding to the complexity of dialogue in academic genres is the practice of writing collaboratively, as we are doing here. Ivanič has always stressed the power of collaboratively produced texts, especially for apprentice writers, and of editing as

---

1. The concept of "discourses" refers to recognisable ways we talk about (represent) self and other practices and events from particular perspectives (see Fairclough 1992).

a dialogic process in which she herself has excelled. Co-writing is one way of sharing the load of the writing and thinking process, and of strengthening the voices of the authors, especially if they are departing from generic expectations (see Part 2). However, joining your words with those of another is not always an easy process. Like travelling companions, co-writers learn to value those precious few others with whom they can navigate this process with sensitivity and respect.

Finally, when a piece of writing has been drafted, it becomes part of another set of dialogues that are not seen by the eventual reader. Academic writing is about making claims of certain kinds, which are subject to the responses of peer reviewers and to the sedimented rules of book and journal editors. Involvement with these evaluative dialogues can be a further source of both difficulty and satisfaction. Some accounts of unequal involvement in these review processes highlight the difficulties for those academic writers who have to write in a second or additional language to break into the powerful Anglo-American writing "markets" (Lillis and Curry 2006; Lu 1994; Belcher and Connor 2001). A. Suresh Canagarajah gives us a detailed picture of this set of relations from the perspective of a writer who has had to negotiate both local and international sets of research and writing practices (Canagarajah 2002). There are, as yet, few accounts of these different, asymmetrical experiences from within the "centre" institutions (using Canagarajah's term), to add to his valuable contribution. Such power laden editing processes tend to be a hidden aspect of professional academic writing, part of custom and practice, confidential and full of sensitivities.

Academic writing involves the writer's sense of identity

Ivanič's work has shown how our writing identities are both individual and collective (Ivanič 1998: 332). The article she co-wrote with Denise Roach, for example, explores the metaphors of trying on and discarding different kinds of clothes, and of academic writing as a form of disguise, to illustrate the way new writers experiment and struggle with a variety of voices in order to find a fit for their emerging sense of authorship (Ivanič and Roach 1990).

Developing "a sense of authorship" is the way that Ivanič has expressed the centrality of identity to academic writing. This idea can be traced back to her involvement with the adult literacy student writing movement (Ivanič and Moss 1991; Gardner 1992; RaPAL 1999; Mace 1995). It has also been an important idea within the feminist and social justice movements where finding your voice through authoring your own texts, crafting new discourses and reclaiming language from majority dominant discourses have been part of cultural and political struggle (Olsen 1983; hooks 1999; Freire 1996). In these circles, developing this sense of control and authorship is seen as an essential part of becoming literate: the implication being that *writing* is central to the acquisition of literacy. Even now, within literacy education, this is a radical position since literacy is so often equated with "the right to read" rather than the "right to write" (see O'Rourke 2005; Woodin 2005).

Becoming and remaining a "writer" within any dominant genre means more than simply understanding and using the expected conventions. The commitment needed to become an author is a high risk venture, as we discuss next – especially when the intention is to voice a new or minority perspective (see Canagarajah 2002). Pamela Richards is another academic who has written about the relationship between the individual and the professional identities wrapped up in academic writing. She reflected on the nature of writing as "risk" when she was experiencing problems with writing about her own research (Richards 1986):

> It's the risk of discovering that I am incapable of doing sociology and, by extension, that I am not a sociologist and therefore not the person I claim to be. The risk of being found out and judged by colleagues is bound up with the risk of being found out and judged by myself. The two are so closely interwoven that it is often hard for me to separate them. How can you know that you are doing OK, that you are a sociologist, unless someone tells you so? It's other people's responses that enable me to understand who I am. (p. 117).

What we write is part of our professional identity: indeed writing is one of the most important products of the academic's profession. So, departing from the expected writing conventions, trying something new, is a double challenge. If it is rejected, or ignored by our colleagues, then it is not just our identity as an author but our whole academic identity and credibility, that is at risk.

Academic writing is high status

One of the central purposes of academic writing is to produce knowledge. Knowledge claims are often legitimated through an authoritative presence. Journal articles, research monographs and plenary conference presentations are examples of authoritative, centralising, powerful "secondary genres" categorised by Bakhtin in his work on genre (Bakhtin 1986; Maybin 2001). However maintaining authority is antithetical to the constant flux and change that is part of everyday language. From this perspective those trying to be creative with such genres are likely to experience protest from those who see changes to the collective authoritative academic voice as an attack on established ideas and practices, and indeed, an attack on the purposes of the genre.

Wolff (2007), in his critique of academic writing referred to earlier, singles out the dominant generic Anglo-American academic convention of giving an outline (or map) of the argument or findings at the beginning of a piece of writing. Wolff argues that this convention takes any "tension" out of the reading, making it less urgent for that reader to want to continue, and is one reason that reading anything in this domain is boring. Writers of detective novels, Wolff points out, don't puncture the suspense by saying "who did it" right at the beginning.

Wolff's use of generic conventions from another field of writing provides a useful stimulus to reflecting on academic writing. One answer to his argument is that the detective novel genre is but one of a diversity of literary genres, and there are many other, literary ways to engage the reader that academic writers might consider. There are also many ways of reading a detective novel, such as choosing to look at the end before getting there – although readers may still choose to read on if the writing and the story capture them. The journey to the end of the story is just as important in literary writing as it is in academic genres.

However, this answer sidesteps the larger issue of the intricate relations between genre conventions and the purposes of any piece of writing (Fairclough 2003). The convention of the "map" of the argument in scholarly work is wrapped up with the aim to give other academics an explicit, detailed set of arguments, research findings or critiques, in which the ideas, and the connections between them, are made as clear and unambiguous as possible. These aims are part of the purpose of knowledge making, and have evolved in the Social Sciences from longstanding and often fiercely territorial traditions of scientific practices (see Bazerman 1988, 1991; Becher and Trowler 2001). If we bring in conventions from, what some would argue, as the less important or serious literary genres, are we not debasing the purpose of the scholar to make new understandings on behalf of the rest of the population? Playing with the way knowledge claims are made can be seen as destabilising the recognised authority of academics to make knowledge, as well as risking the professional identity of the writer.

Change of a convention impacts on purpose, and thus can provoke protest. Canagarajah writes vividly about his experience of unintentionally provoking such protest when submitting his own writing crafted from an Eastern scholarly tradition:

> When a young assistant professor …used his red pen liberally and pointed out that my introduction didn't lay down the outline of my argument or announce my thesis, and that my essay started at one point and ended at another point – I was disturbed. Soon I couldn't take it any more. After carefully choosing my words, I met him in his office to tell him that my strategy of developing an argument had a different logic all its own. I chose the terms inductive and deductive to articulate the difference.
> (Canagarajah 2001: 30)

Canagarajah goes on to explain how it took a lot of argument to get his professor to accept and understand this different logic in its own right instead of trying to change the writing to meet a different set of "high status" expectations.

Part 2: Social change: Loosening the straitjacket of genre?

Despite what we have called the "straitjacket" of genre and the dominance of powerful voices and identities, academic writing, like all genres and discourses, is not an impregnable fortress standing outside social processes. As we will discuss in this section, academic readers and writers have changed over the last decades, as has the value placed on research and practice. These changes have pushed the boundaries of academic genres and have occurred because of forces both inside and outside the academy. We can turn again to Bakhtin's theory that centralising, authoritative genres are always being challenged by the inherent variety of language use, which itself arises from the vast diversity of human beings, and from our social practices.

The changes that have occurred within academic writing in the "West" in the second half of the twentieth century reflect and are part of wider struggles, including reconfigurations of nation, class and gender. As has been widely noted by social theorists, this has been a period of instability and change. Labels such as "late modernity", "post-modernity" and "globalisation" signal attempts to map some of these changes (Chouliraki and Fairclough 1999; Giddens 1991; Graddol 2006). Gunther Kress, who has contributed greatly to the development of understandings of genre, points out that the *"changeability and fluidity of genres"* is one indicator of periods of social change, because genre features arise from the social structures and contexts they are written in (Kress 2000: 5). We discuss some of these changes relevant to academic writing here, and consider how they may open up space for creativity.

Democratisation of the academy in a mass HE system

The growth of mass higher education systems in the west has led to the development of access studies, opening the academy to a greater diversity of people (see Fuller 2001) who have challenged existing academic writing conventions. This challenge, in turn, has opened up new possibilities for the "democratisation" of academic genres. The sociologist Howard Becker's critique of conventionalised academic writing gives an account of a lengthy discussion with a student, Rosanna, about her writing. He described it as *"very wordy and academic"* (Becker

1986a: 27). Rosanna defended this style as *"classier"* than the everyday language and direct style Becker was proposing, reflecting that

> … it is a way to… maintain group boundaries of elitism. ….. Ideas are supposed to be written in such a fashion that they are difficult for untrained people to understand. This is scholarly writing. And if you want to be a scholar you need to learn to reproduce this way of writing. (p. 30).

Rosanna's argument about elitism takes us back to our earlier discussions of identity and authority, and how they are bound up with genre and discourse. For Rosanna a formal prose style, long sentences full of clauses, and the use of technical terms, legitimate the academic writer's claims to knowledge. To bring in the language used in less formal, possibly less hierarchical genres may seem to threaten this legitimacy (however, see Lu (1994) and Vilanueva (1993) for different perspectives on this issue of style).

Nevertheless, as the academic "elite" has expanded and changed, the increased diversity of writers has made an impact on writing style in at least some disciplines. Two writers we enjoy: Howard Becker (1986b) and Donna Haraway (1991) combine vivid everyday words and phrases alongside conventions of rigour and explicitness. They do this in different ways. Haraway blends the "conventional" complex sentence and use of technical terms with a short, informal more spoken style of sentence. Here is an example from a discussion about gender and objectivity:

> We unmasked the doctrines of objectivity because they threatened our budding sense of collective historical subjectivity and agency and our "embodied" accounts of the truth, and we ended up with one more excuse for not learning any post-Newtonian physics and one more reason to drop the old feminist self-help practices of repairing our own cars. They're just texts anyway, so let the boys have them back. (Haraway 1991: 186)

Becker often brings in carefully constructed descriptive detail to his theoretical discussions, which would not be out of place in a novel. For example, he starts off a chapter that aims to define "culture" with a paragraph describing "Saturday night musicians" in Chicago:

> When we arrived at work we would introduce ourselves – the chances were, in a city the size of Chicago (where I did much of my playing), that we were in fact strangers – and see whom we knew in common and whether our paths had ever crossed before. The drummer would assemble his drums, the others would put together their instruments and tune up, and when it was time to start the leader would announce the name of a song and a key – "Exactly Like You" in B-flat, for instance – and we would begin to play. (Becker 1986b: 12)

He then uses this narrative as an example of the conception of "culture" that he was putting forward in this chapter. His sentences are long but easy to read as they flow in a more linear, spoken style.

Increased interdisciplinarity has been a further pressure for change, as disciplinary conventions come into dialogue (and sometimes conflict) with one another. New areas of enquiry like women's studies are good examples of this, where encounters and translations across disciplines have been very productive. The Literacy research that we, and Roz Ivanič, are engaged in, is a further example, as linguists, ethnographers, sociologists, historians and educators have come together to produce new perspectives on written language for new audiences. Here again we see deep connections between purpose, theory and genre conventions.

In the Social Sciences, debates about subjectivity and truth claims have also impacted on genres. Post-modern theories have challenged the conventional objective representation of knowledge, as have arguments about the roles of the theorist and researcher being integral parts of the social worlds they explore. The writer has gradually become visible through the the use of "I" and through a consciously distinctive voice. These shifts open up choices for writers, potentially reducing the distance between academic writer and reader.

As our perspectives on knowledge have shifted, so have some of the ways we construct this knowledge through writing. Academic writers are now much more aware that they are crafting an account that might legitimately be challenged and re-interpreted. The implications of this have been especially well developed in anthropology, a discipline that is built on the project, and challenge, of representing unfamiliar cultures. See for example Clifford and Marcus (1986) and Marjery Wolf's experimental "thrice told tale" where she offers three written versions of the same research study using different theoretical frameworks (Wolf 1992).

This "post-modern" awareness of the contingency of academic accounts and the power relations that underlie their claims to authority has been accompanied by debates, across a range of disciplines, about praxis, the link between research and practice, and between academic and everyday knowledges. In education and other social policy areas such as medical and social work, these debates have been expressed through ideas of practitioner research (PR). The degree to which practitioners are accepted as valid "knowledge makers" is contested and difficult to negotiate because it confronts the power relations of the academy very directly (Cochran-Smith and Lytle 2004; Eraut 1994; Erickson and Gutierrez 2002). Practitioners' accounts are often deemed to be unscientific and to violate the boundaries of academic writing because the knowledge claims they make tend to refer to professional rather than academic contexts, and are concerned with relevance to local conditions rather than universal principles. PR aims for different audiences and questions the relationship between theory and action and how professionals use evidence in making practical decisions.

New writers and readers contribute to change

Changes in the perceived status and role of the academy mean that the audiences for academic writing have changed and that new writers are clamouring to be considered. Policy-makers, research funders, and research practitioners, questioning why academic writing is as it is, demand accessible accounts of findings and short, quickly digestible summaries. They put strong pressures on academic writers asking, "what works?" (see Moss and Huxford 2007). While their reasons differ, they are often critiquing the same features of academic genres as those from within the academy, such as Becker, and Wolff.

Individual's responses to these demands will vary. Each writer synthesises the collective discourses to make their own "voice", which they put back into the discourse collective. Their voices become stronger as they gain power to challenge the gatekeepers. However, approaching claims-making by challenging conventionalised patterns of organisation, or by using informal language, may well get accusations of "dumbing down" from powerful gatekeepers, such as journal editors and publishers (see Haggis 2006).

A new writer has to work hard to gain entry into the publishing field and has little power to argue for new ways of writing, but those who have gained a reputation and a guaranteed audience have more clout and can dictate their terms more easily. If students, especially those from non-traditional backgrounds, are supported to become professional academics then this dialogue with diversity continues. As such writers gain experience and recognition, they, too, can seize opportunities to write differently.

New spaces to publish and communicate findings in different ways

Whilst the elite boundaries of the academy are being challenged, as we have briefly discussed above, there is still work to be done to explore notions of audience and purpose (see for example Ivanič and Weldon 1999). Ivanič has always encouraged academic writers to think more about the reader; for example, her interest in the parallels between written and visual culture has led her to ask why they are not more drawn on in theory and research work (see Ivanič 1998: 2–4). She herself has included visual representations and pursued metaphors through her work with the Research and Practice in Adult Literacy journal (RaPAL), and with mature student writers (see for example, Roach 1990).

We need more discussion about the difficult and contradictory choices writers have to make. The highest status outlets (rewarded by promotion and other forms of academic recognition) are also the most specialist and elite and unlikely to reach a wide audience or to be taken notice of by policy or practice. Publishers of these journals and books are themselves strong gatekeepers of layout, title and presentation. On the other hand, the academic "populariser" is still treated as suspect in the academy – pursued by the media and incorporated into their own agendas. Such contradictions result from diverse challenges to the ownership of knowledge making. Although the academy is being opened up through some of the wider changes referred to here, social change is gradual, and can be fragmented, as those invested in current power relations attempt to maintain them.

For the new writer, the stakes of entering the public debate are very high and spaces where new writers can flex their muscles are few. There are, though, efforts to develop "hybrid" journals and conference formats that retain scholarly rigour and peer review, whilst being more accessible to the wider worlds of policy, practice and the general public. Ivanič has supported such efforts through RaPAL which publishes practitioner research, student and other first time writers (for example see Ivanič and Simpson, Issue 6 1988; Ivanič, Aitchison and Weldon 1996 Issue 28/29).

Most conventional academic writing goes down the black hole of elite journals and conferences. However, as Ivanič has always argued, research can be communicated through a range of different formats adapted for different audiences. One size will not fit all. New conference formats, such as poster displays; new media such as videos, installations, DVDs, blogs, offer new spaces to stretch and change academic genres. Writing that makes knowledge claims can learn from these pioneering forms. These new media offer greater interaction and opportunities for creativity, as we will discuss in the next section.

The challenge of new technologies

The introduction of multi-modal, interactive, digital technologies is having a profound effect on the forms and functions of literacy, including genre change. To be reading and writing on the web is to be interacting in an environment where complex layers of meaning are signalled through layout, images, sound and animation as well as through text itself. The ways in which connections are made between people, ideas, and information, are free from the sequential ordering that printed books impose on writers and readers. A recent research example is a book by Grossman and O'Brien (2007) that documents experiences of migration. It is sold as an illustrated book with a DVD containing sound files, videos and scanned images to be viewed alongside the text in the book. Such packages change the experience of presenting, and of "reading" research data. Communication through email, msm and text messaging has led to the invention of new writing conventions because these media occupy ambiguous and unsettled spaces that are sometimes more like oral communication, sometimes more like formal writing. The shape and potential of these new digital literacies are being explored by many researchers such as Kress (2003) and Snyder (2002). Carey Jewitt has carried out detailed ethnographic work in schools, looking at multi-modality in science and English classrooms (see Jewitt 2007). These multimodal writers will become the next generation of academic writers.

Research in these areas is going on inside higher education itself, especially through e-learning courses where the conventions of academic writing are shifting too (Lea 2001). As an example, Theresa Dobson has shown how the efforts of creative writers to break out of sequential text can be identified and mirrored in a hyper-text environment. She uses stories like those of the author Alice Munro, which move back and forward in time with a complex multi-layered narrative structure. Dobson teaches students how to work on a collaborative critique, gradually building up a common text, as happens in Wikipedia, where each person can see earlier contributions and change and add to these (Dobson 2006).

Implicit in these explorations of multi-modality is the assumption that we use many senses to make meaning and that the traditional focus on written texts for assessment in education distorts and disadvantages many of us. Kress, in particular argues that the digital age is privileging images for the first time in history (Kress 2000). Ivanič has demonstrated through her work on the development of children's projects (Ormerod and Ivanič 2002) how young children initially integrate many different modes of representation in the texts they produce, but over time the images fall away, the texts become more conventional in terms of layout, sequence and linguistic form as the text-focussed practices of schooling take over. Children (and adults) outside school practices, however, do not show the same constraints, moreover immersion in new digital worlds is now pushing hard against the old conventions (see Ivanič and Satchwell 2008). These changes in semiotic practices are becoming increasingly part of everyday practices and offer exciting opportunities for academic writers to continue to expand and change contemporary academic writing.

Conclusion

A deeper understanding of the complex relations between genre and purpose helps us appreciate the real limits to creative approaches in any one genre. Exploring other written genres to get ideas for experimenting is important and fruitful: at the same time, it can make us aware of the intricate connections all genres have with the social practices they are embedded within, and with social change. Challenging the accepted conventions of a dominant genre means challenging its very purposes. This cannot be done lightly, nor can it be done without a power base. But these challenges are integral to the whole project of knowledge making. They are deep in the soul of the scholar seeking to expand and to move on knowledge about ourselves and our worlds. So, change and creativity are also part of academic social practice, and the genres are constantly evolving. As Ivanič says:

> [a]lthough each person's configuration of alignments is unique, people are not isolated individuals……..what seem like individual acts of identification can build up gradually to large scale social change, in for example, views of knowledge or representations of gender. (Ivanič 1998: 332)

We have used the metaphor of a straitjacket to convey our understandings and feelings about the particular set of genres we are part of; that this book is part of. This metaphor accentuates the negative aspects of powerful genres that seek to centralise and perhaps stifle individual voices. But new approaches to writing will still have to pay careful attention to the social purposes of their texts. What this metaphor does not do is convey the attractive and practical aspects of such genres. Stability, recognition, authority and professional identity are all important dimensions of familiar, taken for granted ways of high status writing. In what other ways can we persuade the reader that our knowledge claims are valid if we ditch the easily recognisable forms of academic writing that make up this 'straitjacket'? The metaphor, therefore, has its limitations and we invite you, our readers, to think of your own.

References

Bakhtin, M. 1986. *Speech Genres and Other Late Essays*. Austin TX: Texas University Press.
Barton, D, Hamilton, M. & Ivanič, R. 2000. *Situated Literacies: Reading and writing in context*. London: Routledge.
Bazerman, C. 1988. *Shaping Written Knowledge: The genre and activity of the experimental article in science*. Madison WI: University of Wisconsin Press.
Bazerman, C. 1991. *Textual Dynamics of the Professions: Historical and contemporary studies of writing in professional communities*. Madison WI: University of Wisconsin Press.
Becher, T. & Trowler, P. R. 2001. *Academic Tribes and Territories: Intellectual enquiry and the cultures of disciplines*. Milton Keynes: Open University Press.
Becker, H. 1986a. *Writing for Social Scientists*. Chicago IL: University of Chicago Press.

Becker, H. 1986b. *Doing Things Together: Selected papers*. Evanston IL: Northwestern University Press.
Belcher, D. & Connor, U. (eds). 2001. *Reflections on Multiliterate Lives*. Clevedon: Multilingual Matters.
Canagarajah, A. S. 2001. The fortunate traveller: Shuttling between communities and literacies by economy class. *In Reflections on Multiliterate Lives*, D. Belcher & U. Connor (eds), 23–37. Clevedon: Multilingual Matters.
Canagarajah, A. S. 2002. *A Geopolitics of Academic Writing*. Pittsburgh PA: University of Pittsburgh Press.
Chouliaraki, L. & Fairclough, N. 1999. *Discourse in Late Modernity: Rethinking critical discourse analysis*. Edinburgh: EUP.
Clark, R. & Ivanič, R. 1997. *The Politics of Writing*. London: Routledge.
Clifford, J. & Marcus, G. 1986. *Writing Culture: The poetics and politics of ethnography*. Berkeley CA: California University Press.
Cochran-Smith, M. & Lytle, S. 2004. Practitioner inquiry, knowledge and university culture. In *International Handbook of Self-Study of Teaching and Teacher Education Practices* [Kluwer International Handbooks of Education Vol 12], J. Loughran, M. L. Hamilton, V. L. LaBoskey & T. Russell (eds), 601–649. Dordrecht: Kluwer.
Dobson, T. M. 2006. For the love of a good narrative: Digitality and textuality. *English Teaching: Practice and critique* 5(2): 56–68.
Eraut, M. 1994. *Developing Professional Knowledge and Competence*. London: Falmer Press.
Erickson, F. & Gutierrez, K. 2002. Culture, rigor and science in educational research. *Educational Researcher* 31(8): 22–24.
Fairclough, N. 1992. *Discourse and Social Change*. Cambridge: Polity Press.
Fairclough, N. 2003. *Analysing Discourse: Textual analysis for social research*. London: Routledge.
Freire, P. 1996. *Pedagogy of the Oppressed*, 2nd edn. London: Penguin Education.
Fuller, A. 2001. Credentialism, adults and part-time higher education in the United Kingdom: An account of rising take up and some implications for policy. *Journal of Education Policy* 16(3): 233–348.
Gardner, S. 1992. The Long Word Club. The development of written language within adult Fresh Start and Return to Learning programmes. *Research and Practice in Adult Literacy*.
Giddens, A. 1991. *Modernity and Self-Identity: Self and society in the late modern age*. Cambridge: Polity Press.
Graddol, D. 2006. *English Next. Why global English may mean the end of 'English as a Foreign Language'*. London: The British Council.
Grossman, A. & O'Brien, A. 2007. *Projecting Migration: Transcultural documentary practice*. Columbia: Wallflower Press.
Haggis, T. 2006. Pedagogies for diversity: Retaining critical challenge amidst fears of 'dumbing down'. *Studies in Higher Education* 31(5): 521–535.
Hamilton, M. & Hillier, Y. 2006. *Changing Faces of Adult Literacy, Language and Numeracy: A critical history*. Stoke-on-Trent: Trentham Books.
Haraway, D. 1991. *Simians, Cyborgs and Women: The reinvention of nature*, reprint edn. London: Free Association Books.
hooks, bell. 1999. *Remembered Rapture: The writer at work*. London: The Women's Press.
Ivanič, R. 1994. I is for interpersonal: Discoursal construction of writer identities and the teaching of writing. *Linguistics and Education* 6(1): 3–15.

Ivanič, R 1998. *Writing and Identity: The discoursal construction of identity in academic writing*. Amsterdam: John Benjamins.
Ivanič, R. Aitchison, M. & Weldon, S. 1995. Bringing ourselves into our writing. *Research and Practice in Adult Literacy* 28/29.
Ivanič, R. & Moss, W. 1991. Bringing community writing practices into education. In *Writing in the Community*, D. Barton & R. Ivanič (eds), 193–223. Newbury Park CA: Sage.
Ivanič, R. & Roach, D. 1990. Academic writing, power and disguise in language and power. In *Selected Proceedings of the BAAL Annual Meeting Sept 1989*, R. Clark, N. Fairclough, R. Ivanič, R. McLeod, J. Thomas & P. Meara (eds), London: Centre for Information on Language Teaching and Research.
Ivanič, R. & Satchwell, C. 2007. Boundary crossings: Networking and transforming literacies in research processes and college courses. *The Journal of Applied Linguistics* 4(2): 101–124.
Ivanič, R. & Simpson, J. 1988. Clearing away the debris: Learning and researching academic writing. *Research and Practice in Adult Literacy* 6.
Ivanič, R. & Weldon, S. 1999. Researching the writer-reader relationship. In *Writing: Texts, processes and practices*, C. Candlin & K. Hyland (eds.), 168–192. London: Addison Wesley Longman.
Jewitt, C. 2007. A multimodal perspective on textuality and contexts. *Pedagogy, Culture and Society* 15(3): 275–289.
Kress, G. 2000. The futures of literacy. *Research and Practice in Adult Literacy* 42.
Kress, G. 2003. *Literacy in the New Media Age*. London: Routledge.
Lea, M. 2001. Computer conferencing and assessment: New ways of writing in higher education. *Studies in Higher Education* 26(2): 163–181.
Lillis, T. 2003. An 'academic literacies' approach to student writing in higher education: Drawing on Bakhtin to move from 'critique' to 'design'. *Language and Education* 17(3): 192–207.
Lillis, T. 2006. Readers and writers. In *The Art of English Literary Creativity*, S. Goodman & K. O'Halloran (eds). Basingstoke: Palgrave Macmillan.
Lillis, T. & Curry, M. J. 2006. Professional academic writing by multilingual scholars: Interactions with literacy brokers in the production of English medium texts. *Written Communication* 23(1): 3–35.
Lu, M. 1994. Professing multiculturalism: The politics of style in the contact zone. *College Composition and Communication* 45(4): 442–458.
Mace, J. (ed.). 1995. *Literacy, Language and Community Publishing: Essays in adult education*. Multilingual Matters.
Maybin, J. 2001. Language, struggle and voice: The Bakhtin/Volosinov writings. In *Discourse Theory and Practice: A reader*, M. Wetherell, S. Taylor & S. J. Yates (eds), 64–71. London: Sage.
Maybin, J. & Swann, J. (eds). 2006. *The Art of English: Everyday creativity*. Basingstoke: Palgrave Macmillan.
Moss, G. & Huxford, L. 2007. Exploring literacy policy from the inside out. In *Educational Research and Policy-making*, L. Saunders (ed). London: Routledge.
Olsen, T. 1980. *Silences*. London: Virago Press.
Ormerod F. & Ivanič, R. 2002. Materiality in children's meaning-making practices. *Visual Communication* 1(1): 65–91.
O'Rourke, R. 2005. *Creative Writing: Education, culture and community*. Leicester: National Institute of Adult Continuing Education (NIACE).

Pitt, K. 2008. *Sourcing the Self: Debating the relations between language and consciousness.* Frankfurt: Peter Lang.
RaPAL. 1999. Special Issue on the Student Writing Movement. *Research and Practice in Adult Literacy* 40, Lancaster University.
Richards, P. 1986. Risk. In *Writing for Social Scientists*, H. Becker (ed.), 108–120. Chicago IL: The University of Chicago Press.
Roach, D. 1990. Marathon. (S. Padmore, illus.). *Research and Practice in Adult Literacy Bulletin* 11: 5–7.
Snyder, I. 2002. *Silicon Literacies: Communication, Innovation and education in the electronic age*. London: Routledge.
Villanueva, V. 1993. *Bootstraps. From an american academic of color*. Urbana IL: NCTE.
Wolf, M. 1992. *A Thrice-Told Tale: Feminism, postmodernism, and ethnographic responsibility*. Stanford CA: Stanford University Press.
Wolff, J. 2007. Literary boredom: Academics love a dull read. *The Guardian* 4 September.
Woodin, T. 2005. Building culture from the bottom-up: The educational origins of the FWWCP. *History of Education* 34(4 July): 5–63.

REFLECTION 3

Overcoming barriers

Min-Zhan Lu and Bruce Horner
Bingham Humanities, Louisville University

For many years we knew Roz Ivanič exclusively through her writings. It is readily acknowledged, by any measure, that these have profoundly shaped scholarship on the teaching of writing. Her close attention to students and their writing and the complexity of identity formulated in writing distinguishes her work and makes it exemplary. Her work is also distinguished by her ability to translate "dense" theoretical notions into language that can be used in day-to-day exchanges in classrooms and writing centres, language that students can use to figure out how and why they are experiencing difficulties and how to address them when revising their writing. What is perhaps less visible, and therefore perhaps less recognised, is that these characteristics of her work carry over from her writing to her non-print exchanges with others. We take this opportunity to highlight our experience of that.

Several years ago, we asked Roz to participate in a panel for the U.S. Conference on College Composition and Communication, to be held in San Francisco. She agreed, the appropriate proposal forms were exchanged, the proposal for our panel was accepted, and we looked forward to the ordinary exchange of ideas conferences make possible – the reading of papers, some questions, and some discussion. And all of this did happen, as we expected and hoped. However, at this conference, to support an ongoing strike by hotel workers' unions, the conference organisers had hastily moved the conference from a hotel being picketed to a location where concurrent sessions were held in a large hall divided into approximately 30 x 30 foot squares by thin canvas sheets that made it all but impossible for a particular session's audience, and even panel members, to distinguish what was being said in one panel from the cacophony of what was being said in adjacent sessions.

Not surprisingly, the panel itself – "Writing and Being Written: How Literacy Practices, Genres and Discourses Construct Identities" – would not have been imaginable without Roz's work. And it was clear that most of those attending the session had come to hear her speak. It might be expected that a scholar of her standing would be disturbed by the conditions in which she was being asked to present her ideas. But in fact, she gave her talk as if the conditions were no barrier at all, and she listened attentively to catch what other panel members were saying and answer the many questions posed to her in the discussion period following the presentations.

In light of the time difference between San Francisco and Lancaster, and the heavy lifting involved in delivering her presentation, we expected that she would call it a night. However, as we later discovered, Roz spent the rest of the afternoon and evening talking (and then dining as well) with a number of our graduate students to discuss her work and theirs. We hadn't asked her to do this: she did it on her own. Subsequently, our students regularly referred to the insights they gained from that conversation when working with us to develop their seminar papers and dissertations.

In "Writing and Identity", Roz states that writing is "a socio-political act of identification in which people are constructed by the discoursal resources on which they are drawing, construct their own 'discoursal identity' in relation to their immediate social context, and contribute to constructing a new configuration of discoursal resources for the future" (p. 345). The same is true of non-written discourse as well. Out of the immediate social context of the San Francisco conference and the discoursal resources available to her, Roz contributed to the construction of a discoursal identity as a deeply committed and engaged as well as an insightful writing scholar and teacher that, in conjunction with her writings, is a resource on which we, and our students have drawn to enrich our own work as scholars and teachers.

Reference

Ivanič, R. 1998. *Writing and Identity: The discoursal construction of identity in academic writing.* Amsterdam: John Benjamins.

PART II

Pedagogy

REFLECTION 4

Writing pictures, painting stories with Roz Ivanič

Denny Taylor
Hofstra University, New York

Roz Ivanič might be surprised to know what a remarkable influence she has had upon my life and work. She shifted my positionality and made me see a little differently. In 1998 I attended a meeting of the Literacy Research Group at the University of Lancaster and stayed with Roz and her family. Her husband, Milan, is a painter and his paintings were in every room. Piles of books and papers that had spilled over from Roz's office at the university into her home were mixed with the paintings creating still lifes that it would have been interesting to photograph or draw. I would have been quite content that weekend to read some of Roz's books and contemplate Milan's paintings. It is an extraordinary physical space that made me want to touch and to hold things as well as to think.

At the university faculty, staff and students met to present and discuss the research projects that would eventually be published in *Situated Literacies*, which is edited by David Barton, Mary Hamilton and Roz. I wrote a Foreword to the book in which there is a narrative description of the meeting and I have gone back to it this morning as I write this piece about Roz. It's there on the page, the questions she asked about symmetry and power relationships and social responsibility. These are my questions too, but there were many people speaking and many provocative issues to contemplate before Roz brought me back to the questions she had raised at the beginning of the meeting. With Fiona Ormerod, Roz spoke of the longitudinal study of eight to eleven year old children and the texts they constructed. I wrote in the Foreword, "They have a child's project with them and they talk about the importance of viewing the project as a text which is a material object with distinct physical features. They discuss ways in which texts themselves reveal physically and textually the tools that were used to create them, and the decisions that were made in their construction" (xii–xiii).

I left that weekend thinking about symmetry and power and the materiality of the children's projects and the physicality of Milan's paintings which to me seemed like aesthetic texts. The following summer I developed a course called

"Writing Pictures Painting Stories" which both directly and indirectly focuses on issues of symmetry, power relationships and social responsibility. It is a literacy course that takes place literally in a studio and metaphorically in the interface between functional and aesthetic texts. We focus on illustration as visual story, photography as visual poetry, writing as an art form, lettering as design, and the physicality of written language systems. Our task is to learn more about the ways in which tools and materials influence composition and the production of texts as mindful social practice. We explore the inseparability of reason and emotion, and the ways in which knowledge is inseparable from social practice. And we then read the chapter in *Situated Literacies*, "Texts in practice: Interpreting the physical characteristics of children's project work," that Roz and Fiona wrote. Among the quotes we discuss the following:

- By viewing a text not just as a form of visual and verbal representation, but also as a material object with distinct physical features, we can locate the meanings it is conveying within the physical, technological and social practices associated with its construction [p. 91].
- We see the specific activities ... as instantiations of culturally recognisable and historically situated practices, embedded in broad patterns of social change [p. 91].
- The project as an artifact is very important, in our view, since it embodies, in textual and material form, the whole complex constellation of decisions, actions, feelings, beliefs and processes concerned with focusing on investigating, studying, engaging with and re-presenting the chosen topic [p. 92].
- Each page reveals traces of many different moments in the life of the project, drawing us in and leading us to ask further questions about the surrounding context, and the actors, actions and decisions involved [p. 92].
- Literacy artifacts carry traces of literacy practices associated with their production and life experience so far and their anticipated future use [p. 96].
- Physical characteristics can work, together with the visual, to provide evidence of the ways in which different tools and materials are used in the inscription of words, drawings and other graphic elements [pp. 97–98].
- Physical characteristics reflect attitudes, beliefs and approaches. .... [P]ractices and beliefs are rooted in experience ... the processes are not static, but constantly changing, both in the lives of the individuals and as cultural resources ... [reflecting the] culturally and historically situated values surrounding the production and use of texts [pp. 105–106]

Hundreds of teachers have participated in the studio course and the activities in which they participate have become the basis of many of the activities in which they participate with the children in their classes. Up front our discussions are of symmetry, power relationships and social responsibility. These are not easy conversations for teachers in US schools. Some classroom teachers talk of third grade children who have never held a paintbrush. Others speak of the children in their classes who are not willing to risk drawing because they are usually only allowed to write between the lines information that is copied from the board or is provided for them on a workbook page. Most teacher say illustrations in written texts are not valued. There is no room for creativity, no opportunity to play with writing as something beautiful that connects us with our histories and with our everyday lives. Most teachers concentrate on the tests and recount the experiences of children who cry in class, sleep walk and bed wet. Negotiating a space in which children's projects can take place sometimes causes difficulties and on one occasion a teacher, who is also a doctoral student, was "written up" by the principal for encouraging the seven year old children to draw pictures of themselves on their first day in her second grade class.

In the "Writing Pictures Painting Stories" course there are always traces of the questions that Roz asked and substantiations of the research she conducted with Fiona on children's projects. In the course we play with hieroglyphs and alphabets; iconic and alphabetic writing. We participate in scavenger hunts for fonts. We take our work out into schools and children study different writing systems and write in Chinese, Japanese, Arabic, Hebrew, and Greek. The children are encouraged to create their own writing systems and they are invited to come and participate in projects with our class. When Emma, who is Japanese American, was five she showed us how to write in multiple writing systems, while Ricky, her baby brother, introduced us to the writing of circles and lines.

Each summer when we hold the class we talk about sociocultural knowledge, emotion and embodied meaning, the manipulation of materials in time and space, kids making things when they play, and all the time, through the conversation, Roz continues to reach the teachers who speak. In 2001 the work of the class was published in an edition of *School Talk* that is published by NCTE. Many thousands of copies were mailed to US teachers and, in turn, I have no doubt that at least some of these teachers introduced activities that are based on Roz's research and writing with the children in their classes.

Reference

Ormerod, F. & Ivanič, R. 2000. Texts in Practices: Interpreting the Physical Characteristics of Children's Project Work. In *Situated Literacies: Reading and Writing in Context*, D. Barton, M. Hamilton & R. Ivanič (eds), 91–107. London: Routledge.

CHAPTER 5

Discourses of learning and teaching
A dyslexic child learning to write

Awena Carter
Lancaster University

In her (2004) framework Ivanič identifies six possible discourses of writing and learning to write. I use this framework as a heuristic to examine the genesis of a story written by one of my dyslexic primary school pupils, alongside my own journey from practitioner to researcher. The analysis uncovers the way in which I constructed conflicting identities in order to inhabit conflicting discourses of writing and learning to write. I show how I moved freely among them, and I build on Ivanič's framework of the socially available possibilities for self hood (Clark and Ivanič 1997) in order to explain how this was possible.

An Introduction to the life of the mind

Roz Ivanič was my PhD supervisor. When I first met her I was a peripatetic dyslexia specialist, working with primary school children who had Statements of Special Educational Needs for Specific Learning Difficulties (Dyslexia).[1] I came to her with one over-arching research question which was, "How do the children I teach develop literacy?" Patiently Roz guided me away from the stance of an enthusiastic teacher apt to exclaim, "Didn't they do well?" towards the stance of a researcher who was able to ask, "What is going on here?"; in this chapter I trace part of this journey. It was thrilling to receive my doctorate but I sorely missed (and still do) the stimulation of supervisions with Roz: her excitement in my work and the rigour with which she viewed it. I would leave many supervisions, mentally tired to the state of exhaustion, but always fired to continue because she had

---

1. A Statement of Special Educational Needs is a legal document which is the result of a five-stage process of assessment. When these data were collected statemented children in main stream primary schools were usually assigned a specialist teacher who taught them individually for about two or three hours a week.

made me feel that I could uncover yet more exciting things in my data. What I am most grateful to Roz for is this introduction to the life of the mind.

An introduction to possible discourses of writing and learning to write

In 2004 Ivanič published her framework of the possible discourses of writing and learning to write, reproduced here as Figure 5.1. I am going to use this framework to analyse a page of writing by one of my pupils, Chris; but before I introduce him and his work, I am going to introduce the framework. Ivanič (2004: 224) explains that it is the result of "[working] over a number of years…to and fro between evidence of pedagogical practices, evidence of beliefs, and theories of language and literacy."

The framework is a matrix which brings together and clarifies different, and sometimes conflicting, theoretical and practical notions of: *beliefs about writing; beliefs about learning to write; approaches to the teaching of writing;* and *assessment criteria*. A central concept in the framework is Ivanič's model of the multi-layered nature of language (reproduced as Figure 5.2). In this model, the text is seen as successively embedded in the writer's cognitive processes, the literacy event in which he (and perhaps others) produce it, and the socio-political context which the writer(s) inhabit.[2] The second column in the framework headed, "Layer in the Comprehensive view of Language" refers to this multi-layered view of language. Reading along the rows of the matrix from this column has the effect of identifying relationships between beliefs, approaches and evaluations. These relationships are even more clearly defined by reading along the rows from the extreme left hand column, which is headed *discourses*. Here, Ivanič identifies her six possible discourses of writing and learning to write. As well as mapping horizontally onto theoretical and pedagogical notions, this *naming* of the different discourses has several effects: it compacts the ideas within the discourse, making it easy for the reader to relate to the notions onto which they map; it reveals the socio-cultural attitudes and values in which related theoretical and pedagogical ideas are embedded; and frees the reader to draw together and to reflect on related ideas within her own experience.

---

2. In this chapter I usually refer to adults as "she" and children as "he" to avoid the clumsiness of he/she, (s)he and other ways of avoiding using only one gender to describe every one. Of course, in referring to actual people I use their actual genders.

Discourses of learning and teaching 91

DISCOURSES	LAYER IN THE COMPREHENSIVE VIEW OF LANGUAGE	BELIEFS ABOUT WRITING	BELIEFS ABOUT LEARNING TO WRITE	APPROACHES TO THE TEACHING OF WRITING	ASSESSMENT CRITERIA
A SKILLS DISCOURSE	THE WRITTEN TEXT	Writing consists of applying knowledge of sound-symbol relationships and syntactic patterns to construct a text.	Learning to write involves learning sound-symbol relationships and syntactic patterns.	SKILLS APPROACHES *Explicit teaching* 'phonics'	accuracy
A CREATIVITY DISCOURSE	THE MENTAL PROCESSES OF WRITING	Writing is the product of the author's creativity.	You learn to write by writing on topics which interest you.	CREATIVE SELF-EXPRESSION *Implicit teaching* 'whole language' 'language experience'	interesting content and style
A PROCESS DISCOURSE		Writing consists of composing processes in the writer's mind, and their practical realization.	Learning to write includes learning both the mental processes and the practical processes involved in composing a text.	THE PROCESS APPROACH *Explicit teaching*	?
A GENRE DISCOURSE	THE WRITING EVENT	Writing is a set of text-types, shaped by social context.	Learning to write involves learning the characteristics of different types of writing which serve specific purposes in specific contexts.	THE GENRE APPROACH *Explicit teaching*	appropriacy
A SOCIAL PRACTICES DISCOURSE		Writing is purpose-driven communication in a social context.	You learn to write by writing in real-life contexts, with real purposes for writing.	FUNCTIONAL APPROACHES *Explicit teaching* PURPOSEFUL COMMUNICATION *Implicit teaching* 'communicative language teaching' LEARNERS AS ETHNOGRAPHERS *Learning from research*	effectiveness
THE SOCIO-POLITICAL DISCOURSE	THE SOCIO-POLITICAL CONTEXT OF WRITING	Writing is a socio-politically constructed practice and has consequences for identity, and is open to contestation and change.	Learning to write includes understanding why different types of writing are the way they are, and taking a position among alternatives.	CRITICAL LITERACY *Explicit teaching* 'Critical Language Awareness'	social responsibility?

Figure 5.1 Discourses of writing and learning to write (adapted from Ivanič 2004)

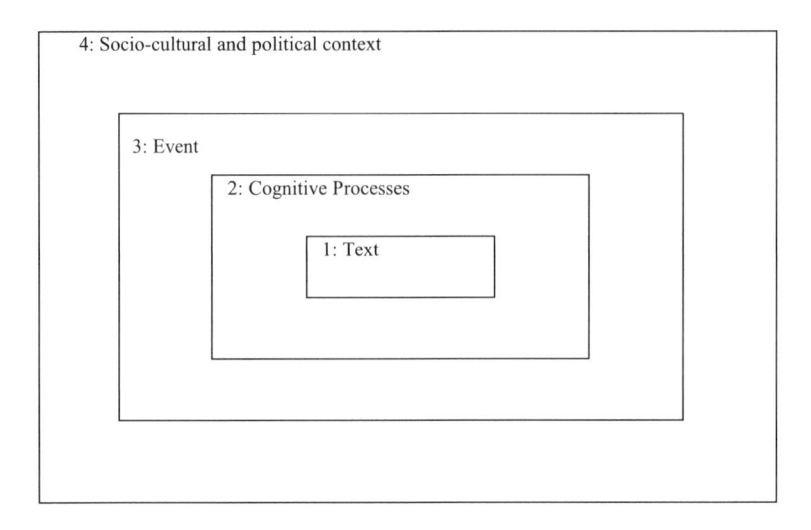

Figure 5.2 A multi-layered view of language (Ivanič 2004: 223)

Some words about Discourses

Drawing on Gee's (1996) view of Discourse, Ivanič defines discourses of writing, as "constellations of beliefs about writing, beliefs about learning to write, and the sorts of approaches to teaching and assessment which are likely to be associated with these beliefs," and that, "participating in one or more of these discourses positions people ... identifying them with others who think, speak, write and act from within the same discourse" (Ivanič 2004: 224). This stance on language and literacy shows that people and groups of people are positioned in social, cultural and political ways that can include issues of empowerment and disempowerment around the way they use literacy.

Ivanič's framework is a valuable heuristic which can be used to uncover different, and sometimes conflicting, discoursal beliefs embedded in educational policy and pedagogical practice, and I use it in this way in this chapter. In talking about particular discourses, Ivanič taught me not to refer, for example to "the creativity discourse", or "the process discourse", but always to refer to "the creativity discourse of writing and learning to write", or "the process discourse of writing and learning to write". She insisted that the pattern in referring to a specific discourse was always "*the ... discourse of ....*" and I have followed this practice in this chapter.

An overview of my practice in teaching writing

My pupils all came from rural schools in which they were usually the only child with a Statementof Special Educational Needs for dyslexia. I usually taught them in 1:1 withdrawal lessons in which I aimed to make the atmosphere relaxed and informal. I was non-judgemental because I wanted the children to be so unafraid of making mistakes that they could begin to understand that reading and writing were not tests, but powerful ways of making meaning. They chose their own subject matter: they wrote stories and non-fiction accounts by hand; drew cartoon strips and wrote the speech bubbles. In all these activities I supported them by discussing what was being written and by supplying the words they could not spell, so that we did not break the flow of their writing. When this first draft of what they had written was finished we would word process, illustrate, and photocopy the text in order to publish a number of hand-made books – one for the school, one for the child, one for me, one for my team and so on. Sometimes the books were activity or puzzle books, or biographies they wrote about each other from information supplied by questionnaires they filled in. Once a year they all contributed puzzles and articles to a magazine which was circulated around the informal group my pupils made. They all read one another's books and then wrote to one another about them; although they did not meet they knew a lot about one another. I discuss the purpose behind these practices in the sections on the social practices and socio-political discourses of writing and learning to write.

A valuable heuristic

In this chapter I use Ivanič's framework as a heuristic to analyse the writing practices of one pupil, Chris. He was 9 years and 5 months old when I first began to teach him and a pupil in a village school, of about 250 pupils, in the North West of England. I saw him for two or three hour-long lessons a week, withdrawing him from class and teaching him in the school staff room. Chris appeared to view reading and writing as disagreeable tasks that had to be done correctly. He seemed to be deeply afraid of making mistakes in speaking as well as in reading and writing. His whole demeanour was that of a passive learner: my aim was for him to become an active learner, able to exercise judgement and to make choices in reading, writing and speaking.

The data I discuss here consist of the first draft and final version of one page of his story book, "Detective Sam Finds the Crystal", as well as my informal and formal record keeping, notes of my liaison meetings with Chris' parents and teachers, and my headnotes (see Sanjek 1990: 93). Figure 5.6 shows page three of the first draft of Chris' story, and Figure 5.7 shows the page in the finished book; I am going to use Ivanič's framework to analyse this data, by looking at the discourses of writing and learning to write one by one. As a teacher, I thought I was using a process approach to teaching writing, and so I am going to start with the process discourse of writing and learning to write. When, as researcher, I used Ivanič's framework to analyse my practice, it became clear that there were other aspects to my pedagogy than I was aware of when I was teaching. It is these other aspects that form the basis of the rest of this chapter.

In each of these discourses I appear to act in different ways as a teacher. I flag these up in the headings to each section and return to them at the end of the chapter.

The process discourse of writing and learning to write: The teacher as an agent of organisation

When I was teaching dyslexic children I separated the process of writing into, what I then thought, were the discrete stages of *gathering*, *selecting* and then *sorting* ideas before *ordering* them into a plan, which then became the basis of creatively *writing* a first draft. This was then *edited* before being *presented* in its final form. This tidy linearity was intended to help my pupils to concentrate on one stage of the process at a time (see Figure 5.3). Sometimes the *gathering ideas* stage took the form of a talk around what the child wanted to write. I often helped reluctant writers like Chris, who had very little idea of how to begin, to brainstorm ideas on a piece of paper. This brainstorming sheet could then be consulted by us at later stages of the writing process. Chris's brainstorming can be seen in Figure 5.4. I scribed his ideas for him because that left him free to think; even so he needed a great deal of prompting and encouragement. In a subsequent lesson I

STAGE IN THE WRITING PROCESS	POSSIBLE ACTIVITY
Gathering ideas	Brainstorming
Sorting and selecting	Underlining words in different colours
Ordering	Making a linear plan
Writing a first draft	Free writing, concentrating on self expression
Editing	Proof reading first (or subsequent drafts), correcting spelling, perhaps altering structure.
Presenting	Illustrating, word processing, photocopying, producing a bound book or books.

Figure 5.3 Writing as a tidy linear process

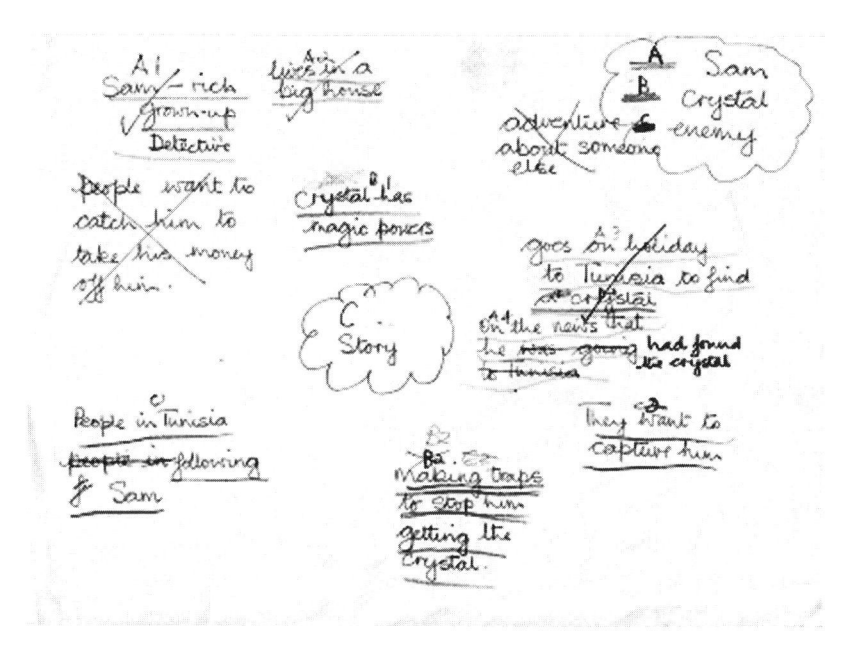

Figure 5.4 Brainstorming ideas for the story

suggested colour coding aspects of the story, and this can be seen in the bubble at the top right hand corner of Figure 5.4. To see the colour version of this figure please go to http://dx.doi.org/10.1075/swll.12.figures.

I then encouraged Chris to use these colours to underline the ideas and to number them. As you can see, in Figure 5.4, one idea was rejected and crossed out. As a teacher I was now satisfied that the *selecting* and *sorting*, and *ordering* stages had been covered Chris then moved to the next stage of the process, creatively *writing the first draft*.

His first attempts, on September 19th, can be seen in Figure 5.5. In my weekly record I wrote that it was "like pulling teeth." By the time he wrote page 3 on the 7th and 14th of November (Figure 5.6) he was writing more freely, as we shall see in the section on the creativity discourse of writing and learning to write. On the weekly record sheet in which I had to record and comment on the lesson content, I wrote "C writing fluently and using own ideas" (7th November) and, "Chris getting the idea of pace (21st November). Figure 5.6 shows that we corrected spelling errors and I shall talk about that in the section below on the skills discourse of writing and learning to write. Sometimes we added words and phrases (see Figure 5.6, lines 11 and 13) but at the time I merely thought of this as a sort of informal editing. What I then saw as the real work of *editing the first draft* took place when we word-processed the story. The process, as I saw it, ended with *presenting* stage:

Awena Carter

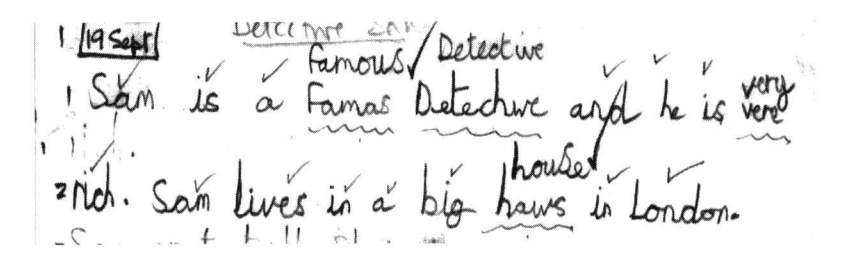

Figure 5.5 The first lines of 'Detective Sam'

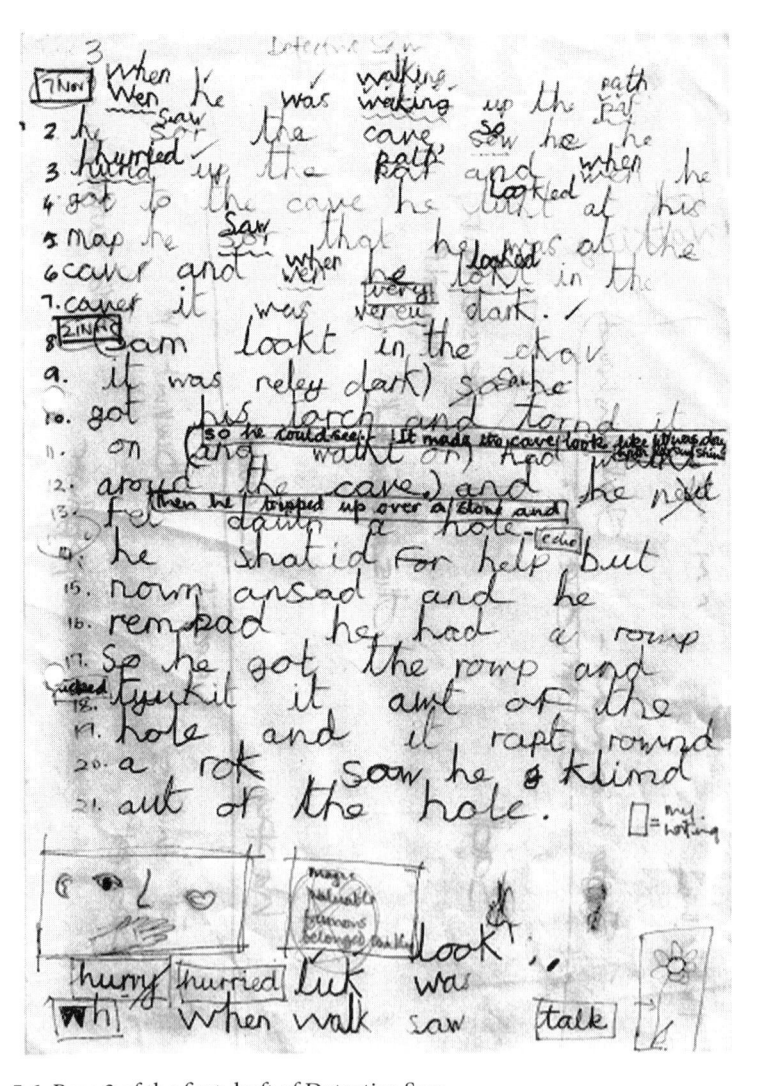

Figure 5.6 Page 3 of the first draft of Detective Sam

the illustrating, photocopying, binding and distributing of the books, as I have described above. Throughout this process I had been the agency through which Chris had negotiated the different stages of writing.

After I had read Ivanič's paper, "Discourses of Writing and Learning to Write" (2004), my view of what actually goes on throughout the writing process changed considerably. In this paper Ivanič writes that "it is best to recognise that "writing processes" can refer to either or both the cognitive and the practical processes" (ibid: 231). In addition, Ivanič, writing with Clark, discusses writing in terms of a "non-linear, recursive process" (Clark and Ivanič 1997: 92). Reading these explorations of the writing process, I began to understand that it was not an exclusively practical technique, nor was it a linear process comprising discrete stages. I realised that my tidy pedagogical plans had ignored the "internalised operations which are often completed without any conscious recognition" (Hyland 2002: 27), because the process approach to teaching writing is really about "stages of planning, drafting, revising and editing, which are *recursive, interactive and potentially simultaneous*" (ibid: 231, my italics).

When I came to analyse what actually happened during the writing of "Detective Sam Finds the Crystal", it appeared that an untidy recursiveness kept asserting itself into the discrete stages of my approach. An example of this is the way the brain-storming sheet (Figure 5.4) – used to gather and sort ideas for "Detective Sam" which, for a time, we referred to as a plan – is annotated and altered. Eventually it was abandoned as a reference because Chris drew a series of drawings at home which altered the course of the story, becoming a new plan which subverted my tidy linearity. Another example of this recursive interaction can be seen in Figure 5.6: it is there in the brackets around lines 8 and 9b and around "*and walkt on*" in the middle of line 11; in the extra lines I have scribed for Chris above lines 11 and 13; and in the crossings out in lines 9 and 12. We inserted these new ideas as a result of talking about what Chris had written that day and the way it meshed with what he had written before. What I had at the time dismissed as a spot of informal editing, now appeared to be a revisiting of the *gathering ideas*, or the creative writing of the first draft stages.

This recursiveness continued throughout the typing of the final draft which was what I then thought of as the editing stage, and you can see this in Figures 5.7 and 5.8. Figure 5.8 shows the changes we made as we talked through the typing: there are some minor ones, such as adding or altering punctuation. Others are more major, such as the placing of added words which significantly expand and explain Sam's actions to the reader. Sam does not merely walk around the cave, he explores it to find the crystal; he falls down a hole because the stone he has tripped over hides the hole from him; he cannot climb out because the hole is deep. These, like the insertions in lines 11 and 13 in Figure 5.6 are revisiting the stages of

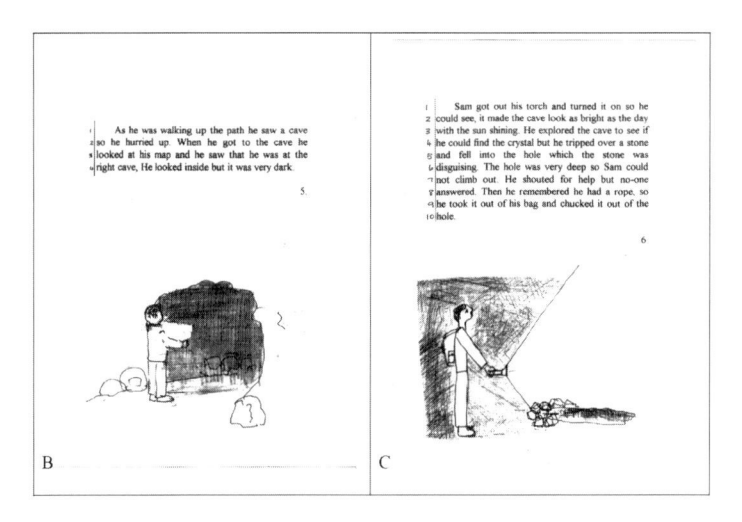

Figure 5.7 The text in the published book

gathering ideas and creatively writing showing that final editing was not a tidily discrete stage in the process of writing but as *recursive* and *interactive* (Hyland 2002:231) as earlier stages, despite what I had thought at the time.

The genre discourse of writing and learning to write: The teacher as an instructor of how to write

On November 21st (Figure 5.9) when I wrote that *Chris* [was] *getting the idea of pace* I meant that he was pushing the plot forward and putting enough of Sam's actions in the story to accord with what I then thought constituted a story writing genre (I explore this view and the reasons for holding it below). When I began to research my practice, however, I began to engage with the debate around the nature of genres. For example I read that Ivanič, writing with Clark (Clark and Ivanič 1997:13) viewed genres as being more readily identifiable by the socially embedded purpose of the writer than by linguistically analysable features. In the paper "Discourses of writing and learning to write" (Ivanič 2004:233) on which I am drawing so heavily in this chapter, I read Ivanič's assertion that the genre discourse of writing and learning to write is "concerned with the written text, but also pays attention to social factors in the writing event." Views like this led me to reflect on what I was teaching my pupils about writing a story. I certainly had no linguistically informed knowledge of the nature of genres on which to draw, which meant that I did not view story writing as one of a set of narrowly defined text types. But when I analysed what I was doing, I realised that I was basing my teaching on my

Discourses of learning and teaching   99

column	EDITED FIRST DRAFT See Figure 6	LINE	FINAL VERSION See Figure 7
		(p. 5)	
6b	when he looked in the	4b	*he looked inside but it was very dark.*
7	cave it was very dark		
8		(p. 6)	
9b	Sam	1	Sam *took out* his torch and turned it on so he
10	got his torch and turned it	2	could see, it made the cave *look as bright as the day*
11	on so he could see. It made the cave look like it was day with the sun shining And walked	3	with the sun shining. **He explored the cave to see if**
12	around the cave	4	**he could find the crystal but** he tripped [ ] over a stone
13	Then he tripped up over a stone and fell down a hole.	5	and fell *into the hole* [ ] **which the stone was**
14	he shouted for help but	6	disguising. The hole was very deep so Sam could
15	no-one answered and he	7	**not climb out.** He shouted for help but no-one
16	remembered he had a rope	8	answered. Then he remembered he had a rope so
17	so he got the rope and	9	he *took it out of his bag* and chucked it out of the
18	chucked it out of the	10	hole. [ ]
19	hole and it wrapped round		
20	a rock so he climbed		
21	out of the hole.		

Note:
- *italics* show text which has been reworded in the final version
- **bold text** shows new ideas introduced in rewriting
- [...] Square brackets show where a word, idea or punctuation mark in the first draft is missing from the second draft
- underlined punctuation marks show added or altered punctuation

Figure 5.8 Changes showing recursiveness in practice

experience as a reader and writer of stories, and on my experience as a member of a creative writing group. From this perspective I thought that a story should be written for the reader's, rather than for the writer's, enjoyment, and written so that the reader could "see" the action from the main protagonist's view point. This is the reason for the drawings, at the bottom of the page in Figure 5.6, of an ear, eye, hand, nose, and mouth. They had been the basis of a discussion with Chris about what Detective Sam could hear, see, feel and so on. In acting in this way I was instructing Chris about what I thought was the right way to write a story.

Some of the ways in which Chris appropriated what I then understood as the genre of story writing, can be seen in Figure 5.6 lines 8–21 which show Chris giving Sam more autonomy:

2. through verbs of movement:
   lines 11 & 12: *and walkt on Aad walkt aroud the cave*
              (and walked around the cave)
   line 13: *Fel dawn a hole* (fell down a hole)
   line 18: *tyukit it* (chucked it)
   line 19: *it rapt rownd* (it wrapped round)
   line 20: *he klimd out* (he climbed out)
2. through showing Sam's reactions:
   line 14: *he schatid for help* (he shouted for help)
   line 16: *[he] rembad he had a rowp* (remembered he had a rope)
3. through showing Sam's vulnerability:
   Line 15: *nown ansad* (no-one answered)

In this short analysis of the story writing genre that was implicit in my pedagogy, it is clear that, drawing on my experience as a one time member of a creative writing group, I expected Chris to be creative in writing about Detective Sam. The genre and creativity approaches to writing were thus intermingled when I taught story writing and this can be seen in the following section where I explore the creativity discourse of writing and learning to write in my pedagogy.

The creativity discourse of writing and learning to write: The teacher as a facilitator of creativity

One reason that Chris was able to appropriate my view of the story writing genre was by having it modelled and scaffolded (see Wood 1999) for him during his writing of "Detective Sam"; another was that reading stories had made him more familiar with the genre. In this section I trace Chris' development as a story writer and link it to his reading.

The first words of "Detective Sam" (Figure 5.5), were written very carefully and with great labour. It was as though the implied reader (Iser 1974: xii) being constructed by Chris was a critical teacher who drew on a skills approach to the teaching of writing. I aimed to help Chris understand that I wanted him to make meaning, not to engage in an exercise in accuracy. Chris was a very stilted reader as well as being a stilted writer, and I felt his writing showed he had little experience of story books on which to draw. My instinct was to share the reading of a variety of books, aiming to make reading a pleasure rather than a task. We talked around the texts, relating them to Chris' experience, and Chris' experience to the texts, in what I later recognised as life-to-text and text-to-life interactions (Cochran-Smith 1984). In an effort to help Chris to think about ways of telling stories, I told him traditional tales, such as "The Three Little Pigs" and "Goldilocks and the Three Bears" and then encouraged him to tell them back to me. Instead of looking at reading as a test of accuracy, Chris began to enjoy stories and began to choose his favourite books to return to.

Just as I scaffolded his reading, I scaffolded his writing, talking with him as he wrote, scribing when he had no more stamina to write, encouraging him to think about what Sam would think, feel, do next. We consulted the brainstorming sheet and the drawings Chris had done at home, constantly discussing the story and ways of telling it.

What I have described above were the practices of a teacher trying to find ways of helping her pupil to write a story – to facilitate his writing in other words. I did not at the time theorise what I was doing: because I loved stories and enjoyed writing, I implicitly felt that the two went together. Reading Ivanič's paper, however, revealed ways in which I could analyse a teaching approach that I now began to see as embedded in the creativity discourse of writing and learning to write. "What counts as good writing in [this discourse]," she writes, "is based on criteria drawn from literature rather than everyday functional literacy (Ivanič 2004: 229). She continues, "the teaching of writing [in this discourse] is likely to be closely allied to the teaching of reading" (ibid: 230). I began to look at the dynamic between the stories Chris was reading and telling and the story he was writing. This dynamic can be traced in the extracts from my weekly record sheet, and you can see these in Figure 5.9.

In September Chris' reading has *"little expression"* and his writing is *"like pulling teeth"*. In October he is starting to enjoy reading, and although his enjoyment in oral and written story telling has not kept pace, by the end of October it appears to have caught up. During November, when he was writing the page you can see in Figure 5.6, he is enjoying both reading and writing. In creating his story, he was no longer confining himself to words he could spell correctly. You can see this in Figure 5.6, especially line 14: *shatid* (shouted); line 15: *nown ansad* (no-one

EXTRACTS FROM MY WEEKLY RECORD SHEET

Date	CHRIS' READING	MY COMMENTS ON CHRIS' READING	CHRIS' WRITING AND SPEAKING	MY COMMENTS ON CHRIS' WRITING AND SPEAKING
19 Sep			Started writing story	like pulling teeth some scribing by me
26 Sep	Started 'George's Marvellous Medicine' (Shared reading)	Good reading but little expression	Interactive writing based on reading 'George's Marvelous Medicine'	Chris still hesitating to write opinions
3 Oct			Story [writing] continued	Chris still diffident
8 Oct	Read 'George's M. M.'	Great enjoyment and good reading	Oral story telling – '3 little Pigs' (Chris and I alternately) '3 Bears' (Chris)	Language still stilted but slightly readier to form sentences and chance his arm
10 Oct	Read 'Fancy That' & 'Mrs Armitage on Wheels'	Latter greatly enjoyed	Story [writing] continued	
11 Oct	Read all of 'Jolly Postman'	Chris had not read it before – greatly enjoyed		
15 Oct	[Read] 'Mrs Armitage'	Chris' choice		
22 Oct	Read 'George's Marvellous Medicine'		Story [writing] continued	C much readier to write, some scribing [by me]. Chris encouraged to tell story [used] good vocabulary
24 Oct	Read 'Nothing'	– great enjoyment – Chris still needs to attend to punctuation [when reading aloud]		Writing much more freely and with good expression
25 Oct	Read 'Slimy Book' & 'Going West'	Attn. [to] context cueing [making] inferences and prediction. Chris readier to advance own opinion		
7 Nov			Carried on writing story	Chris wrote with more fluency and used own ideas
19 Nov	Finished 'George's Marvellous Medicine'	Very good. Much satisfaction experienced by Chris	Book Report on 'George's M. M.'	
21 Nov	Read 'Can't You Sleep, Little Bear?'	Very much enjoyed [by both] Good interaction with text and characters [by Chris]	Continued writing story Discussion [of] books and publishing	Chris getting the idea of pace
10 Dec	Read 'Jolly Christmas Postman'		Discussed [Chris' drawings] and carried on writing story	C writing fluently

Figure 5.9 Reading, writing, and speaking in a creativity discourse of writing and learning to write

answered); line16: *rembbad* (remembered); line 18: *tyukit* (chucked); line 19: *rapt rownd* (wrapped round); line 20: *klimd* (climbed). Chris was not only reading for meaning, he was beginning to write for meaning too.

Ivanič (2004: 230) writes that, in the creativity approach, "[e]xperienced, eclectic teachers of writing recognize the advantage of inspiring learners to write about topics which interest them and the opportunities this provides for implicit learning, alongside explicit teaching about linguistic rules and patterns" (2004: 230). This describes the pedagogic value of the creativity approach for the teacher of dyslexic children because, once a child has learned to write freely, the anatomy of his difficulties is laid out in his writing. The teacher can then see what difficulties to meet, in what order to meet them and in what fashion. I discuss some of ways of doing this in the following section on the skills discourse of writing and learning to write.

The skills discourse of writing and learning to write: The teacher asserting correct practice

When Chris (or one of my other pupils) had finished a sentence or a short passage of text, we would look at what he had written and do two things: I would encourage Chris to retrieve spelling knowledge that he had worked on in some previous lesson (sometimes the process of looking at what he had written would jog his memory) and I would address the lowest category of spelling error in the passage. This hierarchy of spelling needs is shown in the following analysis of Figure 5.6, lines 2–7 which shows embedded work on:

1. *grapheme/phoneme relationships*, (paf/path, lines 1 and 3)
Most of this was to prompt Chris to remember what he already knew.

2. *spelling patterns*, (waking/walking, line 1; lukt/looked, lines 4 and 6)
In my notes for that day (7th November) I recorded that we practised two words using *Simultaneous Oral Spelling*[3] "Look" (Chris remembered he already knew this), and "walk" (we had not worked on this before). Work on these words was done at the bottom of the page where you can see some analogies to "*walk*": *talk* and the drawing of the *stalk* of a flower, using different onsets for the rime "alk". My notes of two days later read "Tested "look" & "walk"".

---

[3] This is a multisensory way of teaching spelling, so called because it uses the kinaesthetic sense and the senses of speech, hearing and sight (see Bryant and Bradley 1985: 24f., 128f.).

3 *high-usage words* (wen/when, lines 1 and 6; sor/saw, lines 2 and 5)
At the bottom of the page is my representation of "wh", as in "when" – drawn to remind Chris of the mnemonic, "Witch's Hats". Chris has also written *was* and *saw* based on talk about the mnemonics "Water And Sand" and "Sand And Water".

The skills approach was also embedded in the process approach to writing at the stage when the first draft was typed. The extract from my weekly record sheet in Figure 5.10 shows how, when I read Chris' work to him as he word-processed it, I could assess how successful I had been in teaching him spelling patterns and high usage words and revise them if necessary. Sometimes, if he started to make an error, the act of typing and my reading would be sufficient to enable him to retrieve the correct spelling. In all this I was asserting correctness as an important aspect of writing.

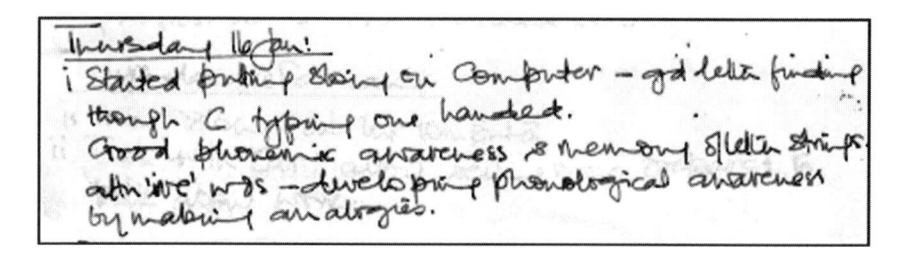

Figure 5.10 The skills discourse implanted in the process discourse of writing and learning to write

Ivanič, in writing about the skills discourse of writing and learning to write, draws attention to the notion of the primacy of "correct" practice over other aspects of writing that are embedded in this discoursal view. "Associated with this belief about writing," she writes, "is a belief that learning to write involves learning the sound-symbol relationships which generate well formed words, syntactic patterns which generate well-formed sentences, and looser cohesion within and between paragraphs which are characteristic of well-formed texts" (Ivanič 2004: 227). She acknowledges that, "there is no question that implicit knowledge of spelling patterns, of what is accepted as grammatical in written English, and of conventional punctuation is an essential part of writing," (ibid: 228) but contests both the ways in which this sort of knowledge is privileged over other understandings of writing, and the ways in which it is taught. When I read this I found myself agreeing that it is this privileging which leads to the hegemony of the dominant discourse of education. As I have indicated, I embedded my teaching of spelling patterns in children's writing; and my strongly held view was that my pupils should write for meaning and that this was more important than accuracy of spelling or of syntax.

However, part of what I was supposed to do as a teacher of dyslexic children, was, as I have written, to address my pupils' spelling needs, to teach them how to punctuate and how to write a "well-formed sentence" to apply "knowledge of sound-symbol relationships and syntactic patterns [in order] to construct a text" (Ivanič 2004, see Figure 5.1 column 3). And I was not unhappy with this. It was partly that I felt I had to equip my pupils to survive in the classroom, but there was also a real sense in which I thought that I should be teaching them to write in what I would now call a dominant discourse. It appeared that I had been holding two conflicting views about writing, that I was quite happy about both of them, and that I was unaware of any conflict. I shall explore this contradiction in more detail in a later section, after I have explored the social practices and the socio-political discourses of writing and learning to write

The social practices discourse of writing and learning to write:
The teacher as a mediator of writing

Using Ivanič's framework as a heuristic has enabled me to reveal how the genre, creativity and skills approaches to teaching writing were embedded in the process approach in my pedagogy. In this section I argue that these discourses were, in turn, embedded in the social practices discourse of writing and learning to write

I have described the way in which my pupils were in touch with one another through reading and writing stories, letters and magazines. In encouraging them to do this, and in putting them in touch with my other pupils, I was mediating writing as a means of communication. I did it because I wanted my pupils, most of whom were the only children in their schools to receive support lessons, to identify with other children in other schools who read the same books and wrote in the same ways that they did.

Ivanič (2004: 235), drawing on theories of learning which position the learner within a community of practice (Wenger 1998), describes the learner, in the social practices discourse of writing and learning to write, as learning "by apprenticeship, by peripheral participation in literacy events and by taking on the identity of community membership of those who use literacy in particular ways. Identification is a key concept for this sort of learning." When I read this I felt that she had made explicit what I had implicitly known when I designed the practices I have described in the previous paragraph. Ivanič continues, "[t]he role of the teacher is to identify situations which contain a high degree of authentic communication, involving the full complexity of writing practices which occur in naturally occurring literacy events" (2004: 236). Viewing my practice through this lens enabled me to describe it as a social practices approach to teaching writing. However, although there was a "high degree of authentic communication" in all that Chris and my other pupils wrote, I am not claiming anything like the "full complexity of writing practices" which Ivanič (ibid.) mentions. My pupils were not engaged in "naturally occurring literacy events" (ibid.): they were writing for a social purpose which I had designed and in which my pedagogical aims were deeply embedded. One of the things I explore in the following section is this hegemonic stance.

The socio-political discourse of writing and learning to write:
The teacher as a protector of pupils' freedom

In teaching Chris I encouraged him to make his own choices about what to read and what to write. In this I was drawing on the pedagogical practices of my 1960s teacher training, when we aimed to capture the interest of the child precisely by starting with his interests.[4] It seemed to me that this way of teaching was very suitable for a dyslexic child with a history of failure in the classroom; he needed to be taken away from the demands of the curriculum, to write in ways which made sense to him so that he would understand why he was being taught to read write and spell.

It was when I read Ivanič's view that "learning to write in [the socio-political discourse] … includes developing a critical awareness of the historical and political factors which have shaped [particular discourses and genres] and shaped the patterns of privileging among them" (2004: 238) that I began to understand that one of the reasons my pupils did not flourish in the domain of school was partly because of the control of the contemporary dominant discourse of education. This control was hegemonic in the Gramscian (1971) sense that it was, and is, open to contestation. The particular dominant discourse of education which exercised hegemonic control in the 1960s, when I first began my teaching career, was centred on the child and his interests, as I have already mentioned. I would argue that such a discourse implied a greater kindness to dyslexic children than the one which challenged and overturned it, with its emphasis on narrowly defined outcomes based on narrowly defined targets.

I did not openly raise my pupils' consciousness about what I am now calling the hegemonic control of the dominant discourse of education, but which I would, as a teacher, have described as an impoverished curriculum. The reason was the delicate balance I had to maintain between sympathy for my pupils' difficulties in the classroom and the professional stance of maintaining my pupils'

---

4. See Pahl and Rowsell (2005) for an interesting revisiting of the ideas which were common currency in the 1960's and 70's.

respect for their teachers – whatever my private views might be. However, in allowing my pupils to make their own choices, I was empowering them in ways which implicitly challenged dominant classroom practices.

It is worth unpicking the reasons for allowing my pupils' choices in what they wrote about because it reveals ways in which we, pupils and teacher, were socio-politically constructed by the dominant discourse of education, and the ways in which we challenged this hegemony. There is no room in the scope of this chapter to explore, in detail, the ways in which I was hegemonically constructed by the team for which I worked, by the schools in which I taught, by the Local Education Authority, and by Government legislation. However, to this hegemony I would add the ways in which I constructed my pupils in their lessons with me, because I had pedagogic purposes of which they were unaware. Their lessons with me, then, took place within a doubly hegemonic environment; however, within that environment, I cleared a space in which my pupils could make choices about what books to read, and what to write about. When they made these choices I was voluntarily disempowering myself for the ideological reason that I wanted them to draw on their vernacular understanding of literacy, and for the pedagogical reason that I wanted them to develop a measure of self determination. It was in this space that Chris wrote the page reproduced in Figure 5.6 and in which he later published his story. Giving my pupils choices in what to write, and the time spent illustrating, photocopying, cutting and sticking and the other processes involved in publishing multiple copies of their books, did not sit well in some of the schools in which I taught. It was especially true of those in which the teaching of writing and spelling was firmly based in the skills discourse of writing and learning to write. Part of my socio-political stance therefore was the determination to guard the space which I had cleared and to defend my pupils' choices from the negative comments of their teachers.

Conflicting identities

In this chapter I have used Ivanič's framework (Figure 5.1) in two ways. First of all I have shown how, in using it as a heuristic, I was enabled to take the stance of a researcher towards a pupil's work. The second way I have used the framework arises out of this because it has revealed that all the discourses of writing and learning to write, which Ivanič has identified, can be traced in one page of my pupil's work. This seems to accord with Ivanič's view that "all six beliefs about writing …. could make a contribution to a comprehensive view of writing, that any one without the others may be an impoverished view of writing, and that the same is true of the beliefs about learning to write" (Ivanič 2004: 241). Ivanič goes on to suggest that "a teacher attempting such an integration would inevitably face some tensions and contradictions" (ibid.) However, if one looks critically at the list of beliefs about writing and about learning to write in columns 3 and 4 of Figure 5.1, this seems a hopelessly idealistic view. Reading down the columns reveals more than "tensions and contradictions": it reveals conflicting, even mutually exclusive beliefs. It seems impossible that someone who truly holds that there is a *correct* way of writing and that you learn to write by "learning sound-symbol relationships and syntactic patterns" can at the same time hold the view that you learn to write in real life contexts with real purposes for writing, with all the notions of apprenticeship, rather than instruction, that that implies.

This appears to suggest that there is a serious theoretical flaw in Ivanič's argument, especially if one considers the view of discourse to which I refer at the beginning of this chapter. However, my analysis of Chris' writing reveals that I did, in practice, inhabit these incompatible discourses whilst teaching him: they are all traceably present in that one page of his writing reproduced in Figure 5.6. In order to unpick this contradiction, I turn to Ivanič's view of identity. She writes that the "socially available resources for identity are multiple, and that an individual's identity is a complex of interweaving positionings" (Ivanič 1998: 10). In using the word "positionings" rather "positions", Ivanič conveys the sense, not only of change but also of the, often unconscious, choice that is implicit in this view of identity.

My analysis of my practice has uncovered some of the interweaving positionings I took as a teacher. Figure 5.11 maps these positionings onto the six discourses of writing and learning to write. It shows how I simultaneously – or at least in rapid succession – took contradictory stances such as mediating and modelling; facilitating and instructing; teaching correct practice whilst protecting pupils' freedom to make writing choices. I was not serially trying out different discoursal identities as a pedagogical experiment. I was holding them together and moving between them in what I now realise was an unconscious tension: subscribing to

DISCOURSE OF WRITING AND LEARNING TO WRITE	POSITIONING
Skills	Teacher asserting correct practice
Creativity	Facilitator
Process	Agent of organisation
Genre	Modeller / Instructor
Social practices	Mediator
Socio-political	Protector of pupils' freedom to make writing choices

Figure 5.11 Subject positions mapped on to discourses

the beliefs underlying each of the discourses in order to address aspects of my pupils' needs.

I am going to express that notion again: I subscribed to the conflicting beliefs underlying each of these discoursal identities in an unconscious interweaving of positionings. It is only now, as I research my practice, that I can see the tensions and contradictions in what I had only assumed was a well rounded approach to teaching writing. To Ivanič's assertion that a person's identity is a complex interweaving of positionings, then, I want to add the understanding that, underlying the socially available resources for identity, are sometimes contradictory beliefs. The individual, in adopting these socially available possibilities can subscribe, often simultaneously, to such contradictory beliefs. This notion of contradictory positionings is a powerful way of explaining the way in which one teacher, teaching one pupil, can inhabit different and contradictory discourses of writing and learning to write in an eclectic pedagogy.

My debt to Roz Ivanič

In this chapter I have used Ivanič's framework, of the six possible discourses of writing and learning to write, as a lens through which to view, not only my practice, but also my development as a researcher. But the analysis of my practice itself revealed a possible contradiction in the framework. I have attempted to resolve this contradiction by exploring the role belief plays in identity, and by bringing this to Ivanič's notion of the socially available possibilities for selfhood. In doing this I acknowledge my unpayable debt to Roz Ivanič: an outstanding supervisor; a piercingly discerning academic; and a most valued friend.

References

Bryant, P. & Bradley, L. 1985. *Children's Reading Problems*. Oxford: Blackwell.
Clark, R. & Ivanič, R. 1997. *The Politics of Writing*. London: Routledge.
Cochran-Smith, M. 1984. *The Making of a Reader*. Norwood NJ: Ablex.
Gee, J. P. 1996. *Social Linguistics and Literacies: Ideology in discourses*. London: Taylor and Francis.
Gramsci, A. 1971. *Selections from a Prison Notebook*. London: Lawrence and Wishart.
Hyland, K. 2002. *Teaching and Researching Writing*. London: Longman.
Iser, W. 1974. *The Implied Reader: Patterns of communication in prose fiction from Bunyan to Beckett*. Baltimore MD: The John Hopkins University Press.
Ivanič, R. 1998. *Writing and Identity*. Amsterdam: John Benjamins.

Ivanič, R. 2004. Discourses of writing and learning to write. *Language and Education* 18(3): 220–245.
Pahl, K. & Rowsell, J. 2005. *Literacy and Education.* London: Sage.
Sanjek, R. 1990. *Fieldnotes: The making of anthropology.* Ithaca NY: Cornell.
Wenger, E. 1998. *Communities of Practice: Learning meaning and identity*. Cambridge: CUP.
Wood, D. J. 1999. Teaching the young child: Some relationships between social interaction, language and thought. In *Lev Vygotsky, Critical Assessments,* Vol. III: *The zone of proximal development*, P. Lloyd, & C. Fernyhough (eds), 259–275. London: Routledge.

CHAPTER 6

Accommodation for success
Korean EFL students' writing practices in personal opinion writing

Younghwa Lee
Sun Moon University, Chung Nam, Republic of Korea

This chapter reports on a study which investigated Korean EFL students' writing practices and the features of their "personal opinion writing". The data comprises a collection of nine students' written texts and interviews with three students. Whilst there were some differences among the students' written texts, for the most part they shared the key elements of a "Claim/Opinion-Reason" pattern, and their content overwhelmingly originated from the textbook. The students adopted the same or similar textual structures and textual knowledge as those of the textbook's model paragraph rather than attempting their own strategies, which demonstrated a pattern of writing as "accommodation". The conclusion indicates that the students' discourse approaches are driven by their efforts to succeed in a recontextualised setting.

Introduction

Writing in English in the Korean context is a challenging task for many students who have had little experience of it before attending university, and their practices of writing in English may be solely constructed in writing courses at university. This immediate environment of writing pedagogy shapes the overall values and pedagogic practices of teachers, and affects the prevailing patterns of teaching and learning to write in English in Korea. Some existing work in EFL writing area (Camps 2000; Lee 2003; Tarnopolsky 2000) approaches student writing from an essentially "skill-based" perspectives, that is, writing in higher education is assumed to be a competence which, once acquired, enables students to communicate their knowledge and understanding in virtually any context. The qualities of "good writing" are assumed to be self-evident, and largely a matter of learning and mastering universal rules of, for example, grammar usage and text organisation.

However, the work of Ivanič strongly challenges this perspective and raises important questions about the need to uncover discourses of writing and learning to write in any specific context (Ivanič 1998).

The study on which this study was based draws on my personal and academic engagement with Roz Ivanič and her work; Roz inspired me during my doctoral study to look beyond conventional understandings about student writing in Korea. In my study of Korean students' personal opinion writing in an English writing course at a university, I developed an analytic model designed to describe how the students construct textual structures and meaning-making in their writing and, I used qualitative interviewing to locate these texts within the contexts of students' experiences and goals. The study was guided by the following research questions:

1. What are the features of the textual structures and meaning-making in students' personal opinion writing?
2. How do these become visible through students' writing practices in the EFL Korean context?

In this paper, I outline the theoretical perspective I developed in the course of my research, give an overview of the study carried out, and summarize key findings from my text and interview based analysis.

Theoretical background

Central to my study was an attempt to gain a deeper understanding of the writing practices that students engage in within the specific contexts of the Korean EFL writing classroom. One underlying purpose in carrying out this study was to consider new theories of writing in order to apply these to the practices of teaching and learning of writing in the Korean EFL context. In this section I summarize three key theoretical insights that became particularly significant for my study.

Writing as social practice

Fundamentally this study which focuses on writing in an EFL context is based on Ivanič's (2004) perspective for thinking about writing and the learning of writing: her framework takes the writer, text, and context- rather than any single element- as the point of departure in teaching and learning of writing. Her approach is part of a broader literacy studies approach (see Barton 1994; Barton, Hamilton & Ivanič 2000; Barton & Hamilton 1998; Baynham 1995; Lea & Street 1998; Street

1995) where writing is construed as a social practice rather than a set of decontextualised skills. The notion of practices, as Barton (1994) argues, offers a powerful way of conceptualizing the link between the activities of reading and writing and the social structures in which they are embedded and which they help shape. Clark and Ivanič (1997) used the term "practices" rather than "procedures" or the even more widely used "skills" to emphasize the social nature of what we do as writers. They believe that:

> Practices are not just what people do, but what they make of what they do, and how it constructs them as social subjects. The physical act of organizing your work in a certain way before starting to write, browsing for ideas in books on library shelves rather than reading set books from cover to cover are, for example, socially and ideologically shaped ways of behaving. (p. 82)

Even the apparently technical aspects of writing, such as the choice of implement, are deeply embedded in socio-historical relations and have ideological implications. Writing practices also vary not only from culture to culture, but also from person to person and from one context to another. In addition, the plural "practices" implies that "there is no one right or appropriate way of behaving or communication, but multiple competing ways of being" (Clark & Ivanič 1997:83).

An "accommodation" view of learning to write

Accommodation refers to one particular way in which students engage in learning. Chase (1988) defines accommodation as "the process by which students learn to accept conventions without necessarily questioning how these conventions privilege some forms of knowledge at the expense of others" (cited in Ivanič 1998:92). The extent and way in which students accommodate in their writing is a complex issue. Thesen (1994) for example argues that learning within this perspective assigns a strong rule to the individual student as agent and that students within this frame are continuously making decisions in their learning. In particular, she argues that:

> This perspective makes it easier to track and understand the way discourses rub against one another, and what individuals do about this. Locating meaning in the individual does not mean that I am downplaying the social, but trying to find a starting point that is more profoundly social, in that it deals with human a action, which must surely be at the heart of the social. (Thesen 1994:56)

In this chapter I point to the importance of understanding learning as "accommodation" for understanding student writing practices in the Korean EFL writing classroom context.

Personal opinion writing and recontextualisation

"Personal opinion writing" is widely used in Korean EFL writing pedagogy. In general, the purpose of a personal opinion paragraph is to express the writer's opinion. However, as Kitao, S. and Kitao, K. (1992) argue, the writer must do more than just express an opinion. The writer must also give support for the opinion; that is, reasons for holding that opinion. One way of writing a personal opinion paragraph is to state the opinion in the introduction, and possibly mention the number of reasons that will be discussed. Then, in the discussion, the writer gives facts, arguments or supporting data for that opinion. In the conclusion, the writer restates the opinion or summarizes the arguments or facts. Another way of writing a personal opinion paragraph is to mention the opinions of other people or groups and then agree or disagree with those opinions in the introduction. Again, in the discussion, the writer gives support for his or her opinion and in the conclusion restates the opinion or summarizes the supporting data.

Teaching personal opinion writing within education can often be based on unreal tasks with inappropriate, and exercise-based content. This is particularly true at the EFL university level. However, even in the distorted world of autonomous university writing practices it is possible for personal opinions to be the source of real, and meaningful writing activities in an EFL context. In the practices of personal opinion writing in English in an EFL setting in this study, recontextualisation takes place when personal opinions are moved into other arenas and used for different purposes. Shifting an opinion from its location in a textbook or other educational materials to a student writer's text is an example of the process of recontextualisation (Barton & Hall 2000). In the assessment of the writing course in this study, personal opinions are recontextualised as educational material, and this transition can lead to a different genre. The imagined social processes of personal opinion writing are recontextualised in the assignment into another social context, the classroom, which has its own ideological purposes in a Korean institution.

The study

The course, participants, and teacher

The data upon which this paper is based were collected in an optional English writing course for non-English major students at a local university in Korea. The aim of the course was to teach basic knowledge about English paragraph writing for beginners. The participants of this study were two groups of students: nine for text analysis and three for interviews. Firstly, nine texts of opinion writing produced by nine students (out of a class of 35) were analyzed for their textual structures and meaning-making. They were selected from three different English proficiency levels, i.e., high, intermediate, and low, in terms of their scores of the mid-exam and writing assignments with the help of the teacher. They came from a variety of disciplines, grades, and English proficiency levels, and their ages varied from 20 to 27.

Secondly, three students out of the nine were interviewed in order to explore, in more detail, their purposes for writing in English and how they produced the particular form their texts took. The three students, Minhee, Haerim and Sangchul, came from different backgrounds in terms of age, discipline, and previous experience of writing in English. Minhee, aged 20 in Year 1, was studying the area of humanities. She had experience of writing in English for 3 years at her middle school. Another female student, Haerim, aged 21 in Year 2, was studying material engineering, and she had never attended English writing course before. One male freshman, Sangchul, age of 21 in law, had attended an English writing course in the previous semester at the university.

The teacher was female, had studied English literature in the US and had been teaching writing in English for three years. When I met her to discuss my research and to request access to her students, she emphasized the importance of creative thinking in students' writing. She considered writing to be very important for students because learning to express their opinions and beliefs could lead them to successful lives in society.

The writing assignments

Students were asked to submit one piece of personal opinion writing, as the first assignment, on the one of the two options as follows:

a. Write your reactions to the ideas about having information from internet websites everyday.
b. Read the newspaper article (reproduced in Appendix A) about two convicted murderers who were put to death for crimes they had been convicted of committing many years before.

Out of the nine students, eight students chose topic (b), and only one chose the issue of (a). The teacher had four elements, i.e., content, organisation, grammar, and coherence, as the criteria to evaluate students' writing products, and the perfect score of the assignment was 40 points.

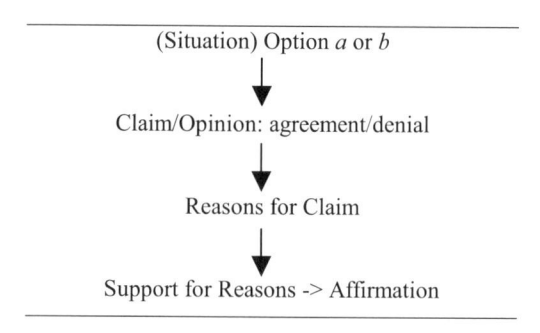

```
┌─────────────────────────────────────┐
│     (Situation) Option a or b       │
│                ↓                    │
│   Claim/Opinion: agreement/denial   │
│                ↓                    │
│         Reasons for Claim           │
│                ↓                    │
│   Support for Reasons -> Affirmation│
└─────────────────────────────────────┘
```

Figure 6.1 Optional stages in 'Claim/Opinion-Reason' pattern

The tool for analysing students' texts

I studied the nine students' writing and applied what I call a "Claim/Opinion-Reason" pattern to the students' writing (see Lee 2003). The "Claim/Opinion-Reason" pattern was developed from Hoey's (2001) "Claim-Response pattern" (p. 179) which had basic components such as Situation, Claim, Reason for Claim, Denial, Correction, and Reason for correction. This perhaps does not represent all the options. That is, a(an) Claim/Opinion may be denied and then corrected with or without Reasons being given for the Claim, the Denial or the Correction. A(an) Claim/Opinion may also be affirmed, in which case a Reason will characteristically be given for the Affirmation, or the Affirmation will reveal itself to have been a feint and be followed by a Denial. Based on this speculation, I build up the "Claim/Opinion–Reason" pattern, since the nine students' texts clearly include a Situation, a(an) Claim/Opinion required, Reasons for the Claim/Opinion, and Support for the Reasons. This pattern is represented diagrammatically in Figure 6.1.

In analysing the students' writing, the options for the writing tasks (a) or (b) are referred to as Situation. The clauses/phrases *"I think", "I believe", "I am in favor of", "I agree/disagree that", "in my opinion", "in my view"*, can be the signals of Claim/Opinion that arguments are being expressed. The list-order transition signals such as *"first, second, third, and finally"* can identify Reasons. The opening expressions *"for these reasons", "therefore"*, or *"in conclusion"* can be categorised as Affirmation which take the role of Supports for the Reasons. As an example of the way the "Claim/Opinion-Reason" pattern operates, Extract 1 represents a full version of the text written by a student, Minhee. Sentence numbers indicate continuity in the text.

Extract 1: A full version of the writing by Minhee

> For Capital Punishment
> (S1) I am in favor of capital punishment. (S2) First of all, what Billy and John did was horrible crime. (S3) Even though they commit crimes twenty years ago, crime is crime. (S4) It is a mistaken idea if you think that time will take care of the test. (S5) Nobody can say for certain that they regretted enough. (S6) Second, victim need time to relieve pent-up feelings. (S7) Think about the raped child's life. (S8) She must have grown up miserably. (S9) John screwed not only child's body but also her life. (S10) What they did was destroying the peace and happiness of families. (S11) Victims and families deserve a compensation for their sufferings. (S12) Third and the most important reason is that society must show what is wrong and what is right. (S13) If law hushes up the convicted murderers on the reason that they had been convicted many years before, who would believe and follow the law? (S14) Capital punishment is a proper measure to give conviction to people that justice is on our side. (S15) In short, I think their death is a natural result, "An eye for an eye and a tooth for a tooth."

The writing focuses on option (b), as a Situation, and begins with a(an) Claim/Opinion with an agreement (Sentence 1) for which a Reason is given in sentence 2; this is then Support for the Reason in sentences 3 to 5. The second Reason is then introduced in sentence 6. The Support for the Reason follows in sentences 7 to 11. Sentence 12 puts the third Reason, and sentence 13 has the Support for the Reason. An affirmation is followed by sentences 14 and 15.

Findings and discussion

Exploring texts

I attempted to focus on what the students demonstrate in their texts and how they construed the form and process of the task in relation to their own understanding of the function of writing in English. The textual structure in the nine samples was analysed in accordance with the Claim/Opinion – Reason pattern. The results show that, except for one (Sample 6), there are few differences among the samples, since they all share the key elements of Claims/Opinions, Reasons, and Supports for the Reasons, which originate from the textbook (Hogue 1996) used in the classroom, as shown in Figure 6.2.

Three pieces of work (Samples 1, 2, and 3) have the perfect score, 40, and the textual structures of these are fairly clear with the specific elements, one Claim/

Sample 1: 40 points	Sample 2: 40 points	Sample 3: 40 points <Minhee>
(Task *b*)	(Task *b*)	(Task *b*)
		(Title)
S1 Claim/Opinion	S1 Claim/Opinion	S1 Claim/Opinion
S2 Reason 1	S2 Reason 1	S2 Reason 1
S3-4 Support	S3-4 Support	S3-5 Support
S5 Reason 2	S5 Reason 2	S6 Reason 2
S6-8 Support	S6 Support	S7-11 Support
S9 Reason 3	S7 Reason 3	S12 Reason 3
S10 Support	S8-9 Support	S13-14 Support
S11 Reason 4	S10 Reason 4	S15 Affirmation
S12-13 Support	S11 Support	
S14 Affirmation	S12 Affirmation	
Sample 4: 37 points	Sample 5: 35 points <Haerim>	Sample 6: 35 points
(Task *b*)	(Task *a*)	(Task *b*)
(Title)		(Title)
S1 Claim/Opinion 1	S1 Claim/Opinion 1	S1-3 Claim/Opinion 1
S2 Claim/Opinion 2	S2 Reason 1	S4-11 Support
S3-4 Reason 1	S3-7 Support	S12 Claim/Opinion 2
S5 Reason 2	S8 Reason 2	S13-15 Support
S6 Reason 3	S9-10 Support	
S7 Support	S11 (Denial)	
S8 affirmation	S12-14 Support	
S9 (Suggestion)	S15 Affirmation	
	S16 Claim/opinion 2	
Sample 7: 30 points <Sangchul>	Sample 8: 30 points	Sample 9: 25 points
(Task *b*)	(Task *b*)	(Task *b*)
	(Title)	(Title)
S1 Claim/Opinion 1	S1 Claim/Opinion	S1-3 Claim/Opinion
S2 Reason 1	S2 Reason 1	S4 Reason 1
S3-4 Support	S3-6 Support	S5-6 Support
S5 Reason 2	S7 Reason 2	S7 Reason 2
S6 Support	S8-9 Support	S8 Support
S7 Affirmation	S10 Reason 3	S9 Affirmation
S8 Claim/Opinion 2	S11 Support	
	S12 Affirmation	

Note: S = Sentence number. The Samples 3, 5 and 7 are the three students who were interviewed and to whom I return below.

Figure 6.2 Textual structures of the nine samples of writing

Opinion, three or four Reasons and Supports, and an Affirmation. Sample 8 does not show a very high mark, 30, even though it includes the same textual structure and obligatory components, i.e., one Claim/Opinion, three Reasons and Supports, and an Affirmation, as Samples 1, 2, and 3.

It is feasible to assume that the teacher's main concern would be interesting content rather than accuracy in Ivanič's (2004) assessment criteria for writing. This is indeed borne out by the fact that the lowest score is given to Sample 9 even though it has a textual pattern that is closer to the model text than other Samples, such as Sample 6.

A central part of the learning process for students is concerned with genre in Ivanič's (2004) framework; in this study it seems clear that the textbook plays a central role in the students' learning of generic knowledge because most of the students closely modelled their texts on this key resource. Indeed, the students seem to be constrained by the model paragraph in the textbook. This can be associated with the socio-cultural context emphasized in Ivanič's framework, in that Korean students who have had passive learning tend to reproduce the knowledge as a power obtained from the textbook rather than creating new ways in the task. In contrast, Sample 5 is situated in the domain which is concerned with the writer's individual knowledge bases rather than adopting the pattern originated from the textbook, since its textual pattern shows a difference from the other eight samples of writing, including two claims in both the first and last sentences.

Here the two approaches which I (2003), after Chase (1988) call "accommodation" and "challenge" can be applied to the nine students. Accommodation captures the way in which the eight students try to reproduce course materials, thereby attempting to "succeed in the assignment", using the course material; in contrast, "challenge" can be used to describe the one student who aims to relate her text to her own life-world context. In terms of content, the eight students who chose the newspaper article show a lack of the *creative self-expression* referred to in Ivanič's (2004) framework. These students adopt the same or similar content to that of the model paragraph on page 176 of the textbook rather than attempting their own linguistic characteristics of text. Expressions such as *"in my opinion"*, *"I am in favor of"*, *"first of all"*, *"second"*, *"third"*, *"indeed"*, etc., are repeated in their pieces.

Samples 1, 2, and 3 include at least three Reasons with Supports for their Claims/Opinions, and this seems to influence their marks- they receive the highest marks. This indicates that these three students comprehend the process approach on how to plan and revise their writing, adopting the material in the textbook to succeed in the assignment. Samples 3, 4, 6, 8, and 9 include a title, and two of them (Samples 3 and 9) adopt the same title, "Capital punishment" as that of the model paragraph in the textbook. Only one student (Sample 5) chooses the option *a* as Situation, unlike the other eight writers. Sample 5 establishes two Claims/Opinions to generate her ideas, including the second Claim/Opinion in the last sentence. Interestingly, one student (Sample 6) adds her own strategy to have two Claims/Opinions and Supports for them without any Reason and Affirmation, bringing in her knowledge of the Bible rather than sticking to the content of the textbook. This reflects that the two students of Samples 5 and 6 are learning writing in English by engaging in their real activities, involving their writing of "real" texts in "real" contexts as discussed by Ivanič (2004).

All of the samples, except Sample 6, use the order-listing transition signals, e.g. *"first of all"*, *"second"*, *"third"*, etc. With respect to content, only two students (Samples 5 and 6) reveal their own understanding about the writing assignment that seems to be derived from their experiences, thoughts and style rather than the knowledge or information derived from the textbook. They produced very different styles of meaning-making which are embedded in their own world of interpretation, unlike the other seven students who used the content from their textbook. The writing practices of the two students of Samples 5 and 6 are associated with what Ivanič (2004) calls "creative self-expression" in learning writing since they explore their own experience and tell their own stories in their texts.

Exploring EFL writing practices

Three examples of personal opinion writing (Samples 3, 5 and 7) produced by Minhee, Haerim and Sangchul are now presented, beginning with statements about brief personal background and the purposes for attending the English writing course. In the interviews, I focused on how these students completed their assignments and what the fundamental elements were to build up their understanding about writing in English. I believe that these writers provide a firsthand picture about each student's perceptions of the writing task and how this shapes their actual practices of writing in English.

> Minhee
> *Minhee is a female student who wanted to study English literature as her major in Year 2. She started to learn English from Year 6 in the primary school with private lessons at a language school. She had a good record of TOEIC scores, 950,[1] and won the first prize in an English speech competition at her high school and university. However, she confessed that writing was difficult for her, and she said that she wanted to learn the logical way of thinking that is emphasized in writing in English.*

Minhee's writing is one of the texts which displays a writer's fairly high sense of personal learning and writing experience derived from the classroom and the textbook rather than from outside the classroom. Her writing consists of the topic sentence for Claim/Opinion, the listing-order signals for each of the three Reasons and Support, and an Affirmation of the Claim/Opinion, as presented in the

---

1. TOEIC (Test of English for International Communication) is accepted by work places in Korea as one of the standard English proficiency tests, and its perfect score is 990.

textbook. The perfect score, 40, given to Minhee indicates that she is able to transfer what she has learned back to her assignment and is well served by the model texts in the textbook. That is, she takes advantage of written models and writing guides in constructing her texts. She learned about the organisation and logic of personal opinion writing by using the textbook:

> In order to produce a logical way of writing, it is the best way to follow the guidelines in the textbook rather than to have my own strategies, I think. We are able to understand the meanings in a text written in Korean although an argument is sometimes vague, implicit, and not clear-cut. But I don't think this works for the case of writing in English.

The above comment shows that Minhee recognises how the linguistic characteristics of text differ according to contexts of writing – English and Korean – which reflects the importance attached to genre in Ivanič's (2004) framework. Minhee also seems to be an example of the a *learner as an ethnographer* described by Ivanič as she is able to tell the different use of writing in two different contexts. The process of meaning-making and accommodation for the logical way of thinking through the writing course are crucial for Minhee. Since she values logical thinking as her purpose for writing in English she can develop and build up her understanding of explicitness and logic within the framework of the classroom pedagogy and the specific textbook resource. The following extract in her Sentences 12–13 reflects this.

> Third and the most important reason is that society must show what is wrong and what is right (Sentence 12). If law hushed up the convicted murderers on the reason that they had been convicted many years before, who would believe and follow the law (Sentence 13)?

She has in effect done what she intended in the learning of writing in the above two sentences because she expresses her own idea in a logical way- that is explicitly sequencing her argument and raising hypothetical questions- which probably leads to her gaining the highest grade. She seems to successfully accommodate to the EFL writing classroom where logical thinking and creativity are privileged and in this sense, Minhee has succeeded in crossing epistemological boundaries on her EFL writing course.

> Haerim
>
> Haerim is a shy and introspective girl who loved to read poems and novels. She went to a private language school to learn English speaking for 6 years before entering university. Very interestingly, she was interested in majoring in material engineering where the majorities were boys. She was planning to take a TOEFL for her future study on a graduate course after finishing the writing class.

Unlike the eight students, Haerim chose the writing task *(a)* which is related to information technology. She wanted to express her opinions about the relationship between a human being and computers from her own experience although she was struggling to write this in English:

> I think writing in English is very challengeable for me, in particular, to express my own thoughts, imagination, and creativity in English is too difficult. When I had the assignment I tried to find something from my own experience and daily life. So I chose the option *a* for the assignment as I sometimes felt that computer caused the loss of human relations.

Haerim applies her concerns about daily life to the assignment context in which she plans to demonstrate her understanding of the impact of computers on human life and critically discusses the relations between human beings and the computer in modern society. She uses Korean composing strategy or processes for writing in English, in that she develops her ideas first in Korean and then translates them into English. She states:

> The experience of writing in Korean during my high school days is very helpful when I write in English. I think of the connection between my reading those days and being a university student who is learning writing in English. These things affected me a lot when I write the assignment. But I used the transitional words I learned in the classroom.

Her approach to the learning of writing that connects her own experience, daily life, and writing in Korean becomes her own strategy in meaning-making in the writing task. She also draws on, however, the available models for personal opinion writing, for example, using the signals *"in my opinion"* for a Claim/Opinion, the list-order *"first of all, second"* for Reasons for Support, *"indeed"* for Affirmation, which derives from the classroom. Interestingly, unlike the textual pattern in the textbook, Haerim puts two levels of strong Claims/ Opinions both in the first and last sentences: *In my opinion, the statement implies that a man lose himself because of a flood of information, and loss of human relations* (1st sentence), and *Depending human life on computer is very dangerous* (Last sentence). Haerim thus partly accommodates to the preferred textual model in her text.

> Sangchul
> *Sangchul is a male student who wished to study political science from Year 2. He wanted to be a civil official through a government exam and hoped to work for his country. Sangchul had been attending the writing course again because he was not happy with the grade he obtained in the previous semester. He thought that writing in English was boring subject for him although he felt that it needed to improve English proficiency through writing.*

Sangchul was extremely keen on gaining a high mark, and it was very important for him to get good records on his bachelor's program as this would play an important role when applying for a job. For these reasons, he always concentrated on what the teacher as assessor focused on in students' writing. He explains:

> I always try to follow up the teacher's taste when I write. For example, if she is a Christian, I attempt to write something about church or Christianity. Also, if she focuses on theme while marking, I make an effort to find some fresh materials from English magazines or books rather than the textbook because my main purpose is to get a higher mark in this course.

The comments show that Sangchul constructs an identity as a university student in Korea in which he demonstrates his deep concerns about the academic achievement. Sangchul believes that a higher score is determined by the teacher's taste or preference. In spite of his strong motivation to achieve a higher mark, his text does not overtly demonstrate the preferred "text knowledge" in his writing about the newspaper article. Text knowledge refers to the knowledge about general characteristics and requirements of the writing task (Victori 1999). This is related to the knowledge about text as a whole and its particular components, i.e., good and interesting content, clarity of ideas, a coherent discourse and grammatical correctness. In this sense, Sangchul's writing reflects a general lack of text knowledge. In his writing, the two Reasons and Supports (in Sentences 2 and 5) are inconsistent with the first Claim/Opinion in Sentence 1 although the listing-order transition signals *"first of all"* and *"second"* are well organised (in Sentences 2 and 5). In addition, the conclusion in Sentence 8 refers back to the first Claim/Opinion. The following is an extract to show evidence of this:

> In my opinion, their deaths are unjust (S1: Claim/Opinion 1). First of all, their crime have no relation with their deaths (S2: Reason 1)… Second, only the death penalty can justify the deaths (S5: Reason 2)…Government should console victims' family and have the right judgment (S8: Claim/ Opinion 2)

It is interesting to note that Sangchul's grasp of logic and coherence seems to be considered poor in terms of the teacher's criteria such as content, organisation, grammar, and coherence in evaluating the assignment. However, the writing task he chose coincides with his purpose for writing in English:

> First of all, I want to improve my general English proficiency. After this semester, I would like to learn how to write an academic essay further.

The above comments indicate his view that academic writing, including general writing, is also valuable and useful for EFL learners, and that general writing acts as a transition in the English curriculum. However, he is not confident about how the nature of the text and requirements of the task of academic writing can be developed.

Conclusion and implications

This study explored students' written texts in terms of both textual structures and textual knowledge shown in the personal opinion writing in an EFL writing course in Korea. I suggest that the primary textual structure and textual knowledge produced by the nine students demonstrate a pattern of "accommodation", as most of the students constructed similar rhetorical patterns and content adopted from the textbook in their texts.

In exploring the purposes for writing in English of three students, Minhee, Haerim and Sangchul, I have argued that the way in which they construct approaches to writing and learning to write, and the contexts within which learning takes place, are crucial to understanding the recontextualisation of the writing task. None of the three students – Minhee, Haerim, or Sangchul – reached the point of comfort and confidence in writing in English. For Minhee, the English way of logic and explicit syntactic structure were challenging and problematic issues. However, she indicates that she was well served by the model texts in the textbook. Haerim transferred Korean ways of writing into writing in English, using the textbook pattern of writing, but then subverts it. For Sangchul, meeting the demands of his teacher was his main strategy to get a higher score.

Teachers need to develop students' critical thought through writing practices, beginning by acknowledging that writing experiences need to be located social-politically. Under the Korean education system, learning is equated with the memorisation of factual information rather than with the development of critical thinking or individual creativity. This situation can be related to the students' writing products in this study where most writers showed limited ability for critical thought, simply reproducing the textbook, and it appeared that it was a problem for them to generate and formulate ideas into sound and cogent arguments. Critical thinking in the learning of writing can be related to the "critical literacy" in Ivanič's (2004) framework, for which students should discuss the interests, values, beliefs and power relations they are becoming party to, by participating in different writing practices, discourses, and genres. Finding the different practices between Minhee, Haerim and Sangchul underscores how important it is for teachers to present a variety of perspectives, approaches, and strategies to their students so that eventually each writer can develop a process that works for her or him in a given writing context.

References

Barton, D. 1994. *Literacy: An introduction to the ecology of written language.* Oxford: Blackwell.
Barton, D. & Hall, N. (eds). 2000. *Letter Writing as a Social Practice.* Amsterdam: John Benjamins.
Barton, D. & Hamilton, M. 1998. *Local Literacies: Reading and writing in one community.* London: Routledge.
Barton, D., Hamilton, M. & Ivanič, R. 2000. *Situated Literacies: Reading and writing in context.* London: Routledge.
Baynham, M. 1995. *Literacy Practices: Investigating literacy in social contexts.* London: Longman.
Camps, D. 2000. Drawing on, adapting and recreating writing practices for their academic purposes: The case of six Mexican postgraduate students at four British universities. PhD dissertation, Lancaster University.
Chase, G. 1988. Accomodation, resistance and the politics of student writing. *College Composition and Communication* 39: 13–22.
Clark, R. & Ivanič, R. 1997. *The Politics of Writing.* Routledge: London.
Hoey, M. 2001. *Textual Interaction: An introduction to written discourse analysis.* London: Routledge.
Hogue, A. 1996. *First Steps in Academic Writing.* New York: Addison-Wesley.
Ivanič, R. 1998. *Writing and Identity: The discoursal construction of writer identity.* Amsterdam: John Benjamins.
Ivanič, R. 2004. Discourses of writing and learning to write. *Language and Education* 18(3): 220–245.
Kitao, S. K. & Kitao, K. (1992). *Basic English Paragraphs: Improving reading and writing skills.* Tokyo: Eichosha.
Lea, M. R. & Street, B. 1998. Student writing in higher education: An academic literacies approach. *Studies in Higher Education* 23(2): 157–172.
Lee, Younghwa. 2003. Alignments and detachments in writing pedagogy: Interface between teachers' practices and students' purposes in two EFL writing courses in Korea. PhD dissertation, Lancaster University.
Street, B. 1995. *Social Literacies: Critical approaches to literacy in development, ethnography and education.* London: Longman.
Swales, J. 1990. *Genre Analysis: English in academic and research settings.* Cambridge: CUP.
Tarnopolsky, O. 2000. Writing English as a foreign language: A report from Ukraine. *Journal of Second Language Writing* 9(3): 209–226.
Thesen, L. 1994. Voices in discourse: Re-thinking shared meaning in academic writing. MPhil dissertation, University of Cape Town.
Victori, M. 1999. An analysis of writing knowledge in EFL composing: A case study of two effective and two less effective writers. *System* 27(4): 537–555.

Appendix A. The newspaper article for the assignment (b)

> What Is Justice?
> Two men were put to death last week in the United States for murders that they had been convicted of committing many years ago. Billy Bailey died in the first hanging in Delaware in fifty years. It was twenty years ago that he murdered an elderly couple after breaking into their home. John Taylor, a child rapist and murderer, was shot by a five-man firing squad in Utah. Polls show that 70 to 80 percent of U. S. citizens favor capital punishment. Many believe that people who commit horrendous crimes deserve to die brutally in return for the brutality that the inflicted on their victims. Others protest the barbarism of the death penalty, be it by lethal injection, electric chair, firing squad or hanging. While there were many people who supported the two deaths that took place last week, there were also many protesters.

Appendix B. The model paragraph in page 176 of the textbook

176 Unit 6

> Capital Punishment[1]
>
> In my opinion, capital punishment is wrong. First of all, I believe that it is wrong to kill. Only God has the right to take away life. Human beings should not kill human beings. Even if a criminal has committed horrible crimes, the government does not have the right to execute[2] him or her. Second, the threat of going to the electric chair or to the gas chamber does not stop criminals. When people commit a violent crime such as murder, they are not thinking about their punishment. In fact, many murders happen when people are angry. They are not thinking about the consequences of their actions. According to a report in the New York Times, the State of Louisiana executed eight men in nine weeks in the fall of 1987. During that same time period, the murder rate in New Orleans rose 16.4 percent. This shows that the threat of capital punishment does not stop crime. The third and most important reason for abolishing[3] the death penalty is that the government sometimes makes mistakes and executes innocent people. In fact, this has happened. According to an article in Time magazine, there were twenty-three executions of innocent people in the United States between 1900 and 1991. In my view, this makes the government itself guilty of murder. For these three reasons, I believe that the United States should get rid of capital punishment, which is really just "legal murder."

[1] capital punishment: the death penalty
[2] execute: kill legally
[3] abolishing: getting rid of; cancelling

REFLECTION 5

Collegiality and collaboration

Karin Tusting
Lancaster University

I have been very privileged to work with Roz Ivanič over the past ten years or so as a teacher, colleague and friend. During that time, I have many times heard her quote Dick Allwright on writing, that: "If you have a problem, share it with your reader." So here is my problem: how is it possible to distil what I have learned from Roz throughout that time into one small piece of writing? Well, of course it isn't. Rather than attempting the impossible, I will just pick out one or two of the most important things I have learned from working with Roz for all this time.

I have to admit, when I first met Roz as one of the lecturers teaching the "Grammar, Genre and Social Context" module of my MA, I was somewhat suspicious. She seemed far too positive about students' work and ideas, treating us all as equal colleagues, rather than lowly first-step-on-the-ladder postgraduates. Very aware of my lowly position in the academic hierarchy, this made little sense to me and I kept waiting for the let-down – but it never came; the enthusiasm about what all of her students were doing was genuine. Roz has the gift of seeing first the strengths of her students' work and developing these, rather than focusing on the flaws and limitations, making her one of the most encouraging and helpful teachers I encountered during my time as a student.

I quickly came to take this equal treatment and enthusiasm for granted, and it encouraged me to see myself as a colleague rather than a student. Participation on this basis in academic events like the *Situated Literacies* seminar, which Denny Taylor mentions in this volume, was crucial in helping me to develop a new identity as an academic with something of my own to contribute. Preparing the book which came out of *Situated Literacies*, I worked with Roz and Anita Wilson in preparing the chapter "New Literacy Studies at the Interchange" which closes the book. Collaborative writing was fairly new to me then, and again, looking back on it, I was rather spoilt in having this experience as my introduction to it. All of our contributions were valued on an equal basis, and the process of integrating them into a chapter was negotiated perfectly smoothly. It was only later, with more experience of the wider academic world, that I realised how unusual it was for students' writing to be considered in this way.

However, to praise Roz' enthusiasm for students' and colleagues' work is not to say that she overlooks problems with it, either. Her forensic attention to detail means that gaps in arguments and errors in reasoning cannot be disguised with fancy rhetoric. I was lucky enough to have Roz as my PhD internal examiner. After introductions, she began by saying that the external examiner would deal with the broad theoretical ideas in the thesis, but she would like to ask just "one or two little nitty-gritty questions" before moving onto that. My relief that the examination would have an "easy start" was short-lived, when her first "little" question identified a crucial contradiction in the way I had summarised critical discourse analysis theory that went right to the heart of the argument in the thesis. A very pertinent lesson there about the importance of rigorous academic thinking! The same attention to detail has always been a feature of Roz' research, and it has many times proved highly revealing to me just how much richness she is able to draw from the detailed analysis of language data.

I would say that the most important thing I have learned in these years of working with Roz has been from her profound concern for people as individuals. It is this deep and natural concern for people's needs and priorities that has driven the research contributions she has made, the way she has approached teaching, and the various responsibilities she has taken on for the wider Applied Linguistics community. This book demonstrates the appreciation that so many people who have worked with Roz feel for both her work and her approach to life, and I am glad to have had the opportunity to be part of this.

Reference

Tusting, K., Ivanič, R. & Wilson, A. 2000. New literacy studies at the interchange. In *Situated Literacies: Reading and writing in context*, D. Barton, M. Hamilton & R. Ivanič (eds.), 210–218. London: Routledge.

CHAPTER 7

Advanced EFL students' revision practices throughout their writing process

David Camps
Tecnológico de Monterrey, State of Mexico

The present chapter discusses advanced EFL students' revision practices as a part of a larger study conducted on the writing process at a private university in Mexico. "Practices" consist of the different ways of dealing with writing and, in this case, the ones upon which students draw to assist them. My theoretical framework is based on Clark and Ivanič's (1997) view of the writing process as a social practice:

1. the writing process is dynamic and recursive;
2. revising takes place throughout the writing process;
3. practices vary from person to person;
4. technology can shape the way we write.

The findings suggest a variety of revision practices and my chapter gives examples.

Introduction

The present chapter examines the revision practices of advanced English as Foreign Language (EFL) student writers, as a part of a larger study of the writing process for composing essays, at a private university in Mexico City.[1] For the purposes of this chapter I am basing my findings on Clark and Ivanič's (1997) view of the writing process as a social practice with the following four dimensions:

a. The writing process is dynamic and recursive.
b. Revising takes place throughout the writing process.

---

[1]. A private co-educational university system with campuses throughout the country. Its students are required to obtain a TOEFL score of 520 for graduation so the teaching and learning of English becomes one of the university's main goals.

c. Practices vary from person to person.
d. Technology can shape the way we write.

I discuss first the four dimensions above mentioned. Secondly, I describe the background of my study, its participants, and data collection method. Thirdly, I comment on the students' revision practices for their compositions; I analyse portions of their responses to the interview questions and samples of the students' practices. Lastly, I discuss the findings and relate them to Clark and Ivanic's dimensions.

1. Theoretical framework

a. The writing process as dynamic and recursive

The writing process has been approached socially and cognitively (Camps 2005b and Hayes and Flower 1980, 1983). The literature on EFL composition defines the writing process as "a sequence of a series of cyclical, recursive, and progressive stages with the purpose of producing a final piece of written work" (Camps 2005a: 14), in contrast to the cognitive approach, which sees the different stages in this process, such as pre-writing, organizing, drafting and revising, as taking place neatly and sequentially. This approach has its roots in the model of the writing process proposed by Hayes and Flower (1980, 1983). In general, these authors suggest that during the pre-writing and organizing stages, a writer triggers the skills of exploring, developing and organizing ideas in order, subsequently, to continue with the drafting or translating, and revising or reviewing stages, where more skills will be employed, so that the writer will make the necessary changes to the draft before s/he reaches the final version of her/his paper (Hayes and Flower 1983; Camps 2005a). The amount of time and effort spent on the process will depend on the experience of the writer and the length of the work (Cassany 2005; Camps 2005a). The writer can employ these same stages of the writing process for any future writing, and apply similar skills acquired from previous writings.

However, Clark and Ivanič (1997) strongly criticize this type of model of the writing process because "it concentrates only on the psychological processes of the individual mind, without relating the writer to the social context in which s/he is writing…the implication is that the cognitive processes that [Hayes and Flower] describe are universal" (p. 92). In reaction to the model proposed by Hayes and Flower, and when discussing an alternative view of writing processes and practices, Clark and Ivanič (1997) point out that there is "a dynamic interplay both between all of the elements of the writing process and between the psycholinguistic and social features... and... there are no prescribed routes through the process" (p. 94). This is the view that I take in this chapter. A social approach such as Ivanič's recognizes that the writing processes is recursive and dynamic and takes place in a particular context where we engage in a set of useful and meaningful practices for a particular purpose (Clark and Ivanič 1997; Currie and Cray 2004; Camps 2005a). I am using the term "practices' to refer to different ways of dealing with writing. In this chapter, they are the ones EFL students draw upon to help them meet the instructor's writing requirements and to solve language problems they encounter when they write an assignment (Barton 1994; Currie and Cray 2004; Camps 2005b). One example of socially situated practices drawn upon and shaped by a specific domain or community can be seen in business students who are involved in an organization-based project. They may be required by their academic department to keep a diary with notes about reflections on a practical aspect so they can write a report (Camps 2000 and 2005a). They can decide if they should keep an electronic or a manual diary, if it should be divided by day or week, what type of reflections they should include, and which ones are useful for their report. The way these students write down their reflections may depend on the instructions given by their academic department or tutor, and the choices they make in order to accomplish the task successfully (Barton 1994; Camps 2005b).

I suggest that the practices I am examining are socially situated, in the sense that each time undergraduate EFL students are asked to write they may bring previous practices; learn something new; decide what to do with the written activity; make changes; leave it as it is; hand it in for marking; ask the instructor for advice; feel confident or unsure; show their work to someone else and meet or fail to meet the instructor's requirements (Ivanič and Moss 1991; Camps 2000).

Thus, the writing process can no longer be viewed as a linear progression of a series of neat and orderly stages where we employ skills. On the contrary, it can be seen as disorderly, recursive, dynamic, and recurrent where more than skills are involved. Practices are drawn upon, feelings are involved, the writers' identity is established, and the purpose and context of the writing activity all play a role. These elements are vital to understanding what steps are taken and why they are taken in such manner during those progressive stages of that particular process.

b. Revising takes place throughout the writing process

In the case of EFL student writers, practices of revising are, as Clark and Ivanic claim (1997:97) "ongoing throughout the process" and they involve ways of examining each part of a composition as many times as the students deem relevant, in order to improve it and to meet the set requirements. Language instructors may think of revision as looking for errors in grammar and punctuation in order to correct them, but this view is too narrow. Students may constantly check their progress throughout the different steps of their writing process based on the demands placed upon them, making choices related to anything they think needs to be changed (Camps 2000). The purposes of revising may vary from correcting grammar or vocabulary with a coloured pen to changing content in a Word document. It all depends on the writers' purpose, or the course requirements, or what student writers want to communicate. Revision practices are not only introduced in the proofreading or editing stage of the writing process, as the cognitive approach would suggest, but they may also be drawn upon in the prewriting stage where an EFL student writer may have to revise the ideas s/he has developed and planned so that they can be organized in short notes to be further developed in drafting the text. It may be the case that the student writers can revise the short notes organized in an outline, and consider it relevant to change their order with the purpose of having a more coherent plan for drafting the paragraphs. They may "revise their plans in the light of new thinking or new information..." (Clark and Ivanič 1997: 97). The revision practices may also take place in the final drafting stages in order to correct typing, punctuation, and spelling errors. The student writers can revise "their understanding of the reader's needs in the light of rethinking or after discussing with an intermediate reader. Writers revise mentally and they revise as a physical 'procedure'" (Clark and Ivanič 1997: 97).

c. Practices vary from person to person

Practices not only refer to acts such as thinking about a topic for writing, or looking for information about that topic in a book or on the Internet; they also refer to "the linguistic and discoursal choices that the writer makes [and] there is no right or appropriate way of behaving and communicating" (Clark and Ivanič 1997: 83). In this sense, EFL student writers may bring an array of practices to their writing in order to assist them in planning, developing, revising and finishing a meaningful piece of work. They may engage in prewriting practices for generating ideas and planning, such as mind mapping (Camps 2005a). They may also simply draw pictures instead of jotting down words or phrases for the development of ideas (Camps 2000) or, as we will see, they may quickly write down anything related to a topic. Hence, the practices may vary from person to person, and are drawn upon differently every time we are immersed in a writing process. They are socially situated in the sense that context and purposes are important components to be taken into account when we compose (Ivanič and Moss 1991; Camps 2000). Students may draw upon practices to respond to a writing task placed upon them. They may see themselves as struggling to develop ideas for an essay topic, trying to give sense of what they write, deciding which ideas to develop in order to meet the instructor's expectations and specific requirements (Camps 2000).

d. Technology can shape the way we write

Clark and Ivanič (1997) emphasize that technology can affect the act of writing, and consequently, different types of practices connected to the writing process so that "the choice of writing technology will have an effect on the cognitive work that a writer does: using a word-processor is likely to lead to a greater willingness to revise and redraft" (p. 84). The utilization of computer technology has definitely made a tremendous impact on the way we engage in practices for writing. For the initial stages of the writing process, we can now create a mental map by simply using a software program. The utilization of computers has also changed the way we engage in the practice of using tables or graphics for our papers. Nowadays, we can open the Word program and choose the tool for designing tables, saving us time and the tedious procedure of using a ruler and a coloured marker (Camps 2004). Any writer using a computer can now simply use a spell checker to correct typos or spelling, or even sentence structures, something which was not possible in the past. Indeed, the utilization of technology has contributed to new practices that assist us with our writing.

2. The background and the methodology of the study

The study of revision practices in this chapter has its origins in the results of two research projects at a private university in Mexico City. The first one examined the comments on EFL student writing made by tutors lecturing in English. The tutors' comments mainly consisted of irritation at the students' carelessness and lack of revision (Camps and Salsbury 2008). The second study explored EFL students' perceptions of the writing process. The findings suggested that not only do students revise, but revising does play an important role throughout the writing process, (Camps 2005b). This led therefore to my posing the following research question: What revision practices do student writers introduce in the different stages of the writing process? In order to understand what and how students revise, I chose an advanced EFL class (a course for first year undergraduate students whose scores on the Test of English as a Foreign Language range from 560 to 597 (see note 1). The participants were first year students from social sciences, business and engineering and they were divided into eight groups of two or three. I asked them to write a four-page composition, and to submit it with a portfolio of their composition process. The portfolio consisted of all the initial parts and subsequent drafts of their writing. The topic chosen was the concept of beauty. The students were asked to write a paper in their groups. They were given a picture of an African woman adorned with jewellery according to her traditions and folklore. Afterwards, I provided the students with a definition of beauty with which they had to either agree or disagree. Their argument for or against this definition should be supported by references.

The eight groups were also interviewed in Spanish[2] because I thought the students would feel more confident and relaxed if the interview were conducted in their native language. I first examined the students' portfolios, wrote comments, and formulated questions according to what the students had put in the portfolios for each of their final papers. Secondly, I conducted the interviews and took notes with the portfolios at hand. Each interview was recorded and transcribed. The transcriptions did not focus on linguistic or conventional features, such as pauses, hesitations, or intonations, but rather on the content of the responses. During the transcribing, I wrote comments about the revision practices that the students had talked about. Finally, I went through each of the groups' portfolios, transcriptions, and my notes again in order to triangulate. All this helped me to understand what type of revision practices the students had engaged in.

3. The students' revision practices

This section refers to the data relevant to the variety of revision practices that each group of students drew upon during the process of writing a four-page composition. Figure 7.1, below, condenses the different practices used in revising. Due to space restrictions, I have only chosen four groups of students, and based my analysis on the information they had provided about the different types of revision they had engaged in. In this section, I include facsimiles of extracts from the students' portfolios and also include transcripts of portions of the students' responses during the interviews. The numbers following the portions from the transcripts refer to the page of the original transcript. Groups 1, 2, and 4, comprised three students each. Group 3 had only two students.

---

2. The transcriptions have been translated into English for quotation here. If you are interested in seeing the originals, please contact the author.

STUDENT GROUP	REVISION PRACTICES	DATA SOURCE
Group 1	Ticks and crosses beside the ideas in the outline	Portfolio
	Annotations in the margins in the outline	Portfolio
	Correction of grammar with a marker in first drafts	Portfolio
	Annotations in the margins of the first paragraphs	Portfolio
	Checking for clarity in the first drafts evidence	Interview
	Looking over the draft	Interview
	Assistance from someone else	Interview
Group 2	Reorganization of ideas	Interview
	Developing the thesis statement	Interview & portfolio
	Checking for coherence in the paragraphs	Interview
	Reading through the draft for errors	Interview
	Assistance from someone else	Interview
	Checking for grammatical errors	Interview & portfolio
Group 3	Selection of ideas from free writing	Interview & portfolio
	Reorganization of ideas	Interview
	Checking for coherence of ideas	Interview
	Looking over and revising drafts	Interview
	Assistance from a tutor and language instructor	Interview
Group 4	Reorganization of ideas in the outline	Interview
	Reorganization of the mind map	Interview
	Rewriting drafts in a Word document	Interview
	Reading out loud for mistakes in form and content	Interview

Figure 7.1 EFL advanced students' revision practices

Group 1

This first group of students began their revision in the initial stages of the composition process. I observed from the students' portfolios that the first part of the process was handwritten (see Figure 7.2 and Figure 7.3). The students had had an initial thinking time and had begun to make corrections and annotations in the

136 David Camps

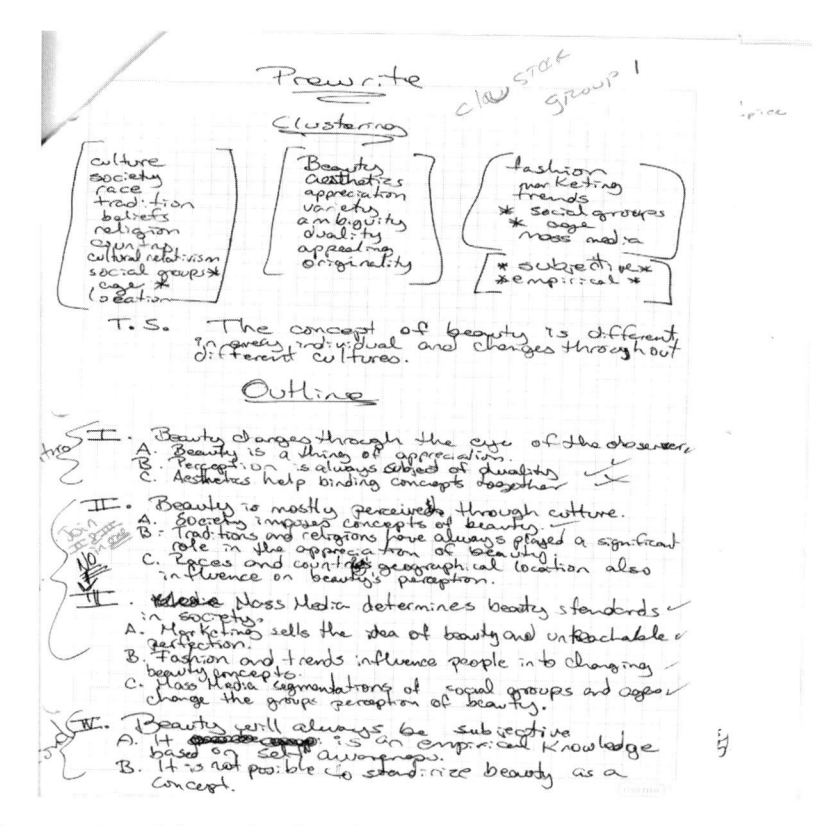

Figure 7.2 List of ideas and outline of Group 1

margins in order to establish their topic for discussion by selecting the most relevant ideas. In addition, I found in the portfolio that the students drafted an introductory paragraph with a thesis statement. The introductory paragraph had some corrections made by hand with a different coloured pen and some annotations in the margins with short comments on what the paragraph should look like.

> Well, we first wrote the essay following the technique called non-stop writing... which is to write all the ideas down that had sprung up. Each member would contribute to ideas, and then we had clusters... We grouped the ideas and designed an outline and in the draft we were putting the ideas we deemed [based on the marks]. Then we had a review and editing. We looked for errors in orthography, subject-verb agreement and the like. And after that I checked the coherence and sense of what we were saying (Group 1: 2).

In the portfolio, I also found what the students called a "cluster" (this is a list of ideas grouped by topic that they had learnt about in high school), as well as the outline and draft (Figure 7.1 and Figure 7.2). In the outline, there were sentences

Advanced EFL students' revision practices   137

with ticks and crosses as well as annotations with a different coloured pen. The marks suggest that the students were selecting the sentences that needed more work. The annotations indicate that they thought that some of the parts in the outline should be restructured. The extensive corrections in the draft and the annotations were related to both form and content. The corrections to form consisted of changes in spelling and vocabulary. The annotations in the margins were instructions for necessary changes to some of the statements that needed to be

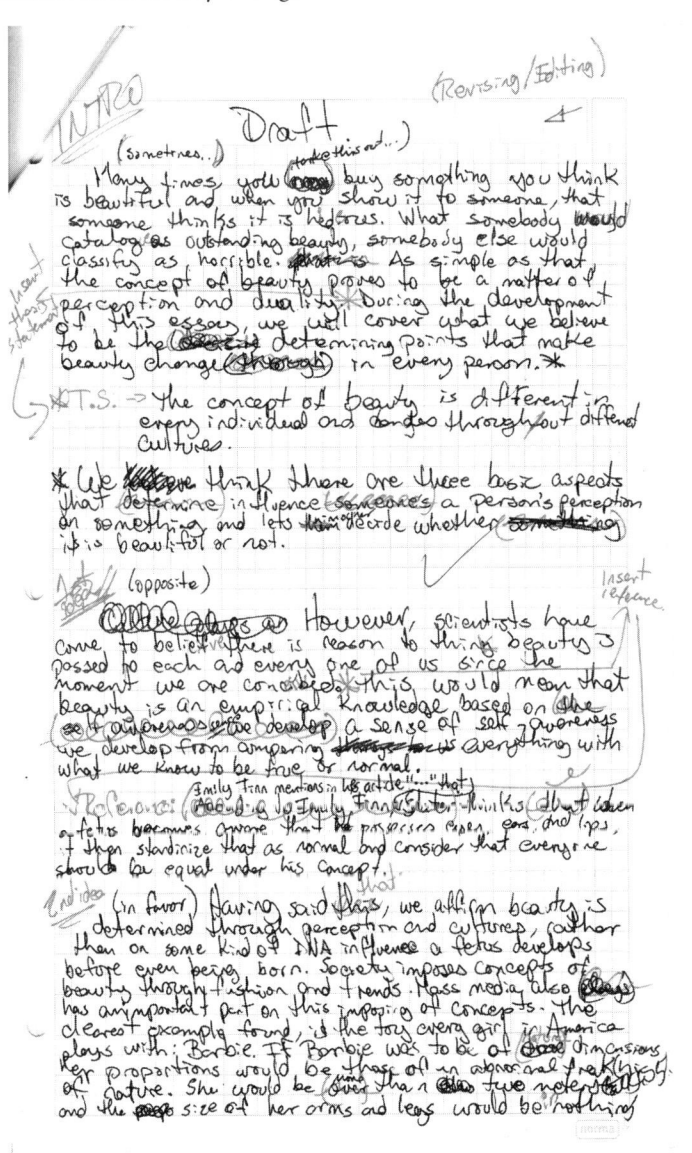

Figure 7.3 Sample of the first draft of Group 1

backed up with a reference. Corrections to content indicate that some sentences should be changed or moved to another paragraph.

According to the interview, only one student was in charge of looking over the draft and correcting it:

> *[Who was in charge of the revision?] Me... and after that my mum. [She's] an English teacher. So I gave her the final product and told her to read it, and she said that when she read it, it was OK ... that the ideas flowed well...* (Group 1: 2).

Besides the extensive revision in the outline and draft shown in Figures 7.2 and 7.3, the student in charge of the revision also looked over the paper at the end, and asked his mother to read it through for errors. After the final reading, he made the changes, and did not deem it necessary to look for more errors. According to the portfolio and the interview, the students understood revision to consist of corrections to the organization of the ideas in the outline, changes to the drafts in grammar, vocabulary and punctuation, with a coloured marker, and some annotations to guide the proofreader as to where to insert new information. The students were aware of the importance of "coherence," (the logical flow of ideas), so they decided to ask somebody else to check the draft in case it was not clear enough. In this way, they could have a reader-friendly, consistent and logical text.

Group 2

This group of students also mentioned during the interview that the revision took place at the moment that the ideas generated by brainstorming were incorporated into an outline, since it was at this moment that the students began to change, select and reorganize them. I also noted in the portfolio that the prewriting and drafting was handwritten (see Figure 7.4).

The students' interview provides the account of how they began the whole process:

> *We 'brainstormed' with complete sentences. Then from these sentences we took the main ideas and put them in the outline to organize them and give them more shape. After that we established our thesis statement and we put it in this paragraph [the introductory paragraph]. Then we wrote a draft and checked it, we read it to see it had coherence ...* (Group 2: 3).

I found a handwritten draft with some corrections in the portfolio. According to the interview, the students drafted almost everything in the same Word document several times, and checked the coherence. The final version in Figure 7.5 demonstrates that the students had actually revised the drafts since there are very

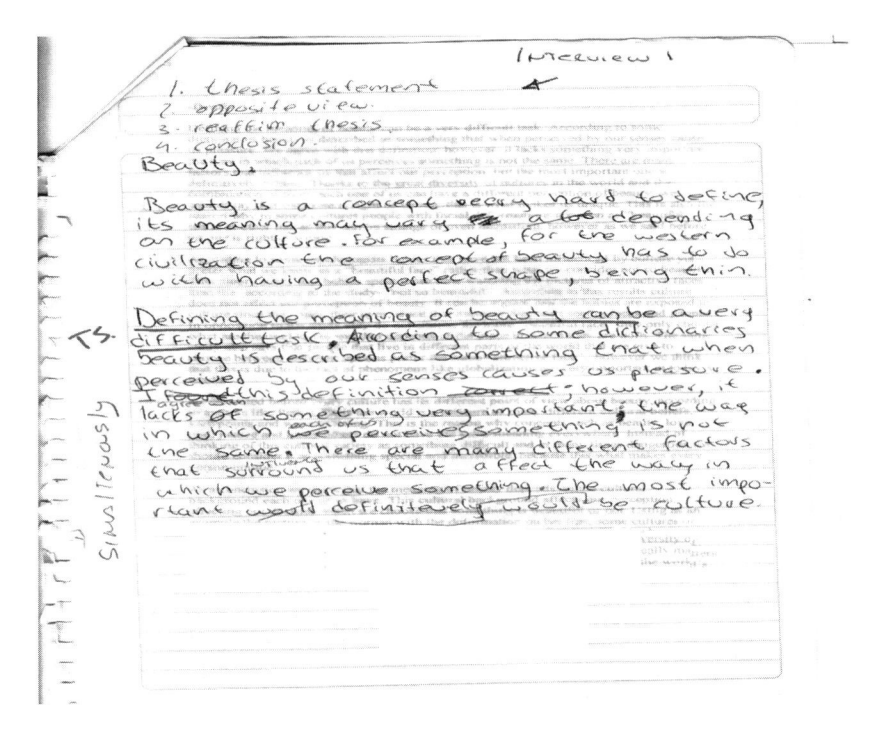

Figure 7.4 The outline and first draft of Group 2

Figure 7.5 The first page of the final version of Group 2

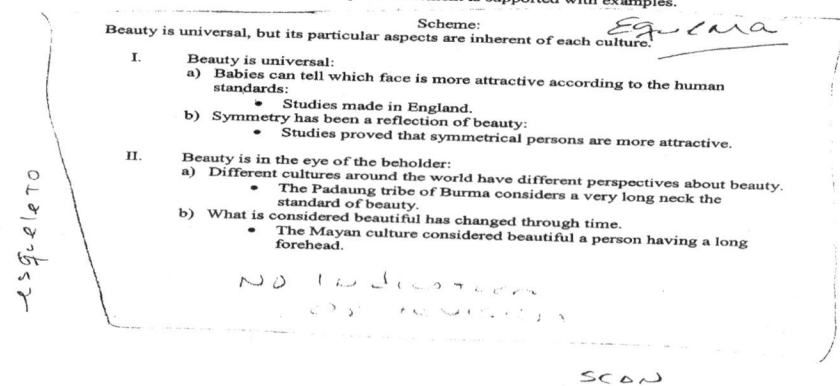

few corrections from the language instructor. The students had typed the drafts up and read them over before they handed in the assignment for assessment. I noticed that the corrections made by the instructor consisted of minor corrections in the language and the need to back up one point of the discussion with references. As in group 1, one student was in charge of the corrections:

> We read it to understand what we had written down because if you don't understand what you've written then from that moment you are wrong. So, you read it and if you understand what you do, you ask somebody else to read it. In this case it was my mum. She read it and said it was "OK, but check the spelling because you have some things that are wrong." So, I began to check the spelling and grammatical errors and this is the final product (Group 2: 3).

Figure 7.6 The two main points of discussion of Group 3

Group 3

Most of the prewriting and drafts in the portfolio were typed up. The interview responses indicate that one of the students began the paper by writing directly in a Word document without stopping for several minutes and without paying attention to errors.

> *I wrote without stopping for several minutes, i.e. without pausing for spelling, punctuation, capital letters. I just wrote and poured out everything I had in my head. After that I outlined the main points … (Group 3: 5).*

He outlined the ideas after choosing the ideas he thought were good to develop. He then continued drafting on his own. Once he had done this, both members met and compared what he had. They wanted to have two contrasting ideas so the other member would draft from a different point of view. They deemed it necessary to select two different points of view for discussion so that they could have two contrasting points (see Figure 7.6).

> *We wanted to have two opposing views and then had a comparison [of these points]. We divided both points of view that beauty is universal and belongs in particular to each culture… We had two main ideas and they had to be supported by examples and statistics… we checked the coherence in the ideas and the drafts… (Group 3: 5–6).*

This group's revision began when they checked, changed and selected the points to be included in the outline, and this was done directly in a Word document. Afterwards, they began to write, and as they wrote, they also examined the contrasting points of view and decided how they should back them up. They checked the coherence, meaning that they wanted to be sure that each of the ideas had a logical sequence, and that these ideas expressed clearly what the students intended to discuss. On the word processor, they decided whether the ideas matched the development of the discussion.

> *We made rough drafts three times. In the first draft you wrote what you had and tried to give coherence to what you did. That is, if the ideas were according to what you thought and to what you wrote…The other drafts are a sequence and you see if you are getting away from the topic and you need to go back… This was the revision (Group 3: 5).*

The students' final draft included in the portfolio showed that they had revised their drafts previously since this final version had very few corrections to grammatical mistakes and hardly any to the discussion (see Figure 7.7). Each of the members of the group took part in the corrections. One member revised the ideas

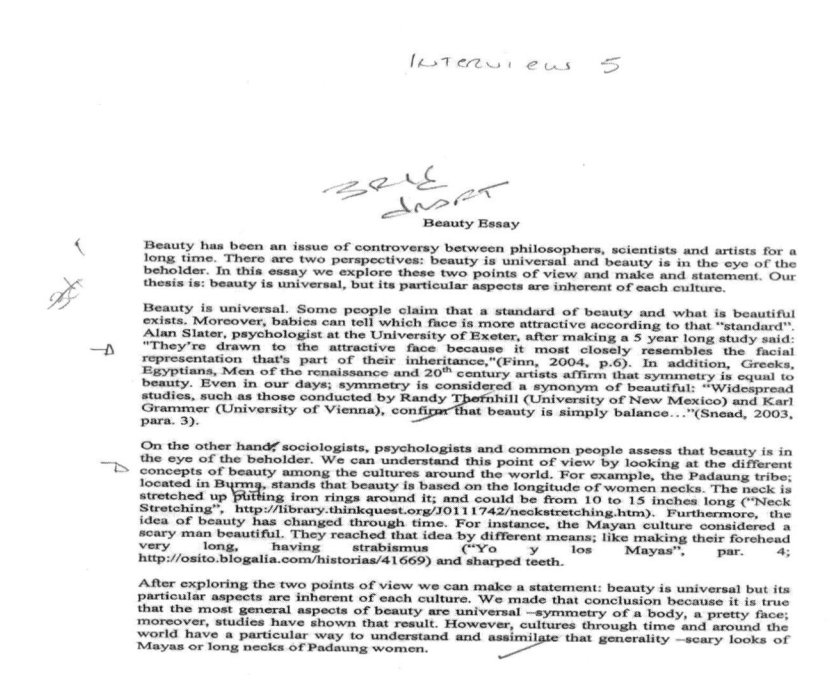

> Interviews 5
>
> BRIEF DRAFT
>
> ### Beauty Essay
>
> Beauty has been an issue of controversy between philosophers, scientists and artists for a long time. There are two perspectives: beauty is universal and beauty is in the eye of the beholder. In this essay we explore these two points of view and make and statement. Our thesis is: beauty is universal, but its particular aspects are inherent of each culture.
>
> Beauty is universal. Some people claim that a standard of beauty and what is beautiful exists. Moreover, babies can tell which face is more attractive according to that "standard". Alan Slater, psychologist at the University of Exeter, after making a 5 year long study said: "They're drawn to the attractive face because it most closely resembles the facial representation that's part of their inheritance,"(Finn, 2004, p.6). In addition, Greeks, Egyptians, Men of the renaissance and 20th century artists affirm that symmetry is equal to beauty. Even in our days; symmetry is considered a synonym of beautiful: "Widespread studies, such as those conducted by Randy Thornhill (University of New Mexico) and Karl Grammer (University of Vienna), confirm that beauty is simply balance…"(Snead, 2003, para. 3).
>
> On the other hand; sociologists, psychologists and common people assess that beauty is in the eye of the beholder. We can understand this point of view by looking at the different concepts of beauty among the cultures around the world. For example, the Padaung tribe; located in Burma, stands that beauty is based on the longitude of women necks. The neck is stretched up putting iron rings around it; and could be from 10 to 15 inches long ("Neck Stretching", http://library.thinkquest.org/J0111742/neckstretching.htm). Furthermore, the idea of beauty has changed through time. For instance, the Mayan culture considered a scary man beautiful. They reached that idea by different means; like making their forehead very long, having strabismus ("Yo y los Mayas", par. 4; http://osito.blogalia.com/historias/41669) and sharped teeth.
>
> After exploring the two points of view we can make a statement: beauty is universal but its particular aspects are inherent of each culture. We made that conclusion because it is true that the most general aspects of beauty are universal —symmetry of a body, a pretty face; moreover, studies have shown that result. However, cultures through time and around the world have a particular way to understand and assimilate that generality —scary looks of Mayas or long necks of Padaung women.

Figure 7.7 The first page of the final draft of Group 3

in the word processor, and the other members checked that they were meeting the instructor's requirements.

The revision in the drafting stages consisted of checking and changing the content to see that the initial ideas were part of the discussion, and that they were consistent with what the students had initially planned. After they were sure that the discussion was coherent enough, and all the ideas were in their proper place, they asked one of their tutors and their language instructor to comment on the draft and make suggestions for any changes.

> …*afterwards, I gave it to a professor so that he could look at it … and comment on it, and we also gave it to the [instructor] …They checked if the ideas did not oppose to each other, and if the text was clear* (Group 3: 5).

The group thought it was extremely important to have external readers involved in this revision process. They wanted to be sure that their two main points of discussion were not confusing or contradictory, and that the final version would meet the instructor's expectations.

Group 4

This group commented during the interview that they looked over and revised their ideas generated from brainstorming, and organized those ideas in a mind map in the computer. When I looked in the portfolio, I found no corrections of the ideas in the mind map made by hand. The response from the interview suggests that the revision at these early stages took place and became helpful because the students were able to have a better picture of what to discuss once they had made changes to the ideas.

> We carried out brainstorming and mind mapping. Once we have our definition [from brainstorming], it was easier to do this and have more order because if you don't start to write you won't make yourself understand as you should (Group 4: 9).

The students' first draft in the portfolio had no indication of any corrections (see Figure 7.8). However, during the interview the students said that each member of the group revised the subsequent drafts for clarity and organization as they typed. They then looked for spelling mistakes and checked that the ideas were well-developed and clear.

> We drafted it and send it to each other so that everything would flow nice, that it had coherence, that the structure would be in order, and all the spelling, and that it was according to what we wanted to communicate. [Who did the final revision?] I read it for the last time and made 2 or 3 changes. I read it aloud from the computer to see how it sounded because I feel that it does change because most of the times when you read it, you are making inferences, the words may not be correctly written. At the moment of reading it aloud you may find errors on grammar and structure (Group 4: 9).

Once each member of the group had checked the composition, one of them read out loud through the final draft in the computer for mistakes. This was also useful because he was able to find more errors. The final version of the paper in the portfolio showed that there were few corrections from the language instructor related to the use of informal vocabulary and errors in mechanics. The handwritten draft in Figure 7.8 suggests no indications of revision. According to the interview, the revision took place as the students typed everything up in a Word document. Afterwards the revision consisted of reading through and correcting in the word processor.

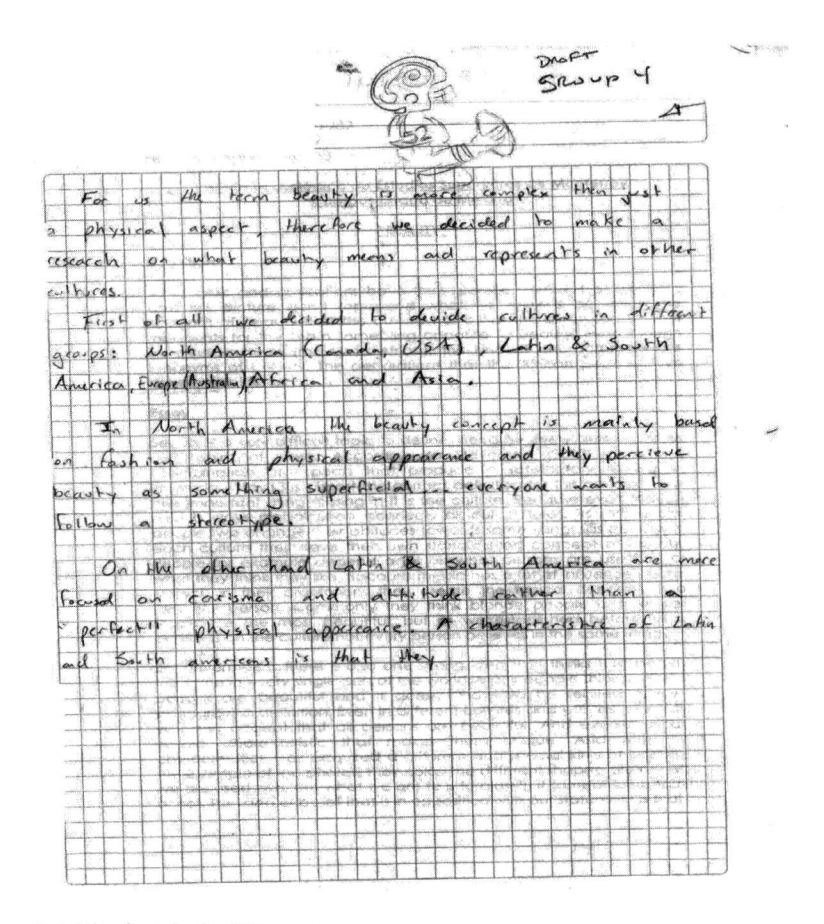

> For us the term beauty is more complex than just a physical aspect, therefore we decided to make a research on what beauty means and represents in other cultures.
> First of all we decided to divide cultures in different groups: North America (Canada, USA), Latin & South America, Europe (Australia) Africa and Asia.
> In North America the beauty concept is mainly based on fashion and physical appearance and they perceive beauty as something superficial – everyone wants to follow a stereotype.
> On the other hand Latin & South America are more focused on carisma and attitude rather than a "perfect" physical appearance. A characteristic of Latin and South americans is that they

Figure 7.8 The first draft of Group 4

4. Discussion and final comments

The findings of this study suggest a variety of revision practices, as can be seen from Figures 7.9a and 7.9b where what the students did is mapped onto Clark and Ivanic's four dimensions.

As can be seen from these Figures, the students started their revision at the moment they began to change the main ideas developed from sharing thoughts. Practices varied: some groups created clusters and outlines which formed part of the revision through which they changed and selected the best ideas they thought worth developing, whereas another group began to mark with a tick or a cross each idea and included annotations in the margins with changes to the ideas, and highlighted them by hand with a coloured pen. This was done with the purpose

Advanced EFL students' revision practices   145

WHAT CLARK & IVANIC (1997) SAY		WHAT THE STUDENTS IN THE STUDY DID
GROUP 1 (three students)		
(a) The writing process is dynamic & recursive	fig.1 p.8	• Selected ideas from the notes page • Went back and forth between the drafts and the outline • Restructured the outline in the light of the draft • Corrected spellings and vocabulary at the same time as changing the order of the sentences
(b) Revising takes place throughout the writing process	fig.1	• Made corrections and annotations in the margins of the notes page. • Began their revision in the initial stages of the composition process.
(c) Practices vary from person to person	p.8	• Used shared thinking • Used of lists/clusters • Non-stop handwritten first draft • Drafted an introductory paragraph with a thesis statement • Wrote notes in the margins about content and to guide the proofreader where to insert new information. • Use of ticks & crosses as well as words • Only one person in charge of revision
(d) Technology can shape the way we write	Figs.1 & 2	• Used of colours.
NEW FINDINGS BY CAMPS	p.8 p.9	• Final draft checked by someone external to the writing process • Needed a reader-friendly, consistent and logical text.
GROUP 2 (three students)		
(a) The writing process is dynamic & recursive	p.12	• Began to change, select and reorganize ideas from the beginning
(b) Revising takes place throughout the writing process	p.11	• Revision started from at the moment that the ideas generated by brainstorming were incorporated into an outline • Checked the first draft for coherence
(c) Practices vary from person to person	fig.3 p.11 p.12	• Brainstormed ideas 'in complete sentences' as a group • Sorted ideas into an outline • Handwrote notes and draft • Made a numbered list for the outline. • Used arrows as well as words • Made notes in the margin • Drafted an introductory paragraph with a thesis statement • One student was in charge of the corrections • Checked the spelling and grammatical errors last
(d) Technology can shape the way we write		• Use of colours to write lists and to underline. • Drafted almost everything in the same Word document several times, and checked the coherence. • Typed the drafts up and read them over before handing the final draft in for assessment.
NEW FINDINGS BY CAMPS	p.12	• Use of reading text to establish understanding • Final draft checked by someone external to the writing process.

Figure 7.9a Practice mapped onto theory, Groups 1 and 2

WHAT CLARK & IVANIC (1997) SAY		WHAT STUDENTS IN THE STUDY DID
GROUP 3 (two students)		
(a) The writing process is dynamic & recursive	p.14	• Examined the contrasting points of view as they wrote and decided how they should back them up. • Went back and forth between drafts
(b) Revising takes place throughout the writing process	p.14	• Revision began with checking, changing and selecting the points to be included in the outline • Checked logical sequence and clarity of ideas as they drafted • Changed the content of the drafts to incorporate original ideas.
(c) Practices vary from person to person	p.13 fig.5 p.14 p.13 p.14	• Non-stop typed first draft • Use of bullet points to outline opposing arguments • Each took one argument and drafted own parts of the essay separately. • Made three rough drafts • Met and compared what they had written • One member revised the ideas in the word processor, and the other member checked that they were meeting the instructor's requirements
(d) Technology can shape the way we write	p.13	• Typed most of the prewriting and drafts from the beginning • Checked development of ideas
NEW FINDINGS BY CAMPS	p.14 p.16 p.17	• Checked that they were meeting the instructor's requirements • Asked one of their tutors and their language instructor to comment on the draft and make suggestions for any changes • Thought it was extremely important to have external readers involved in the revision process because they wanted to be sure they would meet the instructor's expectations.
GROUP 4 (three students)		
(a) The writing process is dynamic & recursive	p.17	• Each member of the group revised new drafts for clarity and organization as they typed. • Checked fro spelling errors at same time as checking content
(b) Revising takes place throughout the writing process	pp.17& 18	• Each member read through all the drafts and corrected them on the word processor • Each member checked the composition of the final draft • One member checked the final draft on the computer for spelling mistakes
(c) Practices vary from person to person	p.17 fig.7	• Brainstorming and mind mapping to establish order • Oral brainstorming, handwritten notes not annotated
(d) Technology can shape the way we write	p.17	• Mind map word processed • New drafts word processed and sent to each other
NEW FINDINGS BY CAMPS	p.17	• Use of writing to promote clarity • Use of reading aloud to aid revision

Figure 7.9b Practice mapped onto theory, Groups 3 and 4

of indicating what ideas in the outline should have been left out and what ideas should be left in so that each group could continue with drafting the paragraphs. Most of the groups assigned someone to be in charge of the corrections at this initial stage, but one group decided that all of the members would be in charge.

I also observed from the data that most of groups sought assistance from other people who were not members of the group. That part was conducted at the final drafting stages. The students wanted to be sure that their paper would not have any errors in the language. It was clear to them that almost at the end of the drafting stage the assistance from a third party would be extremely useful. One group, however, did not look for someone else to look over their final draft. Instead, one member of this group read it aloud, which proved to be useful to him because he was able to find more errors. In any case, the relevance of going over the composition one more time before submitting it was evident.

Based on the data, I found that the revision of content in the drafting stage was mainly centred on the coherence of the paper and the utilization of references. Each group wanted to be sure that the paper would be clear enough, so clarity became the main concern. The composition had to be readable enough so that the language instructor would understand the content of the discussion. I also noticed that the students checked which parts of the discussion needed to be backed up by references. Each of the groups' awareness of having the necessary references became important in order to have a more serious and a more credible discussion and to meet the language instructor's expectations and requirements.

The students employed computer technology in order to carry out the revision. This type of technology was used not only for the drafting stage, but also for the idea generating stage. Some students brainstormed for ideas, and then checked them and outlined them while they made changes at the same time. In addition, as they drafted, they made corrections in the Word document almost simultaneously. Others drafted everything and started to make changes afterwards. The students made the most of the computer technology available, but during the interview they did not mention the utilization of the spell checker although they did proofread spelling and punctuation. In any case, it is most likely that they used the spell checker to help them with the correction of this type of mistakes. Besides the employment of computer technology, other students used a different type of technology, such as coloured pens to highlight errors and changes.

The findings of this study are consistent with the four points of my discussion outlined at the beginning of this chapter. They also suggest that the students engaged in a variety of revision practices in order to have an error-free, clear and meaningful piece of work. First, the students' composition process was dynamic and recursive. The students revised from the moment they began to plan and organize ideas up to the moment they had the final version of their composition.

Second, the way that the students drew upon these revision practices varied from group to group. Third, the use of technology became a vital tool in the students' revision practices.

My analysis, however, has uncovered other practices in which writers may engage. One interesting practice suggested by group 4 (see page 17) is the use of the act of writing itself to promote clarity, in a way that talking about writing seemed not to have done. Three of the groups asked another person, not connected with the writing process, to read and comment on the text and two of the groups used the conscious practice of reading, either silently or aloud, to establish understanding and to aid revision. Although only one of these two practices – asking someone to read the text – appears to draw on the collaborative nature of writing, it is arguable that both these practices draw on the apparent need for writers to separate themselves from the text they have written, in order to be able to evaluate it. In the case of the students in this study, these two practices appear to be intimately connected with meeting the instructor's requirements: one group actually asked one of their tutors and their language instructor to comment on the draft and to suggest changes. This underlines the fact that the social practice analysed in this chapter is situated in an institution in which the teaching of the sort of formal English used in the professions, is the main goal.

Despite this, the findings indicate that the students' revision in the drafting stage of the process was not limited to grammar and coherence. The students revised the structure and content of their essays by discussing and rearranging and making decisions about what to do. However, the language instructor's comments on one of the groups' essays indicated that development of more formal language, or more citing of sources in the discussion, was overlooked. This leads me to point out that the importance of checking for improving the content of these elements should be emphasized more when we teach academic writing in an EFL setting. The focus on checking these points will help students to become more proficient writers of English and prepare for their future careers. For instance, let us say that they will examine the language used; as a result, they will realize the importance of establishing a more formal voice, related to their future professions, through the selection of words and phrases, or even sentences, which are part of standard language usage.[3]

Student writers engaging in a writing process have the capacity or faculty to build on what they have done previously, and they can draw upon practices over and over again, with the possibility of using them differently and abundantly. Students are endowed with openness to new ways of doing things and to a continually

---

3. See Ivanič (1998) and Ivanič and Camps (2001) for further discussion of this point.

expanding collection of practices. These are all practices and attributes which I am sure that Ivanič would celebrate in other writers as surely as she engages with them in her own teaching and writing.

References

Barton, D. 1994. *Literacy: An introduction to the ecology of written language.* Oxford: Blackwell.

Camps, D. 2000. Drawing on, adapting and recreating writing practices for their academic purposes: The case of six Mexican postgraduate students at four British universities. PhD dissertation, Lancaster University.

Camps, D. 2004. The design of visual materials for academic purposes: The case of one Mexican postgraduate student at an English-speaking university. *Revista Estudios de Lingüística Aplicada* 22: 115–133.

Camps, D. 2005a. The process of prewriting of four non-native speaker postgraduate students. *Revista de Humanidades: Tecnológico de Monterrey* 18: 13–33.

Camps, D. 2005b. 'Advanced Students' Visual Representations of the Writing Process. In *Conference Proceedings,* ANUPI, 1–8. Mexico: ANUPI.

Camps, D. & Salsbury, T. 2008. Faculty perceptions of EFL student writing. *ESP World.* Available at: http://www.esp-world.info/Articles_18/issue_18.htm.

Cassany, D. 2005. *Describir el escribir. Cómo se aprende a escribir.* Barcelona: Paidós.

Clark, R. & Ivanič, R. 1997. *The Politics of Writing.* London: Routledge.

Currie, P. & Cray, E. 2004. ESL literacy: Language practice or social practice? *Journal of Second Language Writing* 13: 111–132.

Hayes, J. & Flower, F. 1980. Identifying the organization of writing processes. In *Cognitive Processes in Writing,* L. Gregg & E. Steinberg (eds), 3–30. Hillsdale NJ: Lawrence Erlbaum.

Hayes, J. & Flower, F. 1983. Uncovering cognitive processes in writing: An introduction to protocol analysis. In *Research on Writing: Principles and methods,* P. Mosenthal, L. Tamor & S. Walmsley (eds), 207–220. New York NY: Longman.

Ivanič, R. 1998. *Writing and Identity. The discoursal construction of identity in academic writing.* Amsterdam: John Benjamins.

Ivanič, R. & Camps, D. 2001. I am how I sound. Voice as self-representation in L2 writing. *Journal of Second Language Writing* 10: 3–33.

Ivanič, R. & Moss, W. 1991. Bringing community writing practices into education. In *Writing in the Community,* D. Barton & R. Ivanič (eds), 193–223. Newbury Park CA: Sage.

CHAPTER 8

Reconceptualising student writing[*]
From conformity to heteroglossic complexity

Mary Scott and Joan Turner
Institute of Education, UK / Goldsmiths College, UK

In this chapter we draw on concepts that have been central to Roz Ivanič's insightful analyses of students' writing, viz., writing as social practice; identity; and ideologies of knowledge-making. Roz's demonstrations of the analytical power of these concepts is at the core of our attempt to show how excerpts from student texts enact heteroglossia by negotiating contemporary disciplinary discourses and inter-relating academic conventions such as citation with previous educational values. We argue that the excerpts throw up questions around academic conventions, and hence academic writing pedagogy

Introduction

The perspective developed in this paper lies at the interface between applied linguistic research on academic writing and the various theoretical discourses that feed into academic literacy or academic literacies. Roz Ivanič is a key figure in literacy research in general and academic literacy research in particular. From her literacy as social practice perspective, she looks closely at student work and distinctively, collaborates with students on publishing research into various aspects of academic literacy. These publications include (Ivanič & Roach 1990; Ivanič 1994; Clark & Ivanič 1997; Ivanič 1998; Barton, Hamilton & Ivanič 2000).

In this chapter, we look at excerpts from student texts and how they enact heteroglossia, by, among other things, negotiating contemporary disciplinary discourses which the students are working on, inter-relating academic conventions such as citation with previous educational values, and developing an argument.

---

[*] This chapter is an adapted version of a paper that appeared in: Scott, Mary and Turner, Joan. 2004 Creativity, conformity and complexity in academic writing: Tensions at the interface. In Mike Baynham, Alice Deignan and Goodith White (Eds) 2004 *Applied Linguistics at the Interface* (British Studies in Applied Linguistics, Vol. 19)

These texts throw up questions around academic conventions, and hence academic writing pedagogy. On the one hand, the questions cannot be ignored, but on the other hand, the aim should be to provide understandings not rules.

Academic literacy/literacies as social practice

The field of academic literacy or academic literacies has received a considerable amount of attention from educators, applied linguists, and others of late, and hence the field has been revitalised. Social practice perspectives have been especially influential. Along with Ivanič, the following work among others is particularly relevant to this chapter: Gee (1990); Jones, Turner, & Street (1999); Lea & Street (1998, 1999); Lillis, (2001); Lillis & Turner (2001); Street (1995). A social practice view emphasises the implications for academic writing of the social construction of knowledge (e.g Bazerman 1988; Berkenkotter & Huckin 1995; Geisler 1994; Hyland 2000; Myers 1990) as well as the perspective or position of the student in relation to her/his writing.

From this perspective the boundaries of a text are social not merely linguistic (Kress 1993), and the theoretical focus widens to include the perception of literacy events (e.g. reading a student assignment) as involving sociocultural values, beliefs and power relations (see for example, Ivanič & Roach 1990). Ivanič also foregrounds the importance of social identities, and in analysing student texts, considers the range of semiotic resources and personal knowledge and experience that students draw on. Her book *Writing and Identity* (1998) is a particularly rich resource for this perspective, as she documents extracts from the texts of her student "co-researchers" and conversations with herself about these texts. For example, in her case study discussion of Rachel (1998: 147–48), she shows how punctuation can be a resource for making meaning and does not simply function as a rule-governed grammatical feature. Another influence on student writers' texts, which she highlights, is the notion of the "autobiographical self". This "autobiographical self" is "at any moment in time the product of their past experiences and encounters in all their richness and complexity" (1998: 182). This is illustrated among others in the case of "Sarah" whose background experience working for the nuclear fuel industry feeds into her essay on environmental ethics (1998: 207–8).

Roz's work shows the value of working with individual students, helping them to be successful in their academic endeavours, and at the same time fostering a critical language awareness (cf. Fairclough 1992; Clark & Ivanič 1997) which helps them to project their own voice in their writing. However, there remains a tension between the complexities inherent in doing this and accommodating to institutional norms for academic literacy. At the level of institutional discourse, expectations of academic literacy tend to be normative, a matter of "common sense" (cf. Lillis 1999). Such a monologic position resonates with the values of "the modern consciousness" (Berger et al. 1973), whose distant, disembodied voice, prototypically projected by a European Enlightenment scientist "discovering" knowledge and making it visible (cf. Turner 2004) signals an objectivist relationship to knowledge. While objectivism has of course been challenged in many areas of the social sciences and humanities, its rhetorical effects continue to hold sway in the conventions of academic writing. These are the rhetorical conventions of what the Scollons (1981) called "essay-text literacy", in association also with Berger et al's depiction of the "homeless mind". The assumptions of essay-text literacy, implicit in much institutional discourse around academic writing, remain powerful. Their taken-for-grantedness undermines the complexity involved in academic writing and furthermore, misses an opportunity to read and enjoy heteroglossia (see further, below).

Mediating academic literacy

In this section, we are looking at examples of work from L2 students and the issues of mediation that arise. The function of mediating academic literacy is often called "language support" but drawing on Baynham's (1995) use of "literacy mediators", we prefer to talk of mediating academic literacy. This does not mean that we write for the student, but attempt to mediate between the background assumptions the student is working with and the dominant institutional assumptions that will make the work acceptable, as well as to help the student mediate between the disciplinary discourses s/he is working with and position her/himself within them. The complexity of issues which arise here is well exemplified in Ivanič's (1998: 304) table, found in Figure 8.1, where she contrasts two major epistemological orientations and their textual and positional ramifications.

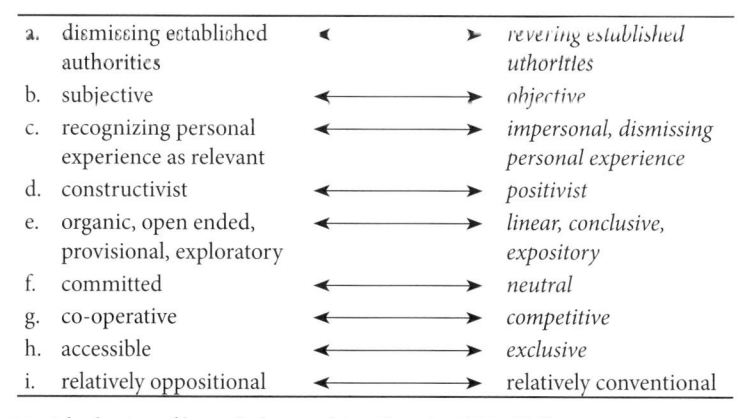

a.	dismissing established authorities	◄――►	revering established authorities
b.	subjective	◄――►	objective
c.	recognizing personal experience as relevant	◄――►	impersonal, dismissing personal experience
d.	constructivist	◄――►	positivist
e.	organic, open ended, provisional, exploratory	◄――►	linear, conclusive, expository
f.	committed	◄――►	neutral
g.	co-operative	◄――►	competitive
h.	accessible	◄――►	exclusive
i.	relatively oppositional	◄――►	relatively conventional

Figure 8.1 Ideologies of knowledge-making (Ivanic 1998: 304)

This table is particularly useful also for teaching purposes, making students aware of how they might write and how this relates to the overarching theories/epistemologies, which they espouse.

Reading heteroglossia in students' work

The following student is working in the area of visual culture, and drawing on the theoretical discourses of postcolonialism and psychoanalysis. She is extremely competent and well versed in those discourses, able to explain or expound at length, orally, on any question asked. However, as the following extract illustrates, the issue of grammatical and lexical accuracy in English, as well as deictic coherence throughout the excerpt, gets in the way of reader accessibility.

> In other words, I discuss the "voice-symptomatic" (un)consciousness with which the sexual slave women spoke in South Korea during the 1990s which appears in the site of contestation within/beyond the "ideological" consciousness and the state of knowledge determined by the ideologically organised normative discursive performative relations between Japan and Korea and its postwar political and economical relations.

Recognising that all texts are the products of heteroglossia (Bakhtin 1981), i.e. of competing voices, the question we would ask of the paragraph above is: What is the nature of this text's heteroglossia? This is a question that can reconfigure the student's "problem with English" especially if it is linked to a view of academic writing as a creative act in which the student writer consciously or intuitively seeks to reconcile the competing voices that beset her. These voices may be numerous; for example, the voices of past instruction; the voices of current tutors; the loud or faint voices of the student's assumptions and expectations regarding writing in English or the demands of a particular course (Scott 2001, 2002). However, in this paper we focus on the echoes of the student's reading in her text, paying particular attention to the heteroglossic tensions that shape it.

The student is researching repressed voices in Korea that are struggling to be heard, i.e. the voices of the Other. Her research involves her in reading texts about otherness by authors who create a "style" or "voice" that seeks to capture "otherness". These writers may demonstrate the conventional features of academic writing (e.g. nominalisation or the passive voice) but they use the features in a particular way. The following example is from De Certeau's (1986: 3 & 4) history of psychoanalysis, an essay that the student had consulted:

> History is 'cannibalistic', and memory becomes the closed arena of conflict between two contradictory operations: forgetting, which is not something passive, a loss, but an action directed against the past; and the mnemic trace, the return of what was forgotten, in other words, an action by a past that is now forced to disguise itself. More generally speaking, any autonomous order is founded upon what it eliminates; it produces a 'residue' condemned to be forgotten. But what was excluded infiltrates the place of its origin – now the present's 'clean' [*propre*] place. It resurfaces, it troubles, it turns the present's feeling of being 'at home' into an illusion, it lurks – this 'wild', this 'ob-scene', this 'filth', this 'resistance' of 'superstition' – within the walls of the residence, and, behind the back of the other (the *ego*), or over its objections, it inscribes there the law of the other.

As is typical of this kind of writing, De Certeau packs the abstractions with ambiguities and paradoxes [*an order founded on what it eliminates*]; he crosses boundaries or creates in-between spaces in metaphors that juxtapose abstraction and the concrete; (*closed arena of conflict; action...disguise; behind the back of the other*); he invents terms ("*cannibalistic*"); uses punctuation in unconventional ways (a comma before *in other words*; a hyphen in *ob-scene*), and he favours the series as a syntactical means of intensifying meaning (e.g. a series of verbs or adjectives or nouns or elaborative and appositional clauses as in *it surfaces resurfaces, it troubles, it turns; "this wild", this "ob-scene", this "filth", this "resistance" of "superstition"*). Generally speaking, this way of writing – this style – enacts "otherness".

A number of the syntactical features are those associated with spoken English (e.g. the co-ordinating conjunctions, *and, but*; the placing of pauses, e.g. before *But*; the parentheses, the juxtaposition of phrases; the use of punctuation to direct the reading). This close-to-speech style conforms to psycho-analysis, the talking cure, in its attempt to capture resonances that evade the rationality of conventional academic argument. It is to this voice, which challenges the conventions of scientific writing, that the text largely owes its readability.

Turning again to the student's text we note that there are echoes of the voices of the authors she is reading. This might be said to be appropriate in view of the fact that her subject is otherness; the return of the repressed. But the student's text represents a problematic hybrid. She is caught between the voice that is required in Ph.D. writing and the voices she encounters in her reading. Her opening sentence (*In other words I discuss*) represents a conformity to the Ph.D. requirement that the writer's purposes be made explicit. The student has also sought explicitness in her syntactically problematic attempt to weld together the different content components of what she wants to say (*with which...; which...*). On the other hand, the voices of her reading are clearly discernible in *voice symptomatic*; in the list of pre-head noun qualifiers – *organised normative discursive performative relations*; and in the slash to suggest ambiguity: *within/beyond*.

We would suggest that the student's perceived problem with language as illustrated in this passage, is rooted in her twofold "otherness", i.e. in the space she occupies in between the expectation that she write for an "intelligent outsider" – to quote advice frequently given to doctoral students – and make her purposes clear, and the style of the texts she is reading, which, for all their complexity of content are readable. The student's text is not; she has created a mosaic – a visual construct in which there is little sense of a writer's voice. To express the problem another way by borrowing Bakhtin's (1981) terms, the centripetal voice of the Ph.D. clashes with centrifugal echoes of the texts she has read.

However, while the student's text is undoubtedly problematic as we have indicated, a question remains. How should students write about topics in fields of knowledge that challenge the view of rationality on which the Ph.D is largely based? How postmodern might a Ph.D thesis be? The conventions of academic writing have, of course, been challenged, especially by Feminist researchers but the focus has tended to be on the explicit inclusion of personal experience and feelings as in the example below which comes from a Ph.D. thesis:

> Teachers setting homework would request us to "look this up in the encyclopaedia when you get home". Not only did this mean I was unable to do the homework, I was constantly constructed as "other" and inferior, for coming from a home where theses and other resources were not readily available. Casual mentions of ski-ing holidays in Switzerland and days out to places of interest in London and elsewhere re-inscribed this sense of outsiderness, and made me long for (and know that I could not have) what looked like a life of excitement beside which mine seemed increasingly tedious and dull.

This view of the importance of the personal in knowledge-making certainly represents a challenge to a view of rationality that is held to express itself in impersonal sentence constructions but it is a long way from postmodern ways of writing which seek to capture resonances in a style that is more usually associated with the poetic or with Deleuze and Guattari's (1994) view of literary style as affect divorced from propositional meaning. In this paper we can only use our example to suggest that there are more questions to be asked about writing and knowledge-making in different fields of study than have yet been addressed.

Widening the focus

The tensions around language in academic writing do not occur only at the doctoral level, however. The question we have asked – What is the nature of this text's heteroglossia? – is relevant at all levels of higher education. The examples that we have selected to make this point are from an assignment by a student on an in-service degree course in Education. The student trained as a teacher in a country where, for economic reasons, training colleges did not have well-stocked libraries. This influenced the modes of teaching and learning and made it impossible for lecturers to set assignments that would require the critical reading of a number of texts.

The student's draft of her first written assignment was seen as demonstrating a "problem with writing in English". In her written feedback to the student the tutor made the following numbered comments

1. You need to write in full sentences
2. Referencing needs care. Consult the course handbook for examples of how to set out references in the body of a text.

Each instance of these problems was underlined and the appropriate number – 1 or 2 – was written in the margin of the student's assignment. The following are three examples of the kinds of sentence that were rightly identified as problematic. Each represents a recurring problem in the student's text.

> (Dave 1975) Explain that lifelong education represents the inner necessity of men to continually exceed themselves
>
> Preparation for life in tomorrow's world cannot be satisfied by a once and for all acquisition of knowledge and know-how. By John Field (2001)
>
> According to the Secretary of State for Education and Employment he wrote that "To cope with the rapid change and the challenge of the information and communication age, we must ensure that people can return to learning throughout their lives".

We acknowledge the need for the student to become familiar with ways of integrating citation into text, and of referencing sources but we would argue that the examples above have a larger significance. As in the case of the Ph.D. student, we read the student's writing as evidence of the student's struggle to reconcile competing voices. The discourses about academic writing that the student has been offered on her course are relevant to our interpretations. The student has been told in seminars that an essential feature of academic writing is an "argument" in which the writer develops her own position – her own voice – in relation to the relevant literature of the field. She has also been advised to acknowledge her sources.

The examples quoted above demonstrate the student's attempt to meet these requirements. However, the student's style of referencing can also be read as articulating her uneasiness regarding the requirement that she position herself in relation to the voices of the "others" that she has encountered in her reading. As we indicate below, a closer look at the examples reveals an interesting pattern. In each case the student has constructed a hierarchy by visually and syntactically marking out a space in which her voice and that of the other to whom she refers are both joined and disjoined.

In the first example the student places the subject of the sentence, Dave, in brackets. She then inserts a phrase of her own: *Explain that*. The use of the capital "E" and of the plural form in *Explain* can be read as mere technical errors. However, we would suggest that they should rather be viewed as the student's intuitive attempt to indicate that the direct quotation of Dave's words which follows – *lifelong education represents the inner necessity...* – do in fact signify a position that is shared by her and Dave. The absence of quotation marks is in keeping with this interpretation. It is not an equal sharing, though. The student's placing of Dave, with date, in brackets at the beginning of the sentence gives his name greater prominence than the conventions of integral referencing would allow. In visually setting Dave apart from herself the student endows Dave, the other, with superior status in the particular field of knowledge-making.

In the second example the student attributes the status of an authority to the cited author by giving him a space of his own that is pegged out by an emphatic, initial *By* and the use of both his first and family names: *John Field*. Interestingly there are no examples of conventional non-integral referencing in the student's assignment. In each case where that would be appropriate she uses the "By" construction. It is as if she needs to emphasise that the quotation she has just used to build her argument comes from someone whose authority transcends hers.

The third example demonstrates a pattern that is frequently encountered in L2 students' academic writing, viz., the anaphoric use of a subject pronoun with verb after "according to...". (*According to..., he wrote....*). However, this instance suggests that it may be relevant to consider who is being quoted. Here the student's syntactically unacceptable use of *he* gives emphasis to the authority of the Secretary of State – the kind of authority which the student said was very highly respected in her country of origin. The Secretary of State's voice of authority is further accentuated by the student's enclosure of his words in quotation marks, a device she did not use in the first two examples above. In thus creating a space between her voice as referee and the voice of the State's representative the student signals the power of the State. It clearly has a voice that needs to be heeded.

Like the Ph.D. student whose writing was discussed earlier, this student occupies an in-between space. In her case it is a space between an institutional past and an institutional present with their different requirements. However, what the examples from this student's writing also indicate is the operation of desire at the centre of student writing. This is almost certainly the case with all writing but it may be especially so when the student is an L2 writer from an educational context with different expectations of student writers from those that characterise higher education in the UK. The student is anxious to meet the referencing requirements but for her this is not merely a technical issue. Desire conflicts with attitudes and feelings towards the Other in the form of the voices in the books she reads – voices that she endows with authority. In fact it might be said that the processes that postmodern writers like De Certeau knowingly try to capture in their writing are being unwittingly demonstrated by student writers like the two whose writing we have considered in this paper.

We acknowledge that our readings of the student's texts are open to question as is always the case with interpretations. We hope, however, that we have stimulated reflection and debate. As we suggested in our initial paragraph this chapter is indebted to Roz's insightful and detailed discussion of student texts (e.g. Ivanič 1998) that challenge conventional assessment-driven readings of student writing. Students, as she has shown, bring with them their autobiographical selves; their linguistic and educational histories and their aspirations. These can "jostle with" the expected voices. Though she has focused mainly on non-traditional students she offers a way of thinking about all students in university classrooms where students represent an increasing diversity of experience and expectations. This way of thinking about student writing includes a new perception of "language" as offering a range of resources for meaning making, such as punctuation, as discussed above. This is however all in the service of a larger aim: being on the side of students in their struggle to achieve authorship (i.e. to write with authority) in the midst of "jostling voices". This does not represent an uncritical championing of the student voice but rather an enlargement of students' understandings of academic writing in its concrete situatedness and of its possibilities and constraints

In the current climate with so much emphasis on training in skills, the proliferation of "how to" books, and narrowly defined criteria, it is good to be reminded by Ivanič that writing is a complex social act to which students and teachers bring past histories and current and future possibilities. On the basis of the discussion above we would argue that it is here that pedagogy needs to begin. Roz suggests a route, in offering the following questions:

> What aspects of people's lives have led them to write the way they do?
> How has their access to discourses and associated positionings been socially enabled or constrained?
> More generally how has the autobiographical self shaped their writing?
> What characteristics of the social interactions surrounding the texts led the students to position themselves in this way?
> How far do they establish an authorial presence in their writing?

What influences shape their disciplinary identity?
How do people establish authority for the content of their writing?
To what extent do they represent themselves or others as authoritative?
(Ivanič 1998: 25–27)

These questions cover the implications of a social approach: the nature and shaping role of the social interactions surrounding the texts; the students' positionings; and establishment of an authorial presence in their texts. The message for the teacher as in our discussion of student texts above is that the focus should be not so much on how to fix this text but rather on recognising the tensions that surround student writing and the assessment of it.

References

Bakhtin, M. M. 1981. *The Dialogic Imagination: Four essays*. M. Holquist (ed.), C. Emerson & M. Holquist (Trans.). Austin TX: University of Texas.
Barton, D., Hamilton, M. & Ivanič, R. 2000. *Situated Literacies: Reading and writing in context*. London: Routledge.
Baynham, M. 1995. Literacy practices. *Investigating Literacy in Social Contexts*. London: Longman.
Bazerman, C. 1988. *Shaping Written Knowledge; Essays in the growth, form function, and implications of the scientific article*. Madison WI: University of Wisconsin Press.
Berger, P. L., Berger, B. & Kellner, H. 1973. *The Homeless Mind: Modernisation and consciousness*. New York NY: Random House.
Berkenkotter, C. & Huckin, T. 1995. *Genre Knowledge in Disciplinary Communication: Cognition, culture, power*. Hiullsdale NJ: Lawrence Erlbaum Associates .
Clark, R. & Ivanič, R. 1997. *The Politics of Writing*. London: Routledge.
De Certeau, M. 1986. *Heterologies: Discourses on the other*. B. Massumi, trans. Minneapolis MN: University of Minnesota Press.
Deleuze, G. & Guattari, F. 1994. *What is Philosophy*. (H. Tomlinson and G. Burchill, trans.). London: Verso.
Fairclough, N. (ed). 1992. *Critical Language Awareness*. London: Longman.
Gee, J. P. 1990. *Social Linguistics and Literacies: Ideology in discourses*. London: Falmer Press.
Geisler, C. 1994. *Academic Literacy and the Nature of Expertise*. Hillsdale NJ: Lawrence Erlbaum Associates.
Hyland, K. 2000. *Disciplinary Discourses. Social interactions in academic writing*. London: Pearson Education.
Ivanič, R. 1994. I is for interpersonal: Discoursal construction of writer identities and the teaching of writing. *Linguistics and Education* 6(1): 3–15.
Ivanič, R. 1998. *Writing and Identity. The discoursal construction of identity in academic writing*. Amsterdam: John Benjamins.

Ivanič, R. & Roach, D. 1990. Academic writing, power and disguise. In *Language and Power*, R. Clark, N. Fairclough, R. Ivanič, N. McLeod, J. Thomas & P. Meara (eds), London: Centre for Information on Language Teaching, for the British Association for Applied Linguistics.
Jones, C., Turner, J. & Street, B. (eds) 1999. *Students Writing in the University: Cultural and epistemological issues*. Amsterdam: John Benjamins.
Kress, G. 1993. *Learning to Write*. London: Routledge.
Lea, M. & Street, B. 1998. Student writing in higher education: An academic literacies approach. *Studies in Higher Education* 23(2): 157–172.
Lea, M. & Street, B. 1999. Writing as academic literacies: Understanding textual practices in higher education. In *Writing: Texts, processes and practices*, C. N. Candlin & K. Hyland (eds), 62–81. London: Longman.
Lillis, T. 1999. Whose 'Common Sense'? Essayist literacy and the institutional practice of mystery. In *Students writing in the university: Cultural and epistemological issues*, C. Jones, J. Turner & B. Street (eds). Amsterdam: John Benjamins.
Lillis, T. 2001. *Student Writing. Access, regulation, desire*. London: Routledge.
Lillis, T. & Turner, J. 2001. Student writing in higher education: Contemporary confusion, traditional concerns. *Teaching in Higher Education* 6(1): 57–68.
Myers, G. 1990. *Writing Biology: Texts in the social construction of scientific knowledge*. Madison WI: University of Wisconsin Press.
Scollon, R. & Scollon, S. W. 1981. *Narrative, Literacy and Face in Interethnic Communication*. Norwood NJ: Ablex.
Scott, M. 2001. Written English, word processors and meaning making. In *Developmental Aspects of Learning to Write*, L. Tolchinsky (ed.). Dordrecht: Kluwer.
Scott, M. 2002. Cracking the codes anew: Writing about literature in England. In *Writing and Learning in Cross-National Perspective: Transitions from secondary to higher education*, D. Foster & D. Russell (eds). Urbana IL: NCTE and Mahwah NJ: Lawrence Erlbaum Associates.
Street, B. 1995. *Social Literacies: Critical approaches to literacy in development, ethnography and education*. London: Longman.
Turner, J. 2004. Academic literacy in Post-colonial times: Hegemonic norms and transcultural possibilities. In *Critical Pedagogy. Political approaches to language and intercultural communication*, A. Phipps & M. Guilherme (eds), 22–32. Clevedon: Multilingual Matters.

REFLECTION 6

Roz and critical language studies at Lancaster

Norman Fairclough
Lancaster University

Roz played an important part in the development of critical language studies at Lancaster University. She was one of the group (with Romy Clark, Marilyn Martin-Jones and myself) that sought to give a critical turn to ideas of "language awareness", leading to early publications on "critical language awareness" (Clark, Fairclough, Ivanič & Martin-Jones 1991, 1992; Fairclough ed. 1992). These ideas attracted a great deal of interest in educational circles at the time (reflected for instance in the LINC project directed by Ron Carter, see Carter 1996). I recall Roz persuading me to do a day school with her for a group of secondary school teachers of English in the face of my protestations that I couldn't possibly presume to address such an audience. She of course could, and she managed to convince me that I might have more to offer such an audience than I thought (a very Rozian accomplishment!), and with her guidance I got through the day in a reasonably creditable fashion. At least that's the way I prefer to remember it. Roz and I also published together a short critique of the Kingman Report on English language education (Fairclough & Ivanič 1989).

Roz of course gave her own particular inflection to critical linguistics and critical discourse analysis in the work that she did on writing, writer identity and writer agency (Ivanič 1998, Clark & Ivanič 1997). She also contributed a great deal to the development of ways of teaching critical approaches to language analysis. I am thinking particularly of an MA course which she and I taught together for a number of years in the 1990s, New Directions in Language Analysis, which was attended by such luminaries as David Barton and Courtney Cazden as well as many enthusiastic and gifted MA students. I learnt much of what I know about how to teach critical discourse analysis from Roz in our co-teaching on that course, and I have her (as well as Romy and Marilyn) to thank for the moves I have made, such as they are, towards a more audience-friendly style of talking about my work.

References

Carter, R. 1996. Politics and knowledge about language: The LINK project. In *Literacy in Society,* R. Hasan & G. Williams (eds). London: Addiso Wesley Longman.

Clark, R., Fairclough, N., Ivanič, R. & Martin-Jones, M. 1991. Critical language awareness Part 1: A critical review of three current approaches to language awareness. *Language and Education* 4(4): 249–60.

Clark, R., Fairclough, N., Ivanič, R. & Martin-Jones, M. 1992. Critical language awareness Part 2: Towards critical alternatives. *Language and Education* 5(1): 41–54.

Clark, R. & Ivanič, R. 1997. *The Politics of Writing.* London: Routledge.

Fairclough, N. (ed.). 1992. *Critical Language Awareness.* London: Longman.

Fairclough, N. & Ivanič, R. 1989. Language education or language training? A critique of the Kingman model of the English language. In *Kingman and the Linguists*, J. Bourne (ed.). CLIE Working Paper.

Ivanič, R. 1998. *Writing and Identity: The discoursal construction of identity in academic writing.* Amsterdam: John Benjamins.

PART III

Methodology

REFLECTION 7

Sharing writing, sharing names

Hilary Janks
University of the Witwatersrand, South Africa

I owe a great deal to Roz Ivanič. She was my friend, my teacher, my writing partner and my doctoral examiner. When I arrived in Lancaster University in 1989 as a mature (the polite word for *older*) student from South Africa to begin working on my doctorate, I joined the research circle on writing for which Roz and Romy Clark were responsible. Little did I know at the time how ground-breaking their work would prove to be. Amongst the researchers working in the area of language and power at Lancaster, they were the only ones working on writing and power and they paved the way for others such as Barbara Kamler (2001; Kamler and Thomson 2006) and Theresa Lillis (2001), by putting questions of identity and power at the heart of a critical approach to writing. In the area of what was then known in the UK as 'critical linguistics' or Critical Language Awareness, the focus was on critical discourse analysis and critical reading.

I think it was Roz's deep concern for her students and her experience in adult education that led to her understanding of the connection between writing and identity. Because she took the alienation experienced by her late-entry (the polite word for *older*) working class students seriously, she gained insight into the effects of powerful institutional discourses, an understanding of issues related to access to these discourses, and a grasp of the impact of both power and access on the identities of students from diverse backgrounds.

Rather than writing about these students, she wrote with them. In institutions which privilege individual scholarly work, collaborative writing is undervalued. For the students, however, this work with Roz was a gift. Not only did she help them to articulate their struggles with writing in the academy, she included them as knowledge makers in the world of scholarly publication. She helped to bring these marginalised students into the centre of the academic endeavour and in the process to deconstruct the language, the genres and the practices of academia. She literally wrote their concerns about academic literacy into our thinking about language and identity in the academy, providing a way forward for teachers in higher education internationally and a point of reference for marginalised students everywhere. Our work in the area of academic literacy and pedagogies in higher education in South Africa, where we work with first generation university students, has been greatly enriched by her pioneering work.

I was one of the lucky ones. Writing with Roz was for me a formative experience. While it was not the first time I had co-published an article, this was the first really collaborative experience that I had had as a writer. Roz was much more experienced than I was, yet she insisted in her characteristically generous way that I be the first author. At the time, I was particularly struck with her ability to signpost the moves we were making and to think about how to assist the reader. One of the ideas we explored while working together was that collaborative writing was a means of making visible to each of us the differently positioned discourses she and I were drawing on. Negotiating our own investments in these positions helped us to understand our own identities and to find a position from which we could speak in a jointly authored paper: 'Critical language awareness and emancipatory discourse' (Janks and Ivanič 1992).

Some years later when I became interested in naming practices in different communities, different families and different religions as well as how these practices were informed by power relations at different moments in history, I told Roz and her husband the story of my surname. When I married I assumed my husband's name, Janks, at the time a naturalised gendered practice. Janks is an abbreviated form of Jankelowitz, a Lithuanian Jewish name. My husband's father anglicised his name, I believe, in order to disguise his origins and to improve his life chances in South Africa. Jankelowitz means son of Jankel; the English word for Jankel is John. Like me, Roz also adopted her husband's name. He too came from Eastern Europe. In Serbian, the suffix 'ič' means son of. So Ivanič means son of Ivan; Ivan is also a version of John. In an English speaking world, the one paper that Roz and I wrote together, was in fact co-authored by Johnson and Johnson. I like to think of this story as emblematic – as a story which suggests that people despite their diverse backgrounds often have more in common than they realise.

References

Janks, H. & Ivanič, R. 1992. Critical language awareness and emancipatory discourse. In *Critical Language Awareness*, Fairclough, N. (ed.), 305–331. London: Longman.
Kamler, B. 2001. *Relocating the Personal*. Albany NY: State University of New York.
Kamler, B. & Thomson, P. 2006. *Helping Doctoral Students Write*. London: Routledge.
Lillis, T. 2001. *Student Writing: Access, regulation, desire*. London: Routledge.

CHAPTER 9

Bringing writers' voices to writing research
Talk around texts

Theresa Lillis
The Open University, UK

This chapter explores how a key methodology developed by Roz Ivanič, "talk around texts", constitutes a fundamental contribution to writing research in three ways; firstly by disrupting conventional researcher-researched positioning; secondly by keeping writers centre stage even whilst using text-linguistics; and thirdly by opening up opportunities for re-examining textual practices, by questioning what should (and could) be valued in formal institutions of learning. I locate this methodology within the particular values Ivanič espouses, as evidenced by both her pedagogic and her academic-theoretical work and illustrate how my own research has been influenced by this work in specific research decisions that I have made and in generating further questions that I am still struggling to address.

Introduction

This chapter focuses on a key methodology developed by Roz Ivanič, "talk around texts", and explores how this approach has made a fundamental contribution to the field of writing research, namely by bringing writers' voices to the centre of any attempt to explore what's involved and at stake in academic writing. The chapter begins by briefly illustrating "talk around texts" and then locates this methodology within the particular values Ivanič espouses, as evidenced by both her pedagogic and her academic-theoretical work. As is discussed in this chapter, each dimension – the pedagogic and the academic – has contributed significantly to the development of the other; the pedagogic engages with specific pedagogic traditions, the traditions of critical pedagogy (Freire 1985) and critical language awareness (Clark et al. 1991), and the academic-theoretical engages with a specific approach to literacy, that of literacy as social practice (Barton, Hamilton and Ivanič 2000). Drawing on connections between both dimensions, Ivanič's development of "talk around texts" has impacted on writing research in significant ways, three of which are discussed in this chapter and each of which I discuss under the following headings;

> *disrupting researcher-researched positioning* – by allowing research participants to contribute to the direction of research and thus the naming of the phenomenon or "problem" being explored;
>
> *placing writers centre stage whilst using text-linguistics* – by paying careful attention to writers' perspectives whilst at the same time bringing to bear the tools of linguistic-discourse analysis;
>
> *opening up opportunities for re-examining textual practices* – by questioning what should (and could) be valued in formal institutions of learning.

Alongside the main chapter sections, I illustrate how my own research has been influenced by Roz's work in specific decisions that I have made and in generating further questions that I am still struggling to address. I also offer some brief reflections not just on what Roz has contributed through her written publications, but on the quiet (usually invisible) but powerful ways in which her generosity as a scholar has supported and encouraged many scholars who have felt (or feel) at the margins of the academy, including myself.

> *I remember my first visit to see Roz as my "academic advisor". The doors in Lancaster's department corridor were decorated with famous names from the fields of applied linguistics, critical discourse analysis, New Literacy studies…there were also, countless posters on the walls advertising interesting seminars and lectures- flaunting (it felt like) the discussions that outsiders would not take part in. Roz didn't take these for granted. She welcomed me into her high status institution with its wealth of symbolic academic capital displayed for all to see, even though I was only there for an afternoon, borrowing from the wealth. Having a cup of tea with her was an invitation to share. She asked me my opinion about current texts I was reading and talked of her interests and her concerns about some ideas in recent works. I felt invited to offer my own ideas; treated like an adult with a past, a present not a "student" who had only reached so far. I think that many academics think they (we) are welcoming and open – particularly to those ill at ease, uncomfortable in what is such a privileged and such a middle class marked space (certainly in the UK) – but actually very few are…Roz is one of those few.*[1]

---

1. Roz was an 'academic advisor' to me in my doctoral research. This meant that she was officially a member of the supervisory team, although she was located in a different institution, and in practical terms meant that we met up two or three times each year for an intense afternoon of discussion and questioning.

What is talk around texts?

The method of talk around text is core to much of Ivanič's research work, particularly her research on writing in higher education (see in particular Ivanič 1998; but also in her recent work in further education (as in Ivanič and Satchwell 2007). As a method, what does it essentially involve? Talk between the researcher and the writer-participant about a text that the writer is writing or has written. Such talk may focus on a text type, text, or section/feature of a text: the specific focus at any one moment in time may be something as small as a specific use of a full stop, to patterns of vocabulary or grammar, such as the use of particular pronouns across a text, to a specific convention emblematic of academic discourse, such as the use of citations. Two further basic points should be noted: (1) The texts around which such talk is based are "real" texts, that is writing that is part of a learning/study activity in which writers are engaging – an essay in a politics course, for example, not a task set up for research purposes; (2) Talk is not a one-off interaction between researcher and writer but is embedded in a "longer conversation" (Maybin 1994) relating to people's life and literacy histories.

As a specific method, at this broad level, talk around texts seems straightforward enough and probably a seemingly obvious approach to adopt in exploring what's involved in academic writing. Here's an extract from such talk between Roz and Rachel, a student on a social work course at the time of Ivanič's study; they are discussing one particular extract from an essay (Ivanič 1998: 154):

> Rachel: – so some of the story's descriptive and some of it's just describing.
> Roz: I don't know what you mean.
> Rachel: Sometimes I'm just telling a story and in my storytelling I'm describing things and then other things it's not like the story plot, it's just, like, I'm describing –
> Roz: For example?
> Rachel: Like this bit here "On our last visit Ms A admitted to me that she had been better off without her cohab"… I am describing what she said.

I will discuss below how this seemingly simple methodological move of inviting participants for their views on the texts represents a radical move in academic writing research. Here it is worth noting how such a move constitutes a response to public discourses on student writing. Public discourse on the state of students' writing in higher education is typically framed in deficit terms – students' can't write – and "writing" is usually reduced to specific ideological framings of text, however vague, such as "spelling" and "grammar" (see discussions in Lillis and Turner 2001; Haggis 2003; Lea 2004). The "problem" is taken as given rather than raised as an issue to be explored and the perspectives of writers themselves, or the processes or practices in which texts are embedded, are usually ignored. Ivanič in contrast focuses on these perspectives and practices, drawing on her expertise as teacher and academic to explore them.

The central place given to seeking out writer perspectives in Ivanič's work reflects and enacts a particular ideological stance towards language, pedagogy, research processes and knowledge making which she merges from what I see as two specific and strongly interrelated interests and commitments in her working life: broadly speaking, the pedagogic and the academic-theoretical. Whilst recognising that these are not completely discrete domains, it is Roz's commitment to both which I think has helped her to forge a research methodology which stays rooted in people's real life concerns.

Locating Ivanič's talk around texts within a critical ideology of pedagogy and academic research

Pedagogy: Collaborative research and critical language awareness

Ivanič's pedagogic interests pre-date her involvement in academia as scholar and researcher. As a teacher in adult basic education (ABE) she was centrally concerned with the relationship between language and participation in formal institutions of education, a concern that is always evident in her work as a researcher. Talking about how she came to be involved in language and literacy research, Roz said:

> I felt there were an enormous number of things about language which I needed to understand in order to improve my teaching. It was through listening to students and realising that their explanations, for why they were doing things the way they were, were often based on aspects of language which I would never have predicted, that I felt the complexities of language much more thoroughly.
>
> (Interview 2001)[2]

The impact of her pedagogic experience on her research approach is evident in her book *Writing and identity* where, in referring to the research on which her book is based, she says:

> In my view, by turning tuition into research we were putting into practice two fundamental principles of Adult Basic Education: maintaining symmetry if not equality among adults, and empowering both learners and tutors.   (1998: 110)

---

2. This is an extract from an interview Roz Ivanič did for an Open University Masters course, *Language and Literacy in a changing world*.

This valuing of participant researchers as collaborators, and the fundamental interconnectedness between research and teaching, where teaching itself is construed as an ongoing research activity (in the sense of the need forever to be exploring with learners what is going on and what is at stake) is a core value and highly influential in academic writing research in the UK, and internationally (see for examples in UK, Gardener 1992; for South Africa Thesen and Van Pletzen 2006; for US Lu 1994). A particularly important contribution to raising the profile of language use in general – rather than of writing in particular – was made by Ivanič with colleagues from the Lancaster research group in their work on *critical language awareness*. Building on critical pedagogy (Freire 1985) and critical discourse analysis (Fairclough 1992b, 1995), their writings on critical language awareness challenged the dominant transmission model of formal education, and raised questions about any top down (researcher-analyst led) model of research – arguing instead for a collaborative problem-posing approach. In Freire's work, learning is viewed as the process of becoming critically engaged with socio-political reality, with specific emphasis on developing ways in which the less powerful in society can become "speaking subjects": language is viewed as central to this emancipation as it is through taking control over "naming the world" that people can occupy an agentive subject position rather than being a (subject) object in a world named by others (Freire 1985: Chapter 3). The Critical Language Awareness (CLA) work takes up this view and, building on Fairclough's work in critical language study (CLS) and critical discourse analysis (CDA), takes up the position that discourse analysis should not be only about describing language practices, but should also have an explanatory goal, to seek to explain how it is that certain forms are privileged above others in specific contexts and why. "The explanatory objective of CLS is to show the connection between discourse and its structural determinants and effects" (Clark et al. 1991: 42). A key contribution Ivanič makes in exploring such a connection in writing research, is to place language users, and more specifically in her work, writers, at the centre of such explanatory objectives as I discuss below.

Academic research: New Literacy Studies and ethnography

The attention to learner perspectives that Ivanič draws from core values as a pedagogue and her work with colleagues on CLA is strongly consonant with what can be described as the academic or scholarly dimension to her working life, which is enthused by a combination of academic approaches, notably ethnography and linguistics. I focus on the linguistic-discourse dimension below but here want to emphasise the strong connection between fundamental values in her pedagogic work in ABE and her academic or scholarly interest in ethnography. A core ethnographic principle is that participants' views be treated as authentic and significant (see Hammersley 2006 for discussion of interviews in ethnography) and that research needs to be empirically grounded in, and theoretically infused by, participants' lives. At a theoretical level, this ethnographic approach to the study of student academic writing reflects Roz's collaboration with colleagues in New Literacy Studies, including Street's contrasting notions of autonomous and ideological positions on literacy which have proved to be a particularly powerful heuristic for opening up a critical exploration of the specific literacy demands and practices in context, including those associated with academia (see Lea and Street 1998). Rather than the dominant position on literacy as autonomous – whereby literacy is viewed as a single and universal phenomenon with assumed cognitive as well as economic benefits – Ivanič draws on Street's view of what he calls an *ideological* model of literacy. Here the focus is on acknowledging the socioculturally embedded nature of literacy practices and the associated power differentials in any literacy related activity (Street 1984, 2004, 2005). This "academic" ethnographic framing of literacy connects strongly with Ivanič's pedagogic values outlined above and indeed gives strong academic credibility to the long standing tradition from practitioner oriented research to taking seriously students' perspectives (see Gardener 1992). In Ivanič's focus on writing, this involved seeking out writers' perspectives, including challenging the "taken for granted" conventions that they are expected to write within (see Benson et al. 1993; Ivanič and Simpson 1992; Ivanič, Aitchison and Weldon 1996; Ivanič 1998).

Disrupting researcher-researched positioning

The value placed by Ivanič on students participants' perspectives amounts to what I am referring to here as one of her key contributions to writing research – that of disrupting conventional researcher-researched positioning. Writers' perspectives are typically backgrounded in academic research on writing (and academic research more generally) in a number of ways: firstly, the dominant tradition in academic research is to – even whilst seeking them out – restrict the significance of the perspectives of participants in research to the status of "informants", rather than collaborators who are participating in the exploration of the "problem" or phenomenon; secondly, in academic writing research where linguistic tools are brought to bear, it is often the linguistic or textualist focus (see Horner 1999 for textualism) as determined by the researcher that remains the central object of focus. In this dominant model of academic research the researcher might elicit participants' perspectives but continues to hold on to her/his position of "interpreter of the world" (Reynolds quoted in Lather 1991: 59).

Ivanič's values from Adult Basic Education, her work in CLA and the emphasis on *emic* (insider) perspectives in ethnographic approaches that frame the New Literacy Studies, challenge any notion that writers' views and perspectives are simply "background" information, or subordinate to the main object – the text. Rather they are central to what the "object" of research is "However interesting and complex the writing process may appear in theory, the observations by writers themselves are even more interesting and reveal even greater complexity." (Ivanič 1998: 115)

Creating spaces where writers can talk about their texts is difficult given that (1) no talking space is ever neutral and, (2) of specific relevance to writing research, talking spaces are shaped by powerful institutional constraints in both teaching and research contexts. There is an unequal power relationship, with the teacher or researcher conventionally controlling the talking space; most obviously in a teaching context, the teacher is usually the assessor too, so s/he has to actively work at creating opportunities for dialogue; in the research context, unless the researcher seeks out ways of foregrounding participants' perspectives, the research agenda and analysis remain firmly controlled by the researcher. Talk around texts as a methodology developed by Ivanič has the specific goal of explicitly seeking out writers' perspectives through ongoing discussions over time. Moreover, it is set within a commitment on the part of the researcher to learn about the writer's interests and desires within the context of their life histories in order to make greater sense of any specific acts of writing.

The use of "talk around text" has been crucial in my own research over the past ten years in two research projects, with student-writers and with professional academic writers. I have been – and continue to be – surprised and excited by writers' responses to what are simple and often quite unsuspecting questions (unsuspecting because although I often think I am asking the most relevant questions, it often turns out that in fact I am actually groping towards meaningful questions). I am also struck by the fact that once a research dialogue has been opened up, writers offer up some of the most interesting and complex comments without any request or prompt from the researcher.

Extract 1.   Comment by student-writer
  See, when I say I think of myself as English [when writing academic essays] what I mean is that I'm trying to imagine how an English person would be writing – to make myself think as if I'm an English person writing this out.
  (Lillis 2001: 89; see also Lillis 2003)

Extract 2. Comment by professional academic writer
Saying something from [Central Europe] which is new is not good, not allowed. Of course it's absolutely their perspective to see [Central Europe] as, I don't know, a tribe trying to do something scientific. (Lillis and Curry 2006)

Both above comments were made by writers in the context of "talk around" specific texts, illustrating the value of the method for opening up discussion about wide ranging contextual – as well as text specific – issues. But whilst I continue to use this methodology, I have also worried that such talk is treated (by analysts) too often as if it were **transparent** and thus analysed quite differently from the ways in which written texts are analysed (in the same research studies). Written texts are pulled apart and theorised for their meanings, yet what people **say** about texts is often treated as straightforwardly transparent. So one question for me is – Can we as academic writing researchers justify our treatment of spoken and written "texts" in such different ways? I think that to a certain extent we can; accepting what people say as meaningful to them is a fundamental principle of both critical pedagogy and ethnographic research. However, accepting what people say as authentic and meaningful does not mean that we should treat them as either transparent or fixed. In grappling for meaningful ways of conceptualising the talk around texts, in recent times I have found it useful to conceptualise talk around texts as always involving three key aspects outlined in Figure 9.1.

---

1   Transparent/referential
Insider accounts/perspective on texts (part of a text), practices including information about the writer – for example, about the person – age, languages spoken, number of papers published, number of assignments written etc.
2   Discourse/indexical
As indexing specific discourses about self, writing, academia, etc.
3   Performative/relational
Researcher and researched performing research, identity, power, specific practices at specific moment/place in time

---

Figure 9.1 Three aspects of talk around academic texts

Whilst the first aspect in Figure 9.1 is important (most obviously there is some information that writers share which is referential – details of age, schooling, languages used, qualifications achieved etc.) the other two aspects mentioned in Figure 9.1 are also always in play. Thus in Extract 1 above, the writer is not only telling a "realist tale" about herself (category 1) (van Maanen 1988) but is indexing (category 2) whole sets of meanings about academia and what is valued in academia – notably here, being English monolingual, monocultural. Similarly, the writer in Extract 2 is signalling the power differential between academics writing out of non-Anglophone centre contexts. Furthermore, all talk around texts needs to be considered for its performative/relational dimension (category 3 in Figure 9.1) at a number of levels: most obviously, the kinds of things that are shared between researcher and participants depend very much on the immediate situation/identities/status of both and how these are perceived by the other. These immediate situations are in turn shaped by broader sociohistorical shifts:

> Some things can only be said at certain moments, under certain conditions. Likewise, and as a correlate of this, some things can only be researched at certain moments and under certain conditions. (Blommaert 2005: 65)

The conversations with the student-writers took place at a time when the problematics of participating in university study were both high on their agenda – at critical moments in their lives – as well as on the public (politics and media) agenda of widening access to higher education in the UK. Likewise, conversations with multilingual scholars were (are) taking place at time when there is marked and increasing pressure internationally on social sciences scholars to publish in English (as well as paralleling changes in the political climate in some countries where there are increased opportunities to engage with Anglophone scholars). The research moments connected strongly with significant sociohistorical moments for individuals, thus making the research possible.[3] So currently I'm trying to work on my own awareness of all three aspects to talk around texts…

Placing writers centre stage whilst using text-linguistics

Whilst placing the subjects of research – writers – centre stage, Ivanič never argues for giving up her specialist analyst role as a linguist and brings an explicit text-linguistic interest to bear in her writing research. Indeed, her "talk around texts" builds on work by Odell, Goswami and Herrington (1983) and the notion of the *discourse based interview* – which as the label indicates involves explicit attention to discourse features. However there are significant differences between the "talk around text" that Ivanič practices and key aspects of the discourse based interview. The discourse based interview by Odell et al. involves the researcher identifying specific features of a text about which s/he wants to elicit the writer's views and was developed as a way of gaining access to the "tacit knowledge" people bring to professional writing. Their approach involved collecting samples of writing from individuals and looking for variations between texts in an attempt

---

3. For fuller discussion of the issues raised here, see Lillis (2008).

to identify alternatives within each writer's repertoire. They looked, for example, at the range of ways in which people referred to clients in their writing, by identifying the phrases they used to sign their names and the phrasing of requests and commands (: 233). Having identified the range of alternatives, they presented these to writers and asked why they might prefer to choose one of the phrases. Their aim was thus to focus the writers' attention on the way in which they used specific linguistic features in order to encourage them to articulate the reason for such use and thus allow the researcher to gain access to this implicit or "tacit" knowledge. The researchers selected the areas for discussion on the grounds that the writers themselves wouldn't be able to identify points where such knowledge was particularly significant because such knowledge was considered to be largely implicit (: 229).

Ivanič draws on this tool of the discourse based interview in three specific ways. Firstly, and most obviously, she adopts the notion of having **text** focused discussions (in contrast to – and in her work, in addition to – the broader and more wide ranging interviews about writing or literacy practices used in literacy studies). Secondly, she takes up the specific practice of presenting alternative linguistic-rhetorical features – a powerful tool for generating discussion with writers – for example in noting that writers used quotation marks or "scare quotes" around some words and phrases and not others and then asking writers about their reasons for different uses (see Ivanič 1998: 195). And, thirdly, she explicitly focuses on a range of linguistic features, as illustrated in her analysis of a section of Rachel's writing in social work course (already referred to above on page 171): she focuses on types of verbal processes, use of pronouns, use of determiners, formulaic expressions, nominalisations, grammatical subjects, modality and choice of lexis. An example of the linguistic commentary of Rachel's' text is as follows, from Ivanič (1998):

> There are two long nominal groups (135)
> The next sentence contains the first action with a human actor as main clause (136)
> The clause structure is typically academic – Yet many of the clauses and embedded clauses have human participants engaged in physical and verbal processes (137)

Of course, as an applied linguist – and someone who loves linguistics – it is not surprising that Roz would focus on the linguistic features of texts. This is after all what linguists do and there is a strong tradition of linguistic approaches to academic writing (see for examples of overviews Bazerman and Prior 2004; Hewings 2001). However, there are important differences between Roz's approach and text-linguistic orientations to writing. Firstly, she dismisses an approach which is text-linguistic only including the (quite common) practice of "counting features across texts" which she views as "unsatisfactory", particularly given her interest in identity and subject positioning (see Ivanič 1998: 118ff.). Secondly, she allows, indeed, actively encourages writer-participants to identify aspects of the text that are worthy of analysis, rather than pre-determining these from her perspective of linguist-analyst. Consider the way in which, in contrast to Odell et al. described above, she allows writers to choose what should be focused on and recognises the importance of this for her own linguistic analysis:

> In the discourse-based interviews my co-researchers had identified parts of their writing which were particularly interesting or troublesome for them – Often they identified discourse types which I may not have noticed alone. – I used what they had said as a lead into texts, helping me to know what else to turn my linguist's eyes on. (Ivanič 1998: 119)

Thirdly, she makes clear the limitations of text-linguistic analysis, and indeed of the analyst, in establishing the functions of text. For example, she points to the importance of emic, that is, insider knowledge (external to the analyst) for the identification of genres;

> It is – interesting that as a linguist I could see it [section of essay] had particular generic characteristics, but in order to identify its genre I had either to be an insider to the particular social work community in which Rachel worked, or to ask her. This shows that thorough discourse analysis is impossible without contacting participants for contextual detail. (Ivanič 1998: 140)

Thus whilst Ivanič uses linguistic analysis for exploring the nature of specific texts, her goal is definitely to reach beyond what linguistic analysis per se can offer. Attention to linguistic categories enables Roz as analyst to ground "discourses" in actual features, and as importantly, in writer's lives. In this way, she puts not only linguistics, but the linguist as analyst in her/his place: this is a very important place from her perspective, but this "expert" analysis is always seen as something to work *with* writer-participants, not *on* them and directly reflects a critical language awareness ideology. Critical language awareness involves building from "existing language capabilities and experience" (Clark et al. 1991: 47) which include spoken, written, multimodal resources and a range of technologies (from pencil, to PC, to text messaging) and recognises that the ways in which these are used are dependent on the sociohistorical contexts of writers' lives. Through talk around text, researchers can explore what some of these resources are, how the writer wants to use these and the extent to which they connect or differ from the resources and practices that are valued in formal education; in the case of academic writing, this usually means practices in higher education and academia more widely. In Ivanič's more recent work on writing in further education, this concern with exploring and identifying resources and semiotic practices involves seeking empirically to explore explicit possibilities and opportunities for "boundary crossing" (see Ivanič and Satchwell 2007).

Furthermore, just as Ivanič puts linguistics in its (albeit important from her point of view) place, she also avoids any easy readings of local or specific data through the lens of macro theorisations of the workings of discourse. Again, her work in critical language awareness is crucial here. CLA adopts an approach to language study which is premised on the assumption that language practices must be problematised rather than taken as givens: conventions underlying practices are not neutral but are sociohistorically shaped involving complex configurations of subjectivity(ies), power, access and identity(ies). There is a recognition that there is no one-to-one fit between wordings and ideology/discourse/subject positioning (Fairclough 1995: 231), and that the task of deciding precisely how wordings, conventions and practices are socially shaped is an empirical question which cannot be answered either through text analysis alone, or through the privileged lens of the researcher-analyst. Ivanič engages directly with the "felicitous ambiguity" in the notion of "subject/ivity" (Fairclough 1989) by ensuring that the "subject" remains centre stage whilst at the same time seeking to explicate the nature of specific discourse(s) in detail.

Consider Ivanič's linguistic-discoursal analysis alongside her critical interpretation of such an analysis in Figure 9.2 below. In the two columns, I have juxtaposed extracts I have taken from an article by Ivanič on writing in further education (Ivanič 2006). In the extracts in the columns, she is exploring the writing of Logan – a student on a course in hospitality (Food and Drink Service) – in relation to issues of identity (see Figure 9.2).

Several moves are reflected in these extracts from Ivanič's work which, in a very concrete way, illustrate why she attaches so much importance to researching writing (and indeed reflects "why writing matters"). In column 1, she provides an analysis of key linguistic features and a labelling and interpretation of the discourses that such features constitute; in column 2, she provides a critical/interpretative analysis of the relationship between such discourses and the lived desires and experiences of the writer-participant. Here then is a sensitive balancing act between the specialist or expert categories (both micro and macro) of the researcher/analyst and the everyday words/feelings/perspectives/actions of participants. Ivanič sets at the centre of her work the aim of eking out emic, "local" personal and individual histories around texts, whilst always holding in play an awareness of what theoretical notions may have to offer in illuminating participants perspectives, researcher critique and interpretation, and pedagogic implications (see Ivanič and Satchwell 2007 for discussion of the relation between all three).

Column 1	Column 2
Linguistic-discourse analysis by Ivanič on written text	*Critical Interpretation of subject positioning by Ivanič*
Several features of the linguistic text carry the 'make people happy' discourse of food and drink service: the high proportion of personal pronouns 'we', 'you', 'everybody' and 'everyone'; the proliferation of politeness markers 'we would like to' (three times) and 'please'; the lexis in the semantic field of pleasure and enjoyment: 'hope' and 'very enjoyable', and the use of the speech act 'thank' (twice). Associated with this is the use of the handwriting font for the phrase 'Speciality Evenings', suggesting a 'personal touch', carrying a friendly, cosy, informal discourse of personal relationships. Together these discoursal resources position Logan as someone keen to serve customers: to 'make people happy'.	And doesn't the deployment of the romantic love discourse of personal relationships inflate [this] commodification and further exploit people and trick them into emptying their pockets? To this I would answer 'yes, but no ….'. Yes, Logan is being colonised by these discourses and contributing to their continued circulation, and hence participating in these social processes, and it would be politically preferable for him and all the students on the courses to develop a critical awareness of the nature and consequences of these belief systems. But, on the other hand, I suggest that it is not entirely sinister that Logan is constructing his identity through participation in these discourses. Logan is a young man who was disaffected by the whole education system and didn't have any future when he left school. I suggest that his finding something to identify with, something which is consonant with his sense of himself who likes to 'make people happy', is a key factor in learning for him, as I discuss further in the section on 'identification' below.

Figure 9.2 Extract from Ivanič's analysis and interpretation

A key issue I have been grappling with is the relationship between different kinds of languages of description; what do certain languages enable the researcher to see and what do they mask? How does the researcher connect emic perspectives and languages of description with etic, in particular here, "expert" languages of description (such as those developed in linguistics)? In terms of the specific "expert" languages of description from linguistics, I think Roz's work illustrates their limitations when used without writer or emic perspectives, but I also think that perhaps Roz is more convinced of the analytic power of available text linguistic categories than I am, although I do use them to a certain extent as illustrated in the following example:

> *We can map out the features which Tara intuitively recognises as -"academic". It has two long sentences which are lexically dense whilst of low grammatical intricacy – the participants in the first clause are abstract – "restriction", "nature" – and the verb processes are relational-is.* (Lillis 2001: 125)

And having such an "expert", rational discourse to hand is certainly essential in moving away from the highly emotionally charged deficit discourse used about student writing or indeed professional academic writing, (for further examples, see Lillis and Curry 2006). But I wonder whether the rational discourse of linguistic analysis can sometimes mask other processes in play. Consider the extract from an article submitted to an academic journal, written by a professional multilingual scholar. Then consider the extract from the reviewer's comments made about it (Figure 9. 3).

If we read the written text extract (in the left hand column) only through the rationalist linguistic discourse conventionally applied to academic texts, we would miss the highly emotive ways in which the (gatekeeping) reader is orienting to the text. This is in large part due to the fact that linguistic analysis alone treats texts in a flat, or one dimensional way. It doesn't tell us anything about what is more or less salient in specific contexts of their use – by writers or readers. So I think I would want to be cautious about claims about the power of linguistic approaches which focus on texts to make visible what **counts** *to both writers and readers of texts in specific contexts. The same concern relates to macro notions of discourse – and I would want to aim to adopt the critical reflexivity in using any such notions of discourse, evident in Ivanič's comments on Logan above. Here, the cycling between emic and etic, external and internal languages of description is crucial in reaching a nuanced understanding of how people manage to position themselves in relation to powerful discourses and subjectivities. Kell usefully reminds us of Hymes' criticism of emic/etic being used as dichotomy and that Pike – original coiner of these terms – talks of three moments (see discussion in Kell 2006):*

> *Etic 1 – a frame of reference with which an analyst or observer approaches data*
> *Emic 1 – the discovery of valid relations internal to what is being studied*
> *Etic 2 – a reconsideration of the initial frame of reference in light of new results*

Extract from paper	Reviewer comment
This paper is situated at the cross-roads of the idea that international surveys serve valuable, although specific, comparison purposes, with the belief that these surveys can gain from incorporating questions based on previous detailed analyses of particular realities.	There are formulations that, in my view, are *a little bit over the top* and *too pretentious* (for instance "This paper is situated at the cross-roads of the idea…with the belief…"; "Theory that has a theoretical and empirical tradition… "social transformations of our times." –) *Maybe it is not the language, but it is just too Latin for a North-West European.* (My emphasis)

Figure 9.3 Extract from a journal article alongside the reviewer's comments

And of course this representation of three moves is an abstraction in that research always involves cyclical multiplies of these three "moves". I think Roz's work has to a certain extent made these moves visible in writing research and more importantly has directed us towards the need for more questioning of such relations – particularly on the relationship between "everyday" languages of description drawn from writers' emic perspectives and "expert" etic languages of description drawn from linguistics.

Opening up opportunities for re-examining textual practices

And, briefly, there is one further important contribution I would like to stress that Ivanič has made both through her methodology and her scholarly writing – and that is the opening up discussion about which textual practices should be valued within academia and why. Once writers are invited to express their views on the academic conventions they are expected to write within, alternative possibilities come to the fore. Consider just one example from Ivanič (1998: 319) where we are presented with an extract from a Communication Studies essay by Valerie and Ivanič's summary of Valerie's perspective on this text (Figure 9.4).

Here the writer values the use of metaphor in her meaning making in academia. Whilst the assessor-reader doesn't share this value, the talk around text methodology that Ivanič develops makes visible this alternative interest. By taking writers' desires for writing seriously, Roz has engaged in the important project of reconsidering textual practices in academia, a process which still has some considerable way to go (see Schroeder et al. 2002; see also the chapter in this volume by Pitt and Hamilton). In some of her own published writings she has taken the opportunity to work in genres other than essayist text, as in for example her use of drawings and cartoons in her published academic work (see Biff cartoon used in Ivanič 1998) and dialogic exchanges in Candlin and Hyland (1999) as indicated in the extract between Ivanič and Weldon.

Extracts from writing by Valerie	Ivanič's summary of Valerie's perspective
Manchester's proletariat may have suffered in the mould described by Engels but they lacked the capacity to wear a revolutionary mantle. If the city is a stage for dramatic performance, with backcloth, lighting equipment and the semblance of a plot, then Engels had marshalled a number of characters who did not know their lines.	Valerie said that using the metaphorical expression *wear a revolutionary mantle* was part of her identity, and she was disappointed by her tutor's advice to write the more literal *realise a revolution* in the exam.

Figure 9.4 Extract from an essay alongside Ivanič's summary

Extracts from Ivanič and Weldon 2000

ROZ: It seemed to me that, in order to study writing as self-representation, I needed three types of data. First, I needed to understand as much as possible about the writer herself – you, in this case, Sue – where you were coming from in all its meanings: what values, beliefs, practices and previous experiences of written discourses and genres you were bringing to writing – the shaping of your identity a writer. These understandings developed from visiting you at home and from our more informal conversations – both when we met and over the telephone.

SUE: Yes, it's interesting to reflect back on the unravelling of my autobiography and to realise how much of one's life history is embedded in each written text. But as you know, the final print-out bore no resemblance to the first set of scribbled notes, and I considered an essay to be a finished artefact only if it kicked over the traces of 'cut and paste', or loose ends spliced together.

ROZ: That brings me to the second type of data. I needed to focus on one particular piece of writing you had done in order to find actual examples of linguistic decisions you had made which I could associate with particular views of knowledge and views of the world, and with particular social purposes, social roles and relations,. In this respect I was drawing from the methodology associated with Critical Discourse Analysis: studying text in order to identify traces of discourses and genres (as described in Fairclough 1992a).

In my research with student-writers using talk around texts it became clear that writers wanted to breach the conventions they could write within. Whilst they – for the most part – valued the use of evidence based argument, and the kind of literal/referential rhetoric that Valerie's tutor preferred, they also expressed the desire to make meaning through logic AND emotion, argument AND poetry, impersonal AND personal constructions of text. This has led me to take seriously the textual practice of juxtaposition so that, in my teaching, student-writers are encouraged to use essayist conventions and texts, alongside/interspersed by a range of other types of commentary – such as an emotional reflection, critical "asides" on the main argument, the expression of doubts or uncertainties about something they might be presenting as quite straightforward in the main body of the text.

Conclusion

My "visits" to see Roz were twice a year and were absolutely special to me (which is often the perspective of PhD students) but more importantly she made them seem as if they were special to her too. She knew I was hungry for any ideas that I could connect with what I was doing and she shared generously. I remember her offering specific books and papers... "here's a copy of a paper that Norman is currently working on – if there's anything in there you want to quote, let me know and we'll ask him how to cite this"; "I think you'll like this (Gardener) it's just been re published"...

Roz Ivanič's development of talk around text methodology has put writers at the centre of writing research. The methodology reflects and enacts a commitment to collaborating with others and in particular a deep respect for students, particularly those who in different ways are on the margins of the academy. Roz knows writers have important stories to tell and she developed a way of bringing such stories to the centre of academic writing research, whilst at the same time continuing to bring outsider 'expert' knowledge drawn from linguistics to the fore. Furthermore, in her own publications, Roz Ivanič has enacted her collaborative research goals, by co-authoring with colleagues and, more unusually in academia, with co-researcher/research-participants. Such sharing in academia – with research participants and colleagues – is something to treasure and to emulate.

References

Barton, D., Hamilton, M. & Ivanič, R. (eds). 2000. *Situated Literacies. Reading and writing in context*. London: Routledge.
Bazerman, C. & Prior, P. (eds.). 2004. *What Writing Does and How it Does it. An introduction to analyzing texts and textual practices*. Mahwah NJ: Lawrence Erlbaum.
Benson, N., Gurney, S., Harrison, J. & Rimmershaw, R. 1993. The place of academic writing in whole life writing: A case study of three university students. *Language and Education* 71: 1–20.
Blommaert, J. 2005. *Discourse. A critical introduction*. Cambridge: CUP
Candlin, C. & Hyland, N. (eds). 1999. *Writing: Texts, processes and practices*. Harlow: Pearson Education.
Clark, R., Fairclough, N., Ivanič, R. & Martin-Jones, M. 1991. Critical language awareness. Part II: Towards critical alternatives. *Language and Education* 5(1): 41–54.
Fairclough, N. 1989. *Language and Power*. London: Longman.
Fairclough, N. 1992a. *Discourse and Social Change*. Cambridge: Polity.
Fairclough, N. (ed.). 1992b. *Critical Language Awareness*. London: Longman.
Fairclough, N. 1995 *Critical Discourse Analysis*. London: Longman.
Freire, P. 1985. *Pedagogy of the Oppressed*. London: Penguin.
Gardener, S. 1992. *The Long Word Club*. Bradford: RaPAL.

Haggis, T. 2003. Constructing images of ourselves? A critical investigation into 'approaches to learning' research in higher education. *British Educational Research Journal* 34(1): 89–104.

Hammersley, M. 2006. Ethnography: Problems and prospects. *Ethnography and Education* 1(1): 3–14.

Hewings, M. (ed.) 2001. *Academic Writing in Context. Implications and applications.* Birmingham: University of Birmingham Press.

Horner, B. 1999. The birth of basic writing. In *Representing the Other: Basic writers and the teaching of basic writing*, B. Horner & M. Zhan-Lu (eds). Urbana IL: National Council of Teachers of English.

Ivanič, R. 1998. *Writing and Identity. The discoursal construction of identity in academic writing.* Amsterdam: John Benjamins.

Ivanič, R. 2006. Language, learning and identification. In *Language, Culture and Identity in Applied Linguistics*, R. Kiely, P. Rea-Dickens, H. Woodfield & G Clibbon (eds), 7–29. London: Equinox.

Ivanič, R., Aitchison, M. & Weldon, S. 1996. Bringing ourselves into our writing. *RaPAL* 28/29: 2–8.

Ivanič, R. & Satchwell, C. 2007. Boundary crossings: Networking and transforming literacies in research processes and college courses. *Journal of Applied Linguistics* 4(1): 101–124.

Ivanič, R. & Simpson, J. 1992. Who's who in academic writing? In *Critical Language Awareness*, N. Fairclough. (ed.), London: Longman.

Ivanič, R. & Weldon, S. 2000. Researching the writer-reader relationship. In *Writing: Texts, processes and practices*, C. N. Candlin & K. Hyland (eds), 168–192. London: Addison Wesley Longman.

Kell, C. 2006. Moment by Moment: Contexts and crossings in the study of literacy in social practice. PhD dissertation, The Open University.

Lather, P. 1991. *Getting Smart: Feminist research and pedagogy with/in the postmodern.* London: Routledge.

Lea, M. R. 2004. Academic literacies: A pedagogy for course design. *Studies in Higher Education* 29(6): 739–756.

Lea, M. & Street, B. 1998. Student writing in higher education: An academic literacies approach. *Studies in Higher Education* 23(2): 157–172.

Lillis, T. 2001. *Student Writing: Access, regulation, desire.* London: Routledge.

Lillis, T. 2003. An 'academic literacies' approach to student writing in higher education: Drawing on Bakhtin to move from 'critique' to 'design'. *Language and Education* 17(3): 192–207.

Lillis, T. 2008. Ethnography as method, methodology, and 'deep theorizing': Closing the gap between text and context in academic writing research. *Written Communication* 25(3): 353–388.

Lillis, T. & Curry, M. J. 2006. Professional academic writing by multilingual scholars: Interactions with literacy brokers in the production of English medium texts. *Written Communication* 23(1): 3–35.

Lillis, T. & Turner, J. 2001. Student writing in higher education: Contemporary confusion, traditional concerns. *Teaching in Higher Education* 6(1): 57–68.

Lu, M. 1994. Professing multiculturalism: The politics of style in the contact zone. *College Composition and Communication* 45(4): 442–458.

Maybin, J. 1994. Children's voices: Talk, knowledge and identity. In *Researching Language and Literacy in Social Context*, D. Graddol, J. Maybin & B. Stierer (eds), Clevedon: Multilingual Matters.

Odell, L., Goswami, D. & Herrington, A. 1983. The discourse-based interview: A procedure for exploring the tacit knowledge of writers in non-academic settings. In *Research on Writing. Principles and methods*, P. Mosenthal, L. Tamor & S. A. Walsmsley (eds). New York NY: Longman.

Schroeder, C., Fix, H. & Bizzell, P. (ed.). 2002. *ALTDis. Alternative discourses and their academy.* Portsmouth NH: Boynton/Cook.

Street, B. 1984. *Literacy in Theory and Practice.* Cambridge: CUP.

Street, B. 2004. Academic literacies and the new orders: Implications for research and practice in student writing in higher education. *Learning and Teaching in the Social Science* 1(1): 9–20.

Street, B. 2005. (ed.) *Literacies across Educational Contexts: Mediating learning and teaching.* Philadelphia PA: Caslon Press.

Thesen, L. & van Pletzen, E. (eds) 2006. *Academic Literacy and the Languages of Change.* London: Continuum.

van Maanen, J. 1988. *Tales of the Field. On writing ethnography.* Chicago IL: University of Chicago Press.

CHAPTER 10

Listening to children think about punctuation

Sue Sing and Nigel Hall
Open University UK / Manchester Metropolitan University, UK

This chapter draws on Ivanič's innovative approach to the study of punctuation. Punctuation is a fairly abstract concept and it is often difficult to understand why it is used as it is, and to account for such uses. Influenced by Roz's methodology with adult students, we illustrate how data can be collected from participants, in our case quite young children, in ways that as closely as possible reflect how they are thinking about their uses of punctuation. We explain how we developed the procedures for our specific interests and goals, and use some of the data from our study to demonstrate how the methodology was so effective for unpacking children's theories of how punctuation works.

Preface

Both authors of this chapter have known Roz Ivanič for many years. In Sue's case it was first as Roz's student on both undergraduate and post-graduate courses. More recently Roz was the external examiner for Sue's (successful) PhD examination. Nigel met Roz through an association with some of the literacy research being carried out at Lancaster University. They soon discovered a joint interest in punctuation, and subsequently Roz contributed a chapter to a book on the topic edited by Nigel and by Anne Robinson, and she also contributed to their international conference on punctuation. For us, Roz is the epitome of academic rigour and integrity, while also being a deeply caring and generous person. It is a privilege for both of us to be able to contribute to this celebratory volume.

Introduction

In 1988 Ivanič published a paper, *Linguistics and the Logic of Non-standard Punctuation*. A modified version of this was later published as a chapter in *Learning about Punctuation* (Hall and Robinson 1996). In this paper Ivanič did something that has seldom been done by other researchers – she explored the beliefs held about the act of punctuation by a group of young adult basic education students, and she did so by asking them to talk about how they had punctuated some of their written texts; she allowed their voices to constitute the primary data in her study. Some readers may think at this point, "What's so special about that? Isn't that what one would normally do?" In fact, where research into learning about punctuation is concerned, the answer has almost always been "no". With rare exceptions most studies of how people punctuate have either collected written texts and subsequently examined these for errors, or devised specific tests to try and examine particular aspects of punctuation. Ivanič's paper was a fresh and innovative approach as for the first time the voices of punctuation learners could be heard in a research study.

One early and brief exception to this was part of a study about children learning to use capital letters, carried out by Pressey and Campbell in 1933. Although theirs was a fairly conventional analysis of capitalisation errors in the writing of adolescents, they did take the trouble to ask their subjects about why they made specific decisions in their writing. As a result they wrote (1970), "The first, rather unexpected point, is that the errors in capitalisation were in large part explainable, logical and understandable; they were far from being random or senseless." Their use of the word "unexpected" is itself a substantial indication that the voices of younger writers in punctuation studies had not previously been considered significant, and there is no way that a researcher would uncover such thinking by simply retrospectively examining written texts. Despite what seems to us a quite fascinating and genuinely original discovery, it did not impact upon subsequent studies of children learning about punctuation. Cordiero, Giaccobbe and Cazden (1983), Edelsky (1983), Cazden, Cordiero and Giacobbe (1985), and Cordiero (1988) examined the punctuation of young children, yet in all cases the actual analysis was carried out retrospectively and does not seem to have involved actual conversation with the children about their choices, nor detailed observation of the children as they wrote. Thus any judgements about the children's underlying theories, beliefs and decisions about punctuation have solely been abstracted from what the children wrote.

It was not until 1988 when Ivanič, quite independently, decided to explore authors' voices that they reappeared in punctuation studies, and yet when her paper was published one of her conclusions was very similar to that of Pressey and Campbell. She wrote (Ivanič 1988:2), "Unconventional punctuation is often a perfectly logical representation of ideas in writing". Thus again, what would seem to many people to be stupid, bizarre or simply incorrect uses of punctuation were revealed as being far from arbitrary and a result of beliefs that even if ultimately incorrect, were based on clearly articulated reasons. What is clear from both the

Pressey and Campbell and the Ivanič study is that these less conventional ways of thinking about punctuation would not have been uncovered without listening to what young or inexperienced writers had to say.

The act of using children's own voices to explain their choices would seem to offer significant increases in the understanding of why certain punctuation decisions might be made. Perhaps one reason that the use of children's voices has not been picked up by other researchers was that Pressey and Campbell were working with adolescents and Ivanič was working with young adult basic learners, and both these groups were reasonably capable of explaining their thinking. Most research into learning and thinking about punctuation has been carried out with young children and perhaps it was thought such explicit explanation could not be obtained from them. In our own work we wanted to challenge such a view, believing that it was not only possible to hear what children had to say about punctuation but that it was critical to understanding how they made sense of punctuation.

Historically, and in particular throughout most of the twentieth century, children were thought of as "incomplete" beings, as "immature, irrational, incompetent, asocial [and] acultural" (Mackay as cited in Prout & James 1997: 13) and always subordinately socially situated in an adult world in comparison to adults (Jenks 2005). Children were interesting because of what they would become rather than for what they were. In more recent times an approach, now generally recognised as "the new childhood studies", has been repositioning childhood, maintaining that children need to be understood as people who think and behave in ways that are appropriate, meaningful and useful to themselves, and who need to be considered as human beings in their own right. The consequences have been fairly dramatic, among them a massive change by researchers regarding both the ethical position of children as participants in research and in the increased recognition that ways can be found which allow even the very youngest children's voices to be heard and acknowledged as worth taking seriously.

These ideas were taken on board in the study considered below, for we took the position that children are intelligent and competent social and cognitive beings, who possess powerful abilities for trying to make sense of the world around them and who will work strategically on whatever issues they encounter, e.g. solving punctuation problems. And though they may be young, and may not have full command of the language needed to be explicit about their punctuation decisions, we believed techniques could be found that would allow them to discuss their ideas about punctuation.

In this chapter we explain the methods and procedures generated to encourage very young children to talk extensively about punctuation and consider an example of the data that illustrates the kinds of discussions that took place.

The project

The project discussed here was one of a number of studies about young children's learning and understanding of punctuation carried out by researchers at the Institute of Education at Manchester Metropolitan University. This particular project, *The development of punctuation knowledge in children aged seven to eleven*,[1] aimed to illuminate the ways in which young children come to understand the nature and use of the English punctuation system. Data was collected from four schools across one full school year. Each school provided four classes, one from each of the Key Stage 2 year groups. The children undertook an initial punctuation assessment and from each class six children, each of whom achieved a score close to their class average, were chosen and divided into two groups. Thus, in all, 24 children from each of the four year groups participated, giving a full cohort of 96 children, in 32 groups of three.

Given that our primary interest was to examine what, and how, the children were thinking about punctuation issues, our main challenge was to create an environment where children could feel they were able to say what they wanted to say and not what they thought someone else wanted to hear or expected them to say. Finding how to achieve this kind of optimal condition presented us with some significant methodological challenges which essentially related to the fundamental issue of power, an inherent feature of any social relationship, but particularly in those relating to children.

Any interaction between an adult and a child, especially in schooling, involves them in a relationship that is socially unequal. For instance, in a classroom context it is the teacher who is in charge, gives instructions and commands, and is the person who can define or limit the parameters of the children's behaviour (for example, see Edwards & Mercer's work in this area, 1987; and Mercer 1995). In addition, much of the talk that may be classified as "acceptable" in classrooms takes place between the teacher and pupil, and not between pupils; again, it is the teacher who dictates the nature and defines the acceptability of these sorts of interchanges (Sinclair & Coulthard 1975). Prior research also made us aware that the children's perceptions of an adult's power and status might contaminate any data by leading them to respond according to how they think they *should* respond rather than how they would *like* to respond (Hill et al. 1996; Mahon, Glendinning, Clarke & Craig 1996; Christensen 2004). Moreover, Simons suggests that "… wanting to please the teacher may extend to wanting to please the interviewer" (1981:39); Hughes & Grieve (1984) and Scott (2000) offer excellent evidence of children

---

[1]. The Development of Punctuation Knowledge in Children aged Seven to Eleven. ESRC Project: R0002383348.

behaving in such a way. Though the "intergenerational inequalities" (Alderson & Mayall as cited in Mauthner 1997:19) between an adult and child can never be eradicated from their relationship (some researchers contest this, e.g. see Mayall 2000), nonetheless it was important we accounted for their probable influence on the research, particularly in the way they might lead the children to form assumptions about the researcher, the research situation (Simons 1981) and the roles they could play (Burgess 1984).

So, how did we set out to encourage children's genuine voices to be heard? These issues are most easily discussed by considering them in relation to the activities we invited them to undertake.

The activities

At two points in the school year, all 32 groups were presented with an activity aimed at encouraging them to discuss what they were thinking about when deciding whether or not to use different punctuation marks in a specially composed piece of prose text. For both tasks, each group worked with one adult researcher. The first activity involved a short passage which included a number of strategically positioned boxes. Some were situated in places where no punctuation would normally be required while others, according to conventional English Language grammar rules, did need to be marked. In essence, the boxes were asking the children to decide whether any punctuation was required at the specified points in the text. The second activity was to identify in a short text whether the punctuation was correct and whether any other punctuation needed to be added or removed. Children could mark their joint decision on the text with a pen, but crucially no mark could be made unless ALL the children agreed on the decision.

The context surrounding these children's experience of these two exercises, and their mode of administration, were designed to facilitate the collection of the children's own views about punctuation.

Firstly, the researcher's role was defined at the outset to be facilitative; it was not to teach the children, nor to judge or mark their responses. Rather, it was to ensure that all participants were offered an opportunity to voice their opinion, keep their talk on-task and "probe" for elaboration where it was felt beneficial to do so; as such, the role was not to "interview" the group but to encourage the talk that went on (Watts & Ebbutt 1987). Perhaps the most important task, and maybe even most difficult, was to listen, a skill that is often lacking in researchers (Albrecht, Johnson & Walther 1993; Russell Bernard 1994). As Seidman points out, the difficulty is this:

> thoughtfulness takes time; if interviewers can learn to tolerate the silence that sometimes follows a question or a pause within a participant's reconstruction, they may hear things they would never have heard if they had leapt in with another question to break the silence. (1998: 77)

Secondly, the researcher would accept the children's language and thoughts as spoken; no expectations were made of them for using metalinguistic terminology. As Williams, Wetton & Moon say, in their discussion of health education issues,

> …it is more profitable to encourage children to use their own language, and their own ways of communicating, and to ask them to clarify where necessary, rather than attempt to understand and reply using other people's words.
> (cited in Mauthner 1997: 25)

So, the language the children used was the language we accepted. But, in encouraging them to use words of their own choosing it was especially important to display an open, accepting and non-judgemental attitude to what the children said as well as "hear" what they were saying. Equally, any decisions they made about the punctuation were accepted. Thus, it was our aim to ensure that the children experienced no negative responses to anything they said or did.

Thirdly, the fact that in their groups of three the children had to come to a joint decision, and that their decision would be accepted whatever it was, meant they needed to negotiate and discuss with each other, and not with the researcher. The choice to have groups of three was designed to facilitate this; a smaller group might have been too easily dominated by one child and a larger group might have led to individuals being able to avoid participating (Frey & Fontana 1991; Lewis 1992). By asking children to work together in a group we hoped to encourage them to say to each other what they were really thinking, which they might not do if the task required them to talk individually to a researcher. We also recognised that in a group situation, it is probable some individuals will think differently to the others and so the need to resolve these differences would encourage children to talk in ways that might not be possible in normal classroom situations. By having to convince each other they would need to move towards explicitness, but in terms and at levels that were comprehensible to the other children.

Finally, and the above factors anticipate this, there was a high level of ethical concern for the children. It was to be their forum for discussing punctuation. Although the groups were initially selected by the researchers, all the chosen children were invited to participate and were told at the beginning of each task that they were free to stop and withdraw at any time (something that happened only once when a child was taken ill). The researcher's first name was used when sitting alongside the children and everything was very carefully explained and explored through a small trial exercise.

The combination of facilitation, acceptance, collegiality and ethical concern was intended to create a rich and supportive communicative space in which the children would feel confident to think aloud and engage in intense discussion with each other. The critical question, given our attempts to create this environment, is, "Did it work?"

The evidence

We believe the answer to the above question is a very strong "Yes". Across the 64 sessions for the two exercises, there was a small number that lasted slightly less than twenty minutes, but in most cases the researchers had to draw the children's discussions to a close so that they could return to the classroom at the times designated by the class teachers. The average number of turns in each discussion was 336 turns. The sessions were marked by intensity of discussion, great humour and considerable reflection. While the participation of each child in each group was never exactly equal, there was only one session where a child hardly participated. The most exciting result was the collaboration of the children, even the youngest, as they worked their way to formulating a decision. Of considerable importance to the researchers was the fact these sessions did work as excellent vehicles for gathering data about children's understanding of punctuation.

As space is limited for this chapter we have chosen a fairly typical extract to illustrate what the discussions were like. This is a Year 4 group (8–9 years old) and the transcription comes from the first exercise. The whole discussion lasted 451 turns and approximately 35 minutes. Nearly a quarter of these turns (110 turns) were spent discussing box 10, which was set in the sentence:

Do you want to go to Tom☐s house?

This time was wholly spent discussing whether or not an apostrophe should be used between "Tom" and the letter "s", and why. However, it should be noted that the *National Literacy Strategy's Framework for Teaching* document does not position the teaching of what it terms the "possessive" apostrophe until the second term of Year 4, thus these children had only just been introduced to this notion and were therefore working at the edge of their knowledge.

The first half of their discussion (58 turns) will be analysed here. In the transcript below "R" is the researcher sitting alongside the children and the other initials indicate the individual children. Any underlining represents an extract from the exercise text, and italicisation indicates a description of some action by a child or the researcher. Meaningful units are marked by slashes (/) in the transcription.

Transcript Extract
Group DY4Ta discussing box 10 in Exercise 1: *"Toms"*

288	K	I know that one/it's easy that one
289	R	"<u>Do you want a lift to Toms house</u>"/what about this box here? *(points to box 10)*
290	S	it's an apostrophe *(points to apostrophe in box 2)*
291	R	you want an apostrophe?
292	K	yeah/'cos it's "Tom's"/you know I've noticed on/you know when it has apostrophe/at the end of the word it's either an "s" or a "t" or/I don't know/mostly "s" or "t"
293	S	apostrophe/full stop/apostrophe/full stop *(S repeats this, wanting these marks in the last two boxes of the text)*
294	K	I'm not even sure if there's any other letters that go at the end I'm just saying that that's what I've seen...
295	R	...that/that's what you've seen
296	K	yeah
297	R	what do you think about here N?/why you going to put an apostrophe there/what's it going to do?
298	K	it's gonna/it's like that *(referring to box 2)* /it's going to hold a letter or two
299	R	what letter d'you think's missing then?
300	N	"e"
301	R	an "e"
302	N	if you said without the apostrophe and an "s" it would say "Do you...
303	S	...it wouldn't sound right if it was an "e"
304	K&N	"<u>Do want a lift to Toms house</u>"
305	N	it would have said if we didn't have the apostrophe and the "s"/it would've said "<u>Do you want a lift to Tom house</u>" *("Toms house" said with emphasis)*
306	K	so it wouldn't make sense so you need the "s"
307	R	you could have/you can still have the "s" there but no box/well/just imagine the box isn't there/ "Toms" with no space/what would that...?
308	S	no that wouldn't look right
309	R	it wouldn't look right
310	K	I'm not sure actually/now you've said that/I'm not sure/I don't think it's a/...
311	N	...actually/...
312	K	...trick box
313	R	oh go on N/you're changing your mind

314	N	yeah/it's either apostrophe or a trick box/...
315	K	...trick box/I think it is/now you've said that it springs to mind
316	N	apostrophe
317	R	you're still sure about your apostrophe?/yeah? *(S nods)*
318	K	yeah/but you could/if you didn't have that box there it be/it'd still make sense wouldn't it
319	N	'cos some letters you don't have to have them...
320	K	..."<u>Do you want a lift to Toms house</u>"/'cos they're still the same without the apostrophe
321	N	'cos with some letters...
322	K	...and I don't think you have them in your names/oh you do don't you?
323	N	'cos with some letters/you don't have to have the apostrophe where the "s" is
324	R	right
325	S	when it's explaining your name out
325a	K	I think it's a trick box that
326	N	yeah I think/yeah
326a	S	no it isn't
326b	N	it is
327	S	it's an apostrophe
328	K	it's not
329	N	I've changed my mind again
330	R	what do you think now N?
331	N	apostrophe
332	R	you think an apostrophe now?
333	N	yeah
334	K	I don't/I don't care
335	R	you don't?
336	K	I'm not sure
337	S	two against one
338	K	no but you've got to change my mind to get it on there
339	R	or you've got to change theirs *(said to K)*
340	K	yeah
341	S	I'll keep repeating it over and over again *(S seems to be getting annoyed now)*
342	K	no but listen if Tom/even if the box wasn't there/forget it/say it isn't there/it would still make sense without the apostrophe there

This group's deliberations are not about whether any other punctuation mark might be more appropriate or correct for the box; they are based on trying to ascertain the reason why an apostrophe might be needed in box 10.

At the outset, two of the three children in the group (child S and child K) confidently assert that an apostrophe is what they should write. However, this is the point where much of their certainty seems to end. Child S gives no reasons for her choice; it is only later through both her arguments and defence of different possible explanations raised, that they become apparent. Child K however, has noticed that words which use apostrophes are spelt with either the final letter "s" or "t":

292	K	yeah/'cos it's "Tom's"/you know I've noticed on/you know when it has apostrophe/at the end of the word it's either an "s" or a "t" or/I don't know/mostly "s" or "t"
294	K	I'm not even sure if there's any other letters that go at the end I'm just saying that that's what I've seen...

Whether she derived this thought from observations she had made prior to the task or if it had arisen as a result of studying other examples in the text that pertain to the possible use of an apostrophe, is difficult to determine. However, it was the researcher's impression that she had formed this hypothesis after reflecting on where the apostrophe had been used elsewhere during the exercise.

Despite having just talked about what she had noticed from word spellings, the same child then introduces the idea of omission:

298	K	it's gonna/it's like that *(referring to box 2)* /it's going to hold a letter or two
299	R	what letter d'you think's missing then?
300	N	"e"
301	R	an "e"
302	N	if you said without the apostrophe and an "s" it would say "*Do you...*"
303	S	...it wouldn't sound right if it was an "e"

Twelve turns into the discussion child N joins in and proposes what she thinks is the missing letter being represented by the use of an apostrophe in box 10. However, child S rejects omission as a plausible explanation on the basis that if "e" is the missing letter this will make the word "Tomes" and for her the sound of this word is wrong.

Just two turns after making her suggestion (turn 302), child N appears to be thinking about something besides omission. Now, and elaborated on in a subsequent turn, she thinks that if they don't write an apostrophe this will mean there will be no letter "s" in the spelling of *"Toms"*. So, at this point the need to maintain the letter "s" in its spelling so that *"Toms"* will "make sense" and the letter "s" will not be rendered an independent grammatical entity, is especially influencing the child's thinking. The researcher explains that the spelling of *"Toms"* will not change irrespective of the box's presence or absence but S still objects and confidently states that this "wouldn't look right". For the others however, this introduces a fair degree of uncertainty into their thinking:

310	K	I'm not sure actually/now you've said that/I'm not sure/I don't think it's a/...
311	N	...actually/...
312	K	...trick box
313	R	oh go on N/you're changing your mind
314	N	yeah/it's either apostrophe or a trick box/...
315	K	...trick box/I think it is/now you've said that it springs to mind
316	N	apostrophe
317	R	you're still sure about your apostrophe?/yeah? *(S nods)*

Child N then begins to talk about an idea first raised by K at the outset of their debate:

319	N	'cos some letters you don't have to have them...
321	N	'cos with some letters...
323	N	'cos with some letters/you don't have to have the apostrophe where the "s" is

From this, she concludes that box 10 is a trick box. But five turns later, she changes her mind again and reverts to wanting an apostrophe but this time offers no justification for her change of heart. Child K however, is still undecided. Her deliberations shown below make clear that essentially she is concerned for the word *"Toms"* to "make sense":

318	K	yeah/but you could/if you didn't have that box there it be/it'd still make sense wouldn't it
320	K	..."*Do you want a lift to Toms house*"/'cos they're still the same without the apostrophe
342	K	no but listen if Tom/even if the box wasn't there/forget it/say it isn't there/it would still make sense without the apostrophe there

If by "make sense" we accept that she is referring to the sentence being grammatical because it will "sound" right, then her struggle seems to be with the fact that writing an apostrophe (or not) will make no difference to the way the sentence sounds. Like child N, she displays a great deal of uncertainty and hesitation about making a final choice and changes her mind several times during the discussion. After turn 342 above, neither she nor her peers consider any other possible explanations; even so, the group debates for a further 49 turns.

Conclusion

The first question is whether the team were successful in encouraging the children's ownership of the discussion. For almost two thirds of the time, the children are interacting with each other rather than specifically with the researcher, and the length of their exchanges tends to increase as they pursue their discussion of box 10. A simple numerical analysis reveals that the average number of turns per speaker is almost 15 and that the researcher's turns total exactly 15. One child (K) has 19 turns, one 14 and the other only 9, with one joint utterance from the children. Thus there is a fairly equal distribution of turns, with 75% of them being the children's. It is also the case that the length of each speaker's turns is relatively equal, although child K's are longer than everyone else's. The researcher's comments contain nothing negative, and overwhelmingly are of a repetitive, verificative, inviting nature, etc.; in other words, they are facilitative rather than controlling contributions. Clearly, the researcher does not dominate these activities and the richness that emerges from the discussion is a result of the children feeling secure enough to discuss what is critical to them rather than the researcher. They engage with each other repeatedly, confidently and without hesitation or the need to be instructed to do so by the adult researcher; all of these factors imply that the children did feel relatively "free" to make comments, to say them out aloud and to share them with one another and with the researcher.

The second question is whether in these discussions the children actually talked about the apostrophe. The data shows very clearly that at no point in their discussions, both in this extract and the whole session, did they fail to stay on-task. All their talk was about punctuation. It still seems to us to be amazing that the children in this study, some only seven years old, spent so long completely focused on something as abstract as punctuation, and not only stayed on-task but did so with great interest and enthusiasm.

The third question is whether the discussions provided information about how the children were thinking about the apostrophe. The engagement demonstrated, the way they sustained their discussion and the energy they employed in their talk, coupled with their generally unhesitant contributions, suggests their remarks were fairly natural, spontaneous and genuine, i.e. they were saying what was in their heads as opposed to editing their thoughts before voicing them out aloud. Sometimes the comments they shared were ideas they seemed to be thinking about at that particular moment, which often appeared to be disjointed and uncompleted thoughts, see turns 294, 310, 314, 319 and 322, for instance. On the one hand, this can be interpreted as simply characteristic of spoken language, on the other and particularly when taken in context it seems more likely that these were examples of "vocalised real-time thinking", i.e. what the children were saying were reflections of what was going on in their minds at that point. The children seemed to be making mental and vocal evaluations of different possibilities in their bid to work out the reason why an apostrophe should be written. In some senses, the decision to share such information might be viewed as a relatively "risky" move; "risky" because it exposes the uncertainty and provisionality behind the speaker's thoughts. Moreover, as soon as they are uttered they become open for judgement by others, thus potentially rendering the speaker in a vulnerable position. One could say the children would not have made such disclosures had they not felt reasonably comfortable and at ease with the situation with which they were faced.

The analysis of the data presented reveals that this group were not arbitrarily deciding to write an apostrophe but were using their intelligence and strategic reasoning to arrive at a sensible choice. Despite their logic not always being founded on grammatical information, it was clear that all three children were taking the activity seriously and were working hard to find a solution to the problem they faced: this was not whether they should punctuate the box but was about finding an appropriate explanation for why an apostrophe should be written. The qualitative richness, the amount of time the children spent debating and deliberating and the duration of this interchange reflected their diligence and determination to seek an answer and an explanation with which they each could feel satisfied; it was clear they were not happy to give just any response. The children were working with an object that was relatively new to them, so possibly were lacking resources for explaining why their first intuitive response might have been correct. However, they desperately tried to use their existing knowledge about apostrophes to provide a rational explanation for this choice, but this resource was not always sufficiently convincing for them. It was as if they knew there had to be a different kind of explanation but just could not find it. The methods used in other studies for gathering data about young children's understanding of punctuation, specifically the apostrophe, did not and could not demonstrate these kinds of insights.

In 1996 Ivanič wrote that "learners should have a say in research about them", and that "learners' perspectives are essential to an understanding of their learning process". (Ivanič 1996: 153) In her own work she aimed to "get as close as possible to the processes they used to decide where to put full stops in continuous composition." Our study was with much younger people and set out to consider reflection on punctuation rather than composition, but the principles used by Ivanič are as critical to us as they were to her. She pioneered such an approach in studying how people learn to punctuate, and we were very pleased to be able to reinforce how important those principles are in studying all learners of punctuation, even the very youngest ones.

References

Albrecht, T. L., Johnson, G. M. & Walther, J. B. 1993. Understanding communication processes in focus groups. In *Successful Focus Groups. Advancing the state of the art*, D. L. Morgan (ed.), 51–64. London: Sage.

Burgess, R. G. 1984. Methods of field research 2: Interviews as conversations. In *The Field. An introduction to field research*, R.G. Burgess (ed.), 101–122. London: George Allen and Unwin.

Cazden, C., Cordiero, P. & Giacobbe, M. 1985. Spontaneous and scientific concepts: Young children's learning of punctuation. In *Language and Learning: An interactional perspective*, G. Wells & J. Nichols (eds), 107–123. Brighton: Falmer Books.

Christensen, P. H. 2004. Children's participation in ethnographic research: Issues of power and representation. *Children and Society* 18: 165–176.

Cordiero, P. 1988. Children's punctuation: An analysis of errors in period placement. *Research in the Teaching of English* 22(1): 62–74.

Cordiero, P., Giacobbe, M. & Cazden, C. 1983. Apostrophes, quotation marks and periods: Learning punctuation in the first grade. *Language Arts* 60: 323–332.

Edelsky, C. 1983. Segmentation and punctuation: Developmental data from young writers in a bilingual program. *Research in the Teaching of English* 17(2): 135–156.

Edwards, D. & Mercer, N. 1987. *Common Knowledge. The development of understanding in the classroom*. London: Methuen.

Frey, J. H. & Fontana, A. 1991. The group interview in social research. *The Social Science Journal* 28(2): 175–187.

Hall, N. & Robinson, A. (eds). 1996. *Learning about Punctuation*. Clevedon: Multilingual Matters.

Hill, M., Laybourn, A. & Borland, M. 1996. Engaging with primary-aged children about their emotions and well-being: Methodological considerations. *Children and Society* 10: 129–144.

Hughes, M. & Grieve, R. 1984. On asking children bizarre questions. In *Early Childhood Development and Education. Readings in psychology*, M. Donaldson, R. Grieve & C. Pratt (eds.), 104–114. Oxford: Basil Blackwell.

Ivanič, R. 1988. *Linguistics and the Logic of Non-standard Punctuation* [Lancaster Papers in Education, No. 51]. Lancaster: Department of Linguistics and Modern English Language, Lancaster University.

Ivanič, R. 1996. Linguistics and the logic of non-standard punctuation. In *Learning About Punctuation*, N. Hall & A. Robinson (eds), 148–169. Clevedon: Multilingual Matters.

Jenks, C. 2005. *Childhood*, 2nd edn. London: Routledge.

Lewis, A. 1992. Group child interviews as a research tool. *British Educational Research Journal* 18(4): 413–421.

Mahon, A., Glendinning, C., Clarke, K. & Craig, G. 1996. Researching children: Methods and ethics. *Children and Society* 10: 145–154.

Mauthner, M. 1997. Methodological aspects of collecting data from children: Lessons from three research projects. *Children and Society* 11: 16–28.

Mayall, B. 2000. Conversations with children: Working with generational issues. In *Research with Children*, P. Christensen (ed.), 120–135. London: Falmer Press.

Mercer, N. 1995. *The Guided Construction of Knowledge*. Clevedon: Multilingual Matters.

Pressey, S. & Campbell, P. 1933. The cause of children's errors in capitalization. *English Journal* 22: 197–201.

Prout, A. & James, A. 1997. A new paradigm for the sociology of childhood? Provenance, promise and problems. In *Constructing and Reconstructing Childhood: Contemporary issues in the sociological study of childhood*, A. James & A. Prout (eds.), 7–33. London: Falmer Press.

Russell Bernard, H. 1994. *Research Methods in Anthropology. Qualitative and quantitative approaches*, 2nd edn. London: Sage.

Scott, J. 2000. Children as respondents: The challenge for quantitative methods. In *Research with Children,* P. Christensen (ed.), 98–119. London: Falmer Press.

Seidman, I. 1998. *Interviewing as Qualitative Research. A guide for researchers in education and the social sciences,* 2nd edn. New York NY: Teachers College Press.

Simons, H. 1981. Conversation piece: The practice of interviewing in case study research. In *Uttering, Muttering*, C. Adelman (ed.), 27–50. London: Grant McIntyre.

Sinclair, J. McH. & Coulthard, R. M. 1975. *Towards an Analysis of Discourse. The English used by teachers and pupils*. Oxford: OUP.

Watts, M. & Ebbutt, D. 1987. More than the sum of the parts: Research methods in group interviewing. *British Educational Research Journal*, 13(1): 25–34.

REFLECTION 8

Ivanič and the joy of writing

David Russell
Iowa state University

I first met Roz when I went to England in the Spring of 1994 to do research on what we in the U.S. call "writing across the curriculum" (WAC). I had hoped to meet James Britton, the man who, with his wonderful group of researchers in the Schools Council Project, had in the 1960s and 1970s done the hard theorising and investigating of "writing to learn" that inspired the WAC movement in the USA. He had unfortunately just passed away before my visit. Those who carried on that work told me that Language across the Curriculum (as their reform effort was called) had not made much headway in the schools, which were then embroiled in brutal curriculum and assessment wars. And they told me also that higher education had not at all taken "writing" on board as a way of thinking about learning.

But, they said, you must visit Romy and Roz in Lancaster. They are doing what you are looking for, they said. So I did.

I spent three wonderful days there with Roz and Romy Clark, who ran their writing centre. And they were indeed doing what I was looking for. And with a kind of unabashed joyfulness that one rarely sees in academe.

They had taken what was a study skills centre serving overseas students and transformed it, through the alembic of writing, into a deeper kind of centre, one that was attracting home students – because the students knew they would improve their learning in deep ways. And, Roz told me, it was especially useful to home students from working class backgrounds. Clearly writing held a key, for Roz, to unpick the complex workings of identity and class among what we call in the U.S. first generation university students – and perhaps help to unlock the fetters that hold many of them back.

They were also working with some departments, mainly in the sciences, as I recall, who wanted to rethink their teaching and the students' learning by focusing on the hidden obvious: writing. Romy and Roz were consulting and collaborating with teachers – what we call in the US doing WAC work – to integrate writing for learning.

I continued to correspond with Roz and to meet her occasionally at conferences, in the US and UK – especially after her book on writing and identity made such an impression in the US and she was a frequent visitor. I always looked forward to her presentations, not only because she gave me new ways of seeing students' writing and learning, but because there was that same unabashed joyfulness, in a riot of slides of student texts and diagrams and digressions.

I didn't visit Lancaster again until 2005, when Roz invited me to present at a meeting of the project directors of some eight different research projects on further education, funded by the Teaching and Learning Research Project (TLRP). She thought my work on activity theory and writing to learn might be useful to the project directors. The all-day meeting with researchers in various fields from around the UK was intellectually stimulating. But what was even more stimulating was the afternoon I spent with Roz and others talking about her own TLRP project, Literacies for Learning in Further Education, trying to think it through in activity theory terms. She was working at many institutional sites with many teachers in many courses and disciplines in the hope of connecting their students' knowledge of life with their school knowledges – all through writing and other literacies. They had mounds of data, from catering, childcare, multimedia, and so on. And though they were feeling at the time a bit overwhelmed by it (as researchers almost always do at that point in their research), I got the powerful impression in talking to them that there was no one in the world more able to do this project than Roz. And that she was revelling in it.

The next spring, when I attended the 2006 Writing Development in Higher Education conference in Milton Keynes, her plenary talk simply amazed me. She absorbed and transformed activity theory into a series of insights into not only her data but also the basic problems of writing and learning. I was glad to have made a little contribution to her thinking.

But when I next saw Roz in February 2008, at the Writing Research across Borders conference in Santa Barbara, and saw her multi-media final report, the activity theory had disappeared into the most clear-headed and clear-sighted explanations of what it is to learn through literacy. And the analysis was combined with a how-to guide to doing WAC work with teachers – creating assignments, developing materials, and so on. And there were cases and stories and diagrams and images, all laid out in the most useful way (for a taste, see http://www.lancs.ac.uk/lflfe).

When I heard that she was retiring, I could see that her Literacies for Learning in Further Education was the culmination of all those years of thinking and working with teachers and students. What she did in Lancaster in those early years with departments and teachers and students was very much of a piece with what she did with those teachers and students in LfLFE. This kind of work holds tremendous potential for transforming higher and further education. I hope that she will inspire many others, in the UK and elsewhere, to do WAC work. And I have no doubt that her work will inspire WAC professionals in the U.S. to look more ever more deeply, in ambitious research projects, at the relation between writing (writ large as literacies) and learning (writ large as our life journey together).

And it struck me that, in a deeper sense, the work she is doing is a continuation of the work of James Britton and Language across the Curriculum, in her search for ways to understand communication in education as something worth taking seriously, as something that opens out the humanity of teaching and learning. Britton said two things that Roz exemplified for me: that education must never be either teacher-centred or student-centred, but always teacher- and student-centred; and that teaching and learning are always personal. And for Roz, apparently, always joyful.

CHAPTER 11

Recontextualising classroom experience in undergraduate writing
An exploration using case study and linguistic analysis

Zsuzsanna Walkó
Centre for English Teaching and Training,
College of Nyíregyháza, Hungary

This chapter shows how case study and textual analysis can be combined as a methodology to investigate writers' representation of the contexts they research. The specific writers discussed are two undergraduate teacher trainees and their contexts in, and for, writing are *"classroom practice"*, *"research"* and *"thesis writing"*. Case study data gives insights into the writers' perspectives of themselves as participants in these contexts; textual analysis, using Van Leeuwen's (1995, 1996) framework of recontextualisation, shows how the writers foreground and background different elements of the contexts in their texts and what kind of weighting they give to each context. Together the case study and text data and analysis enable the researcher to track instances of "voice types" (Ivanič 2004) in discourse.

Introduction

The aim of this chapter is to illustrate the value of combining case study data about writers with a close linguistic analysis of their texts. The analysis is part of a longer study comparing novice and professional writers' recontextualisation of classroom experience as "research reports", based on a framework which highlights the relationships between the contexts of *"writing"*, *"research"* and *"classroom practice"* in the examined texts (for a full discussion of the analytical framework and methodology see Walkó 2007). The present chapter focuses on the insights provided by two angles of the original analysis: a case study approach to two undergraduate thesis writers' participation in the three contexts of *"writing"*, *"research"* and *"classroom practice"*; and examining the representation of these contexts in the writers' texts using Van Leeuwen's concept and methods of recontextualisation analysis.

The present chapter is organised around the following sections:

- Focus on the two writers as participants in the three contexts;
- Focus on recontextualisation analysis as a research instrument;
- Focus on the representation of *social action* in the two writer's texts;
- Focus on the representation of *social actors* in the two writers' texts;
- Conclusions and implications.

This study was inspired by Roz Ivanič in at least two ways: through her own work in exploring the situated nature of writing, the representation of self and the discoursal construction of the writer's identity, and through her constructive feedback on drafts of my PhD as well as her constant encouragement in introducing me as a newcomer to the field.

As I found detailed textual analysis – the original, tentative focus of my thesis – an attractive but, somewhat limiting perspective, I welcomed Roz's suggestion to broaden and dynamise this focus by looking at discourse as representation of social practice and to include the writers' accounts of their process as well as their texts. She drew my attention to Van Leeuwen's work on recontextualisation analysis, which – very appropriately for my double focus on both text and context – combines the "neatness" of linguistic categories with the underlying "messiness" of sociosemantic analysis. Roz directed me to readings which led me to reflect on the complex and conflictual nature of the text – context relationship in academic discourse practices and on the position and struggles of student writers within them. And, at least as importantly, she helped me find my way out of these explorations through her constant support and positive feedback.

Two case studies

The two theses in the focus of this study were written by two Hungarian undergraduate teacher trainees, Edit and Csaba (pseudonyms), at the Centre for English Teacher Training (CETT) of ELTE University, Budapest,[1] in 1999. The two

---

1. CETT was an English-medium teacher training department, functioning within the School of English and American Studies at ELTE University, Budapest, between 1990–2006. It ran a practice-oriented and highly innovative teacher education programme leading to a B.Ed. in English Language Teaching.

theses were written in English and were based on the writers' final-year teaching experience in a Budapest secondary school, where they taught a class for a whole school year.

Csaba's thesis focuses on developing his students' speaking skills through different types of fluency activities. Both graders of his thesis described it as an "outstanding piece of work". The written comments stress the qualities of Csaba's thesis as a piece of research ("a thorough, well thought-out, systematic research process"), as evidence of his professional development ("a valuable developmental process shines through the final product"), and also at the level of language and discourse ("clarity of structure and expression"). Edit's thesis investigates the problem of two dyslexic students in her class and focuses on finding appropriate ways of testing them. In her case there was a disagreement between the two markers' grades and assessment. While both markers stress that she chose an "absolutely genuine problem", i.e. managed to identify a real "gap" both in the literature and in classroom practice and emphasise Edit's courage and dedication in handling this difficult topic, the second marker finds the thesis somewhat lacking in depth and originality.

The case study data includes three interview sessions with both thesis writers: two while they were in the process of producing their theses, and one after they had handed them in, as well as one interview with each writer's supervisor and second grader (also a CETT tutor).

Background and focus

The main aim of the interviews was to gain insight into the motives, processes, and expectations involved in the two writers' production of their theses, into how these motives, processes and expectations were perceived and responded to by their supervisors, who guided their research and writing, and how they were reflected in the second graders' impressions of the texts and their writers, formed solely on the basis of the final products. For the purposes of this chapter, the outcomes of the interview data will be summarised under the following headings:

- the writers' background, their aims and motivation in writing the thesis;
- the writers' attitude to writing, their writing process and their awareness of expectations and requirements;
- the image the two trainees create as writers, novice researchers and teachers.

Csaba[2]

Background, aims and motivations

Csaba was a very motivated, dedicated and highly autonomous language learner, who had invested a lot of time and effort into achieving his high level of proficiency in English. He chose to do the interviews in English, and kept to this throughout the process. He had come to the decision to develop this interest in English into a professional career a few years after leaving secondary school, not thinking of going to university at first. He made this decision and started his studies at CETT because he realised that getting a degree was a major motivating factor and the source of a strong sense of achievement for him, since, as he explained, nobody in his family had a university degree. When starting on the thesis, he was strongly focusing on producing "something really, really good", and this caused him to start off with very ambitious plans and writing in an awkward, highly formal style. His supervisor observed that he was lacking in self-confidence at this stage, and needed repeated reassurance that his plans were good and that his readings relating to the thesis were sufficient.

The fact that he had to write the thesis in English was a major source of motivation for Csaba. He pointed out that he would have found writing a similar thesis in Hungarian less motivating, as using English was "the fun part of it", "the part that's interesting". With hindsight, commenting on his successfully completed project he also added the topic itself, writing about language teaching, as a motivating factor.

Csaba as a writer and his awareness of expectations and requirements

Asked about the kinds of writing he did in general, Csaba said he did most of his writing in English and very little in Hungarian. He described writing as very hard work, and didn't see himself as especially good at it. While working on his thesis he made many changes to his drafts, struggling hard till he was satisfied with the outcome each time. He had formulated and reformulated his text so many times that at the end of the process, as he said, he couldn't see any more what his sentences sounded like, what they meant, or how they worked in the text.

In the process of trying to find his voice, he cut down on the overcomplicated, impersonal structures he tried at first and gradually made his writing more informal. He asked his supervisor for "models" of a more personal kind of writing

---

2. Inreviews with Csaba were carried out in English.

about classroom work before he managed this change of approach. Interestingly, he observed that many other students also needed to "readjust" their style as they were revising their drafts, but typically they were working from the opposite end, finding that their style was too simplistic or informal and struggling to reach the required academic register.

Throughout the whole process of thesis writing Csaba focussed very hard on trying to find out what the expectations were and how he could best fulfil them. His supervisor described him as being over-conscious of the requirements at the beginning, focusing not so much on "how [the thesis] could be done, but on how it should be done". However, his final text and his own comments on the process show that he had managed to gain considerable insight into the nature of the writing that was expected, he had found his voice within it, and that he had made conscious decisions to shape his process and his evolving text to these expectations. In his relation to the authors whose work he relied on in his research, he saw his perceived outsider status both as an advantage and a difficulty. He said he considered the sources he consulted as examples, or models of writing:

> I see those as examples and then it's good because I'm not competing with them […] I think it's good because it also helps you become a better writer.

He found the Background Research chapter easier to write than the rest of his paper because he felt that his sources, published in expensive volumes and relying on long years of experience, had a kind of credibility which he didn't feel he had when writing about his own classroom experience. In the final interview, looking back on the process, however, he described the two kinds of authorship present in his text – i.e. the kind involved in establishing the background and that involved in writing about his own contribution – in a different light:

> [in the Literature Review] this was the structure I designed so I knew that this is something that I created, but it was very indirectly me … in the Results bits and the Final Reflections it was more like my voice

This shows Csaba's awareness of the author's role of construing the background of the field as a conscious design strategy (cf. Kaufer and Geisler 1989) providing him with a framework for presenting and discussing his own findings. This kind of "genre awareness" (cf. Coe 1994) needs to be acquired – it is not directly contained in the department's thesis writing guidelines (CETT 1998), or in other sources of explicit information about the requirements. However, it was also this assumed knowledge that led Csaba to give up the idea of referring to the literature again as a means of comparison when interpreting his findings because, as he said, he wasn't sure "how it would go down with the people who read it". This shows that in Csaba's, and possibly in many other student writers' interpretation the relevance and value of referring to sources is restricted to the literature review (see also second grader's comment on Edit's text below). This is a clear indication of the way student writers position themselves outside the context of the "discipline", seeing it as a data source in their investigation, but not as a social practice within which they can formulate their findings.

The image of Csaba as a teacher, researcher and thesis writer

Asked about the teaching experience itself Csaba described it as an exciting process of discovery and reflection, helping him to get to know himself better. Initial feedback about his teaching suggested that he lacked in confidence, but in fact he had very clear aims and made principled decisions, which – possibly – he didn't always see the necessity to explain. He courageously set aside the course book and experimented with new activities, changed the focus of the lessons from grammar to speaking, and consciously gave his students more freedom than they were used to in other lessons, which, as he said, they sometimes used "for other reasons than intended", not realising that he "does things for a reason". His focus on reasoned choices and principled decisions were mentioned both by his supervisor and the second grader as an obvious characteristic of his approach to teaching. The second grader also described him, based on the impression created by the thesis, as very attentive to detail; a trainee who has the uncommon ability of "building up a lesson from small steps". This principled, analytical approach is also evident in his text.

As regards the research process and representing it in his text, the second grader stresses the distanced stance Csaba takes in discussing his topic, and the clear sense of direction he creates by the successful selection of relevant aspects. She emphasises this as a specific strength of Csaba's thesis. In her words:

> I envy him for being so good at selecting those little drops of the vast ocean that are relevant for his purposes […] other trainees get suffocated by their topic, they cannot isolate the subtopics that are directly linked to their research but stay embedded in the whole field, and he doesn't fall into that trap.

This ability of relating the "background" of his topic to the "novelty" of his project in a variety of relevant ways will emerge as a characteristic feature of his text in the analysis.

Edit

Background, aims and motivation

Edit was a very focussed and conscientious thesis writer, but on the whole she seemed much less introspective or analytically-oriented in the interviews than Csaba. Probably for this reason, she wasn't conscious of any explicit "aims" in writing her thesis. Having always been a hard-working and successful student, and having gone to university straight after finishing secondary school, getting a degree seemed more of a natural process for her than for Csaba.

She described herself as a "practical person", someone who preferred hands-on tasks and problem-solving to elaborating on a topic in the form of, e.g., an essay. She seemed to approach the thesis, too, as a series of concrete tasks with clearly definable aims, several of which she considered completed when we started the interviews, and this sense of completion was evident in her description, as shown by the following examples:

> The literature review is finished; it's a bit short though…
> It's a case study of two learners … I know everything about them already.

This clearly focussed, linear approach was an important criterion in her choice of the topic of testing the two problem learners in her class. With this sense of clarity, she felt confident and in control throughout the process, keeping to her original outline and deadlines without major problems or changes of direction. At the same time, this focus on clarity and completion also indicated that she saw the thesis in terms of *closure* as regards the problems or tasks it presented rather than in terms of *complexity*.

Edit as a writer and her awareness of expectations and requirements

Edit said that apart from university assignments and some e-mails, she did most of her writing in Hungarian. When writing in English, she always had the dictionary at hand, but tended to use it less often now than at the beginning of her studies. She felt frustrated by the fact that her writing in English was not up to her expectations. She did the interviews with me in Hungarian; where I quote her I translate what she said into English.

Like Csaba, she also considered the examples of professional writing she had to read during her studies at CETT as models to learn from in her struggle of finding the kind of register and style she considered effective for her purposes in writing the thesis. However, she used these models in the very concrete sense of actual borrowing: while reading, she made lists of the phrases she found useful.

In other words, she confronted the challenge of trying to find her "voice" in the thesis as a straightforward lexical problem, looking for appropriate "fillers" for the slots in the sentences she formulated.

Apart from replacing the odd word to avoid repetition or other small details, Edit did not tend to make major changes to her text once she had written it. She described herself as a "brief" writer, focusing only on the main points, unable to use long-winded expressions even though, as she said, sometimes one needs to "fluff things up". This "conciseness", as she saw it, had caused her problems in some of her previous courses at the university. While she seemed to consider her "briefness" as a strength, she also expressed her uncertainty about how to expand on her statements in writing:

> I'm good at grabbing the essence, and I do not focus on details […] I don't expand it because then it would be too much and I'm not sure what to expand on and what not, so I rather just focus on the main points.

Edit found that the other theses she had read had "nicer words, used more complex expressions" and thought her own writing was too "shallow" in comparison. She pointed out that working on problems of register and style (in her words, learning how to "embellish your sentences") would be useful preparation for the thesis and should receive more emphasis during the training.

The second marker's comments confirmed the above characteristics of Edit's writing. She found the text on the whole clear and easy to follow, but observed that Edit's collocations were sometimes inappropriate, but this didn't interfere with understandability. She also pointed out that Edit had made some unjustified judgemental statements, such as, e.g. referring to one of the sources in her literature review as providing "the most accurate definition of dyslexia". Such formulations are probably manifestations of the problem that she as a writer perceived as "lack of elaboration" or "lack of linguistic refinement". My interviews with her seem to suggest that this feature of her writing is also related to her focus on closure and completion when investigating her topic, an approach that might deprive her of a motive for looking for more complex explanations.

Similarly to Csaba, Edit was also both anxious and unclear about how to satisfy the requirements successfully. According to her supervisor, her dissatisfaction with her "simplistic" style caused Edit to want to rewrite the whole text at the end until she reassured her that this wasn't necessary. Edit also described doing the lit. review as an easier task than writing about her own work, but she did not see herself present as an author throughout the text in the way Csaba did: she found she was "really talking" only in the final parts where she described her results and reflections, and not where the focus was on the literature or on the two learners she was investigating.

Edit retained a large degree of uncertainty concerning the expectations and requirements throughout her writing process. For her there seemed to be some kind of an impenetrable barrier between her goals in writing which she tried to reflect in her text and the nature of the criteria on the basis of which it was assessed, or in Ivanič and Moss's terms (Ivanič & Moss 1991; Pardoe 1993), between the "self-generated" and the "imposed" purposes in her writing, even when – as in the case of the thesis – these criteria were explicitly described and explained. In her previous encounters with academic discourse she noticed some contradictions between what she perceived as the rules and requirements of such writing and particular instances she came across in her readings where these rules seemed to be broken, but had not reached the stage of being able to resolve these contradictions by "overwriting" rules.

The image of Edit as a teacher, researcher and thesis writer

Edit's interest in children and commitment to her work with her class was obvious for both readers of her thesis. Her supervisor, who had known Edit as a shy student in class, was surprised by this obvious confidence in both her classroom work and in designing her research project tackling a novel field with very little literature to rely on.

When choosing her research topic, she immediately narrowed it down to the problem of testing her two dyslexic students, which provided her with the kind of clear framework she needed. Nevertheless, later on she noticed that the topic was possibly too narrow and that the data she had collected gave her very little to write about. Commenting on her overall impressions of the thesis, the second grader said that Edit "had not dug deep enough" and that she could have got more out of her topic with a stronger, more thorough research design. While appreciating her courage in addressing this topic and her obvious dedication, and noticing that she probably had a good relationship with her learners, the second grader, interestingly, had the impression of the writer of this thesis as lacking in self-confidence and thoroughness, or attention to detail, in carrying out and writing up the research. This, in a way, reflects the mismatch between the confident teacher persona and the more unsure thesis writer working to some extent in the dark, both represented in Edit's text.

However, much of what might seem to the reader as a lack of "thoroughness" in Edit's text is also part of her uncertainty. In discussing her results, Edit refers to "a research" about the number of dyslexic children in Hungary without specifying her source. The second marker pointed out that this is the kind of problem the writer would have surely noticed and corrected if she had proofread her text more carefully. In actual fact, Edit spent several hours proofreading her finished thesis and making last-minute adjustments, even phoning her supervisor several times to make absolutely sure everything was in place. The fact that she still didn't notice this problem seems to show that she probably didn't realise that references were necessary in other chapters than the literature review, and this reflects the degree of her "genre awareness" rather than her attention to detail.

The two writers' approach

The interviews give insights into the kind of problems the writers were faced with in producing their theses and into the causes of some of the similarities and differences that will be discussed when analysing their texts. While both writers were dedicated to their projects and produced successful theses, Csaba's more analytical mindset, his higher degree of language competence and his very high degree of motivation, autonomy and creativity in using English provided him with better prospects for an outstanding outcome. While a clear sense of direction was important for both writers, Csaba seemed more ready to explore and investigate within the framework he set for himself, more flexible in accepting alternatives or modifications. As regards topic choice, Csaba ventured to explore the relatively broad area of developing speaking skills and kept his focus carefully on his specific aims within it, while Edit narrowed her topic substantially at the start to the point where it was difficult to expand in other directions.

In Edit's thesis the link between the background she explored (about dyslexia) and her project (testing her two dyslexic students) was less organic; she did not succeed to the degree that Csaba did in establishing consensus "with novelty in mind" (cf. Kaufer and Geisler 1989) – partly because her topic was less explored, but also because she seemed less attracted to exploring complex relationships. Edit's need for linearity and predictability and her focus on completion seemed to be an important component of her drive and ambition to accomplish the task she set for herself.

These glimpses into the ways the two writers experienced the practices of *teaching*, *research* and *writing* and their position within them raised my interest in how these contexts are represented in their texts, realising that this might constitute a powerful perspective in analysing genre as social action. Van Leeuwen's analytical approach to discourse as representation provided a coherent framework for this type of analysis.

Recontextualisation analysis as a research instrument

The concept of recontextualisation and van Leeuwen's framework

In this section I discuss Van Leeuwen's (1993a, 1993b, 1995, 1996) framework and methodology for analysing discourse as representation examining how "traces" of other activities and practices represented in discourse are present in the lexicogrammar of texts. The focus here is on the framework itself, on the kind of insights it provides into the nature of representation in texts, and on how it will be used in the present analysis.

The starting point of Van Leeuwen's approach to discourse is the basic assumption that all texts, not only narratives, represent other actions, but they crucially differ in the weight they give to these actions in the representation:

> ... all texts must, in the end, connect with "what people do" – it's just that in some the weight shifts towards discussion of the purposes and legitimations, while the activities themselves are more or less taken for granted, or referred to in truncated, abstract, and generalised ways. (1993a: 16)

With his analytical framework, these differences in representation can be investigated in a way to highlight important features of the examined discourse. The central focus of the framework is on analysing the *field structure* of texts, using the Hallidayan term "field" for ideational content, but investing it with the more overarching sense of "ideology". This shows that his approach has its roots in systemic-functional theory, reinterpreted from the perspective of Critical Discourse Analysis.

A basic characteristic of "field" in this fundamental sense of ideology is how it represents or transforms other social practices "into the discourse of an institutional practice other than in which it is actually done" (1993a: 19). Van Leeuwen uses Bernstein's concept of *recontextualisation* to describe this ideological embedding of one social practice into another. The purpose of recontextualisation is to "legitimate and maintain" (ibid.) the institutional practice within which the other social practice is represented. This happens by means of a set of linguistic transformations as a result of which the original activity sequences – the *recontextualised* practice – acquire the properties of the kind of institutional discourse – the *recontextualising* practice – into which they are "inserted". The ideological nature of the recontextualisation, i.e. the assumptions, values and goals on which it is based, can be studied from the "traces" of the recontextualised social practice in the text.

In this way, while becoming explicit through recontextualisation, the recontextualised practice is also made to "pass through the filter" (Van Leeuwen 1993a: 49) of the practice within which it is represented, i.e. it is made explicit in a way that conforms to the goals, values, beliefs, etc. of the representing context. Van Leeuwen's framework and methodology reveals these characteristics of the representing context by exploring the specific *"perspective"* used in the discourse, i.e. the ways in which the represented participants and their actions are foregrounded and backgrounded in the text.

Van Leeuwen's method of recontextualisation analysis highlights the kinds of transformations that the "original" practice undergoes when it is represented within, and from the point of view, of another practice. This analytical "backtracking" process can be performed on any key element of the represented practice, such as the *participants* involved in the practice and the *activities* they engage in. Van Leeuwen's elaborate "systems network" focuses on how these two key elements of the original practice, i.e. the *social actors* (1996) and the *social action* (1995) are present in the lexicogrammar of the text where they appear. This analytical instrument is based on Halliday's (1985) theory of transitivity, but departs from systemic-functional frameworks in its emphasis on the *sociological* as opposed to the *linguistic* aspect of the analysis. Van Leeuwen's framework and methodology, as he points out, aim to outline a "sociological grammar" (Van Leeuwen 1995) of representation in discourse, in which critical analysis of particular modes of representation is related to their specific grammatical and rhetorical realisations in texts.

The texts focused on in the present study, as stated at the beginning of this chapter, are expected to bear the traces of three different kinds of context: *teaching, research* and *writing*. The latter one of these is clearly the *representing context*, or *recontextualising social practice*, and the other two are represented within it. A special feature of the recontextualisation process in these texts is that it takes place in what van Leeuwen refers to as a "recursive" manner (1993a): the teaching practice is represented within, i.e. recontextualised into the research context, which, in turn, is recontextualised into the context of writing. Therefore the three practices involved can be best imagined as constituting *three levels of context that build on each other*, each incorporating the one below.

The present analysis is expected to highlight what kind of "perspective" the two novice writers create in their texts: which aspects of the representing/represented practices they foreground and background in their representation and in what ways; and how this compares with what I learnt about them as writers, researchers and teachers through the interviews.

Focus on the representation of *social action* in the two writers' texts

In this section Van Leeuwen's concept of recontextualisation and his framework for analysing the representation of social action and social actors will be applied to Csaba's and Edit's thesis. The comparative analysis of the ways social action and social actors are represented in the two texts was carried out on six, approximately 220 word-long extracts of Csaba's and Edit's thesis.

Figure 11.1 shows those categories of van Leeuwen's (1995) framework for describing the different types of transformations *social actions* can undergo in discourse which will be made use of in this section.

Actions and reactions

Reference to this distinction will be made in describing the writers' presence in the two texts in the next section.

Material and semiotic actions

The number and distribution of *material* and *semiotic actions* is similar in the two texts, but there is a marked distinction within the types of semiotic actions: in Csaba's text significantly more of the semiotic actions are *behaviouralised*, i.e. the meaning conveyed through the semiotic action is not specified, while Edit has a much higher number of *renditions* and *quotations* than Csaba. This high number of renditions indicates a heavier reliance on sources and a weaker authorial presence in Edit's text.

Transactive and non-transactive actions

Csaba's text contains a significantly higher number of *non-transactive* actions than Edit's. This difference becomes evident from the following examples from Extract 1 of both texts. In the examples, all identified actions and reactions are *italicised*, non-transactive actions are also <u>underlined</u>, transactive actions are in **bold**; "instrumental" and "interactive" are indicated in brackets.

Part of Extract 1 of Csaba's text:

> At the dawn of a new millennium more and more people *understand* that the role of <u>communication</u> has become exceedingly important for a <u>successful and happy life</u>. Therefore it *seems* that the *need to be able* <u>to communicate</u> in foreign languages, and in English especially, <u>has been dramatically increasing</u>.
>
> When I first **entered the classroom** (instr.) with these notions in mind I *was looking forward* to *hearing* my second-year students <u>speak</u>. Within a few weeks, *having reached an overall impression* of my students' average level of language competence, it *seemed to me* that despite a generally adept *knowledge* of grammar and vocabulary most students *were rather diffident* about their <u>speaking</u> skills.

CATEGORY	DESCRIPTION
Action/Reaction:	*Actions* largely correspond to Halliday's (1985) 'material', 'behavioural' and 'verbal' processes, i.e. are processes of "doing" or of "meaning". *Reactions* largely correspond to Halliday's (ibid.) 'mental processes' (i.e. those of thinking and feeling), and subdivide into *unspecified, cognitive, perceptive* and *affective*. Reactions, as van Leeuwen (1995) points out, constitute an important part of the participants' represented social roles and identities, and can also indicate the power relationships between them: cognitive reactions are likely to be associated with more powerful, affective reactions with less powerful social actors.
Material/Semiotic:	*Actions* can be further divided into those with a *material* purpose/effect ('doing') and actions representing *meaning*. The latter largely correspond to Halliday's 'verbal processes'.
Transactive/Non-transactive:	*Actions* can also be divided into those which have an effect on others, involving two participants ('Actor' and 'Goal'), and actions without such effect, involving only the Actor. *Transactive actions* entail more power on the part of the actor(s) involved than *non-transactive actions*.
Interactive/Instrumental:	This is a further distinction of *transactive* actions: *interactive* transactions can only take a human goal (e.g. 'hug', 'deny entry' [van Leeuwen, 1995, p. 90]), while *instrumental* transactions can take a human as well as a non-human goal, and can therefore represent people as interchangeable with objects.
Meaning represented/not represented:	This distinction is used between *semiotic* actions which specify the content of the conveyed meaning, and those which do not. If the content is not specified, the semiotic action is *behaviouralised*: these actions do not "reach beyond the here and now" (van Leeuwen, 1995), do not use the potential of semiotic actions to record other actions taking place outside its bounds. If the content is specified, the further distinctions refer to the degree of closeness to the original wording; in this sense there is *topic specification* (content conveyed in an abbreviated form), *rendition* and *quotation*.
Activation/De-activation:	If the action is *activated*, it is represented dynamically (i.e. in a verbal form); if it is *de-activated* (*objectivated*), it is represented statically, through nominalisation.

Figure 11.1 The representation of social action

Part of Extract 1 of Edit's text:

> … One of the most alarming ones [i.e. problems] was how I would be able to see if they <u>had made any progress</u>, if they needed **some extra help** (inter.), in other words how would I be able to **test them** (inter.)? In <u>writing</u>? But that particular skill may be especially difficult for them **to acquire** (instr.) and **perform** (instr.), moreover, the results **may not at all reflect** (instr.) their real achievement. <u>Orally</u>? But <u>would there be enough time</u> for that in the classroom? And how would the other students react? Would they not consider **my special treatment** (inter.) unfair to them? What would be the most ideal way by which I **could get** (instr.) a realistic impression about their knowledge without **taking time and energy away** (instr.) from the others?

Comparing the two extracts above shows that Csaba starts his thesis by establishing an "outsider's perspective" in representing a complex phenomenon. All but one of the actions are non-transactive: "living happily" and even "communicating" and "speaking" are represented as having no direct purpose, content or effect. The only transactive action ("entered the classroom") is instrumental, i.e. one that takes an object as its Goal. The extract from Edit's text, on the other hand, is an insider's representation of a problem in the classroom, with mostly transactive actions two of which ("some extra help" and "my special treatment") are interactive, i.e. directed at people.

On the whole, as the examples indicate, Csaba's main focus is on *the teaching process as such*, from the teacher-researcher's perspective: his tendency of using non-transactive actions places learners at the "receiving end" of the process, representing them as the relatively less powerful participants. Edit, by contrast, takes a case study approach, focusing on *two of her learners* in her thesis, their background and reactions rather than on the whole teaching process. In this way she stays closer to her participants, and creates less of a distance from the investigated context, examining some of its particularities rather than its entirety. This goes together with a more personalised, more "one-to-one" focus in the description as well as in the investigation. Within this higher percentage of *transactive* actions, Edit's text also contains a higher proportion of *interactive* (as opposed to *instrumental*) actions which, again, indicates this difference between her approach and Csaba's: most of her investigation happens at the level of the individual, through personal interactions (with the two learners, their families, their teachers, etc.) rather than at the more holistic level of the group or even above it, as is the case in Csaba's thesis.

Activation/de-activation

Perhaps the most noticeable difference between the two texts concerns the number of activated and de-activated actions. While in Csaba's text the number of de-activated actions exceeds that of activated actions, Edit uses more activated than de-activated actions. In the following short examples from the two writers' lit. review chapters all actions are *italicised*, activated actions are also <u>underlined</u>, de-activated actions are in **bold**.

Part of Extract 3 of Csaba's text:

> ... In addition, <u>*investigating*</u> the role of the teacher in **this process** *may*, in my view, <u>*highlight*</u> **further factors** which *influence* **the success** of **our project**.

Part of Extract 3 of Edit's text:

> She [i.e. source] also <u>*suggests*</u> that it is useful if a teacher <u>*has some lessons*</u> with the **dyslexic** students on a one-to-one basis, so he or she <u>*can pay attention*</u> to the specific **needs** of the individual. [...] It <u>*has been proven*</u> that although this method <u>*was originally designed*</u> for *teaching* disabled students, it <u>*works*</u> for the general population, as well.

These examples, again, highlight the same kind of difference between the two writers' representation of their research and teaching context that was discussed above: by using nominalised and other non-verbal forms to express actions, Csaba creates a clear shift of perspective between the investigated and investigating contexts; manages to "downrank" the researched actions in order to highlight causal links, add evaluations, legitimations etc. (cf. van Leeuwen 1995). In this way he establishes a multi-layered perspective in writing, which enables him to move back and forth between the contexts with relative ease. Edit tends to focus on the represented actions one by one, rather than embedding them into each other. As a result, her text is based more on accounts than arguments (cf. Coffin 1997), giving her less opportunity to move back and forth between the represented contexts.

The representation of *social actors* in the two writers' texts

In the analysis of how *social actors* are represented in the texts, the following of Van Leeuwen's categories will be used (see Figure 11.2).

CATEGORY	DESCRIPTION
Activation/Passivation:	An *activated* participant is represented as an "active, dynamic force in the activity" (1996, p. 43); a *passivated* participant is represented as 'undergoing' the activity (*subject*) or being the recipient of it (*beneficiary*).
Participation/ Possessivation/ Circumstantialisation:	Social actors can be represented by *participation* (through grammatical participant roles), *possessivation* (e.g. by the use of a possessive pronoun), or *circumstantialisation* (by prepositional circumstantials, such as 'by', 'from'). The three alternatives differ in the degree to which they foreground the social actor, participation being the most foregrounded form of representation.
General/Specific reference:	*Genericised* social actors are represented as classes (e.g. by mass nouns without article and 'universal' present tense); *specified* actors are present as specific, identifiable individuals.

Figure 11.2 The representation of social actors

Activation/passivation

A comparison of the two texts shows that there are significantly more passivated actors in Edit's texts than in Csaba's. The tendency for passivating actors highlights a basic characteristic of Edit's topic and approach: the dyslexic learners are represented as *subjected* to their disability, to past and present diagnoses, to tests in the class, and to teachers "handling them" in different ways; on the other hand they are *beneficialised* in relation to the writer "teaching" and "helping" them; at the same time, their teachers and family members are *subjected* to interviews and questionnaires.

Participation

In Edit's text there is also a significantly higher percentage of social actors represented as *participants* as opposed to being possessivated or circumstantialised. As Van Leeuwen (1996) points out, participation is the major way of foregrounding the actor's active role. This is most often done by placing the actor in the "unmarked" grammatical position of subject and theme of the clause. The lower percentage of actors represented as participants in Csaba's text includes several examples where the actor is shifted out of this unmarked, sentence-initial position into a "non-participant" role, enabling the writer to use various means of emphasis in his text:

> The role of speaking as a means of communication is considered <u>by many learners</u> (circ.), and <u>by most of my students</u> (circ.), of primary significance. Therefore it could be said that the main objective of language learning <u>for most of my students</u> (circ.) is acquiring communicative competence. (Csaba p. 4)

Non-participant roles make it possible for the writer to include a variety of actors within a statement, create complex links between them, and in this way distance himself from the represented practice by viewing it from an "outsider's perspective". In the extract above five kinds of social actors are indicated: people in general (those who speak and communicate), "many learners", "most of the writer's students", the writer as the teacher of those students, and the writer as "writer" who hedges the degree of certainty of his statement ("could be said").

In the extract below, the variety is in the number of actions (appreciating, giving attention, the student's personal views, what is happening in the classroom) represented within one statement through the possessivation of the actors:

> … students also appreciate the <u>teacher's</u> (poss.) attention to their (poss.) personal views on what is happening in the classroom. (Csaba p. 49)

Generic/specific reference

Edit's text divides into distinguishable sections as regards generic or specific focus: Extract 1 (the Introduction) is fully specific, while Extracts 2 and 3 (lit. review) are mostly generic; the other extracts consist of generic and specific "chunks" reflecting the shifts of focus between the writer's own context and general aspects of her topic. In Csaba's text, on the other hand, Extracts 4 and 5 (Research Design and Data Analysis) are fully specific, but the other extracts are more mixed in their focus, generic and specific representations alternate more frequently than in Edit's text, giving evidence of the variety of links the writer creates between the "general" and "specific" aspects of his topic.

The writers' presence in the two texts

Another interesting difference between the two writers' representations concerns the number of ways the writer as social actor is present in the two texts. In the extracts from Csaba's thesis there are 18 references to himself as writer, while Edit refers to herself in this way on only two occasions. Apart from these, both texts contain two references including both the writer and the reader.

In Csaba's text the presence of the writer as social actor seems to fulfil two kinds of functions. One is a *metadiscoursal* function, that of previewing the content to be discussed, e.g.:

> In this part of my thesis I will focus upon…
> … I would like to present…

The other is a *"reasoning"* function, with the help of which the writer highlights links of justification, cause and effect, evaluation or emphasis through his (often implicit [Ø]) presence in the text, e.g.:

> When concentrating on all four areas of communicative competence <u>it seems evident Ø</u> that focusing exclusively on either accuracy or fluency … (: 10)
> The role of speaking as a means of communication is considered by many learners, and by most of my students, of primary significance. Therefore <u>it could be said Ø</u> that the main objective of language learning, for most of my students is acquiring communicative competence. (: 6)

In Edit's text the writing, or representing context is less present than in Csaba's, and her presence as writer is also somewhat different. The following example contains two references to herself as writer:

> The article <u>I have found</u> (1) on the internet gives practical suggestions. The ones <u>I cite</u> (2) here are in connection with language teaching. (: 12)

The second reference (2) has a previewing function similar to the examples in Csaba's text. In the first one (1), however, the writer is a participant in the action of "finding the article", i.e. in "doing" the action rather than in giving a retrospective account of it. In the terms of Van Leeuwen's framework, the actor in (1) is involved in a material action, while all the other examples quoted in this section above represent the writer in relation to either a semiotic action ("presenting", "citing", "saying", etc.) or a reaction ("in my view", "it seems evident", etc.). This shows that semiotic actions and cognitive reactions are important characteristics of representing the "writing context" in research reports.

Conclusions and implications

The interviews with the two thesis writers and their graders yielded interesting information about the *sort of task* they set themselves in writing their theses and how their perception of this task changed through the process. Both writers' accounts showed how they tackled – and to what extent they solved – the paradox of having to "take on a voice of authority" (Ivanič 1998) in a reversed situation where, untypically of most other kinds of writing, the reader is more powerful than the writer. They also gave evidence of how they were trying to transform their "primary discourse" (Bartholomae 1985), i.e. the discourse they were familiar with, into what they perceived as "disciplinary discourse" (ibid.).

The data shows that the key contextual factors underlying and reflected in the two students' writing that account for characteristic features of their texts can be usefully grouped around the way the writers positioned themselves in relation to the three different practices of *writing, doing research* and *teaching*. The information gained in direct, face-to-face interaction about the writers' aims, approaches and beliefs provides an interesting basis of comparison for the ways these contexts are represented in their texts.

The *writing* aspect is very strongly present in Csaba's account of his process, and is also an important part of his overall motivation in carrying out his project: he is motivated by the challenge of producing a piece of extended academic writing in English, and by the wish to "prove himself" and gain status in his family. He managed to internalise the requirements of a successful thesis through a gradual process of matching his ambitions and intentions with the requirements of the genre, realising the importance of the explanatory focus of his text. This conscious focus is recoverable from the relatively forceful presence of the "writing context" in the analysed extracts, featuring semiotic actions and cognitive reactions. In the interviews he differentiated between an indirect presence of himself as writer in the lit. review and a more direct, more personal presence in the final sections of his thesis. The analysis of his text bears out this distinction: while in the rest of his text he uses various ways of impersonalisation and backgrounding techniques, in his final chapter, where he reflects on the research process, this more direct and personal presence is signalled by a high percentage of activation, participation, personalisation and individualisation of actors, a very high percentage of cognitive reactions and material actions.

Edit, on the other hand, did not see the writing aspect of her project as a primary source of motivation, and even though she produced a successful thesis, she did not completely manage to match her agendas in writing up her project with those of the requirements. Her expressed preference for predictability and a clear sense of direction, and her view of the research process as a series of concrete tasks, which became evident in her account of her research and writing process, is visible in the linear, "single-focus" manner of development of her text. She makes less use of non-participant roles as a way of backgrounding actors than Csaba. She also shifts less frequently between the generic and specific aspects of her topic, in other words, creates fewer links between the specific context of her investigation and its background in the discipline.

Both writers clearly positioned themselves outside the *discipline* of ELT research, as less powerful actors than the sources they cited. Csaba's description of his two kinds of authorship (one constituted by establishing the background of his investigation, the other by reporting on his research process and results) shows a conscious attitude in integrating these two aspects of his thesis, creating organic links between them. Evidence of this are the frequent shifts of focus between "generic" and "specific" representations of actors in his text.

In the *teacher's* role, Csaba seems principled, open-minded and highly reflective, these qualities blending in well with his presence as researcher and as the writer of his text. Edit's teacher persona is more directly present both in the interviews and in her text than Csaba's; her actions, puzzles, decisions and those of the other participants in her teaching context are immediately in the foreground, constituting her primary focus.

The analysis of the representation of *social actors* and *social action* provides a lens through which these differences between the two writers' handling of their subject matter can be systematically investigated, along with a variety of other interesting aspects of the represented contexts and the representation itself. This lens seems particularly useful because it does not simply show the extent to which the writer makes use of typical features of academic writing such as, e.g. *nominalisation, impersonal constructions* or *high lexical density* (cf. Hyland 2004), but it also highlights how these features "work" in foregrounding and backgrounding particular elements of representation and how they enable writers to achieve perspective in their texts.

The combined methodological focus of this chapter on participants' actual experience of the different kinds of social practice and on their textual representations of these practices can be a useful instrument in systematically exploring how writers make their choices from various voices, "voice types" (Ivanič 2004) and subject positions when representing their experience in writing.

Roz's work on the social dimensions of writing and on the role of writer identity did not only help me shape the analytical focus of my thesis, it also shaped the way I think about teaching in very concrete terms. In her work she often represents the highly complex issues she explores in the form of simple-looking, easy to handle charts or figures (such as, e.g. "Aspects of writer identity" [1997], "Different types of writer positioning" [2001], or "A multi-layered view of language" [2004]). In this way these concepts can easily be turned into teaching instruments, can be taken into class and employed to shift the focus from texts to literacy events and practices.

And a final note: the experience of support and encouragement I received from Roz – I notice now with hindsight – has also heightened my awareness of how to formulate comments on students' writing or when to put in a "good word" so that the writer stays positive and motivated.

References

Bartholomae, D. 1985. Inventing the university. In *When a Writer can't Write: Studies in writing block and other composing problems*, M. Rose (ed.), 25–30. New York NY: Guildford.

CETT. 1998. *B.Ed. Thesis support booklet*. Budapest: Centre for English Teacher Training, Eötvös Loránd University.

Coe, R. M. 1994. Teaching genre as process. In *Learning and Teaching Genre*, A. Freedman & P. Medway (eds), 157–169. Portsmouth NH: Boynton/Cook.

Coffin, C. 1997. Constructing and giving value to the past: An investigation into secondary school history. In *Genre and Institutions: Social processes in the workplace and school*, F. Christie & J. R. Martin (eds), 196–230. London: Cassell.

Halliday, M. A. K. 1985. *An Introduction to Functional Grammar*. London: Arnold.

Hyland, K. 2004. *Genre and Second Language Writing*. Ann Arbor MI: University of Michigan Press.

Ivanič, R. 1998. *Writing and Identity: The discoursal construction of identity in academic writing*. Amsterdam: John Benjamins.

Ivanič, R. 2004. Discourses of Writing and Learning to Write. *Language and Education* 18(3): 220–245.

Ivanič, R. & Camps, D. 2001. I am how I sound: Voice as self-representation in L2 writing. *Journal of Second Language Writing* 10: 3–33.

Ivanič, R. & Moss, W. 1991. Bringing community writing practices into education. In *Writing in the Community*, D. Barton & R. Ivanič (eds), 193–223. Newbury Park CA: Sage.

Kaufer, D. S. & Geisler, C. 1989. Novelty in academic writing. *Written Communication* 6: 286–311.

Pardoe, S. 1993. *Learning to Write in a New Educational Setting: A focus on the writer's purpose* [Centre for Language in Social Life Working Paper Series 58]. Lancaster: Lancaster University.

van Leeuwen, T. 1993a. Language and representation – the recontextualisation of participants, activities and reactions. PhD dissertation, University of Sydney, Australia.

van Leeuwen, T. 1993b. Genre and field in critical discourse analysis: A synopsis. *Discourse and Society* 4: 193–225.

van Leeuwen, T. 1995. Representing social action. *Discourse and Society* 6: 81–106.

van Leeuwen, T. 1996. The representation of social actors. In *Texts and Practices: Readings in critical discourse analysis*, C. R. Caldas-Coulthard & M. Coulthard (eds), 32–69. London: Routledge.

Walkó, Zs. 2007. Genre in use: The recontextualisation of classroom practice in research articles and undergraduate theses. PhD dissertation, ELTE University, Budapest.

CHAPTER 12

Researcher identity in the writing of collaborative-action research

Samina Amin Qadir
Fatima Jinnah Women University, Pakistan

The purpose of this paper is to explore issues related to the location of "the researcher" in the writing–up process of collaborative action research. The paper will discuss issues arising at the writing-up stage of two small scale research projects carried out in two different institutions in Pakistan. Both research projects were conducted with co-researchers focusing on the grafting of certain skills onto an existing and tightly prescribed curriculum. In both cases the planning of the process of research, the designing, selecting and adapting of materials, and maintaining records of the progress of the students went smoothly. Problems occurred however at the writing-up stage when researcher identity became a significant issue.

Preface

I started working under the supervision of Professor Roz Ivanič at the University of Lancaster in 1993, about the time that she was completing her own PhD. I had been reading, thinking and exploring what I wanted to investigate for my PhD before leaving Pakistan for Lancaster. I had it all planned in my mind in a very linear fashion. Roz's softly uttered probes challenged me to think in a more multi-lateral manner. She encouraged me to use collaborative research for getting a more holistic view of what I was trying to investigate. Using collaborative research for my PhD was a novel idea for me but reading her thesis resolved some of the ambiguities that existed in my mind. Going through the process of research with my co-researchers added a completely new dimension to my work that was satisfying both academically and personally. I had wanted to write a conservative PhD thesis, as I am part of an academic culture where conventions are rigidly pursued; any deviation from the norm is dismissed as "not a contribution to academic knowledge as they know it" (Ivanič 1993: 146). I therefore faced problems in fitting my "unconventional" method of research into the conventional patterns of academic writing. Here Roz facilitated me to think about locating myself in the ethnographic tradition of writing. The decision was a liberating choice that made the writing of my PhD a pleasure rather than a chore.

The focus of this chapter

Since completing my PhD I have collaborated twice with co-researchers to investigate different issues related to English Language Teaching [ELT] in Pakistan. Roz encouraged me to do so in the first place and I have tried to give confidence to my colleagues to work collaboratively in their efforts to find answers to their pedagogic questions and issues. The first project centred on the introduction of new reading and writing strategies; the second project centred on the introduction of cloze tests to teach the correct usage of definite and indefinite articles. In both cases, a key goal was to introduce change that would enhance students' learning, but without disrupting the tightly prescribed curriculum.

Both research projects were conducted with co-researchers in Pakistan and centred on the grafting of certain skills onto the existing curriculum. In both cases the following stages of the research were successful; the planning of the process of research; the designing, selecting and adapting of materials; the maintaining of records of the progress of the students. However, problems occurred in the writing-up stage and documentation of the research, raising issues of identity, some of which are the focus of this chapter.

The methodology used in the research projects

Collaborative action research

The two projects involved what I am referring to here as collaborative action research:

> Action research can be defined as the process of studying a real school or classroom situation to understand and improve the quality of actions or instruction… It is a systematic and orderly way for teachers to observe their practice or to explore a problem and a possible course of action… Action research is also a type of inquiry that is pre-planned, organised, and can be shared with others.
>
> (Johnson 2005: 21)

Nunan (1992: 18) suggests that for "Kemmis and McTaggart (1988) the essential impetus for carrying out action research is to change the system". Cohen and

Manion (1985:219), however, suggest that action research may in fact be "concerned with *innovation and change* and the way in which these may be implemented in ongoing systems" (authors' italics). Compared to the more revolutionary approach of Kemmis and McTaggart 1988, Cohen and Manion's more integrative approach, which engages in change within an existing system, is of more direct relevance to the action research I have been involved in. Of specific interest to the research projects described in this chapter is the work by Lieberman (1986) who has defined collaborative action research as a tool for staff development and an opportunity for teachers and university researchers to work together to investigate and to solve school and classroom challenges. In addition, Finnan (1992) states that interventions can succeed if they are designed to help members of the school community (culture) make the changes they have identified as important. McCarthy and Riner (1996) argue that the obvious strength of action research is that it creates an environment where assumptions are opened up for questioning. They reiterate Oja and Pine (1989) by stating that teachers participating in action research become more critical and reflective about their own practice and attend more carefully to their methods, their perceptions, and their approach to the teaching process. A key dimension to action research is collaboration, which minimises the distinction between "researcher" and "researched", and in which all participants work together as co-researchers (Ivanič 1998). It is a participatory process in which teachers are ... "creating new data and new interpretations as they struggle to understand each other" (Johnston 1990:180). Teachers involved in collaborative research

> usually feel empowered both professionally and personally and there is a decrease in their feeling of frustration and isolation. ... These outcomes are typically attributed to the collaborative nature of teacher research. (Henson 2001:821)

Firestone and Pennell (1993) also reiterate that collaboration becomes an intrinsically reinforcing activity that builds commitment to teaching.

Ethnography

The kind of action research that interests me also builds on ethnography. Fetterman (1998:11) defines ethnography "as the art and science of describing a group or culture". Hammersley and Atkinson (1983) state that "What the ethnographer attempts is the reconstruction of an observed reality. This requires selection, translation and interpretation."

Students and teachers create patterns over a time in the way they interact, understand and believe. This classroom culture becomes invisible and inaudible because it is so routine and ordinary. Ethnography can be used to make this culture visible and audible so that the situation can be viewed from both etic and emic perspectives, as I explain below. Using ethnography, as a method for looking at classrooms, teachers can understand that what might be common in one classroom is not common in another (Green and Dixon 1993). Gordon et al. (2005) refer to the position of the ethnographer in the classroom as contradictory and vulnerable. "She is required to have sensitivity and methodological, positional awareness of herself and her actions in the field" (: 128). She has to highlight "the complex in the routine" and "the routine in the complex" Smith (2001).

Holistic and *emic* are key tenets of ethnographic research. The holistic characteristic implies that "any aspect of a culture or a behaviour has to be described and explained in relation to the whole system of which it is a part" (Watson-Gegeo 1988: 577) and a key goal is to reach out towards participants' perspectives;

> emic refers to culturally based perspectives, interpretations, and categories used by members of the group under study to conceptualise and encode knowledge and to guide their own behaviour.... An analysis built on emic concepts incorporates the participant's perspectives and interpretation of behaviour, events, and situations and does so in the descriptive language they themselves use.
>
> (Watson-Gegeo 1988: 580)

However, ethnographic analysis is not exclusively emic. It may precede and form "the basis for etic extensions that allow for cross-cultural or cross-setting comparisons" (Watson-Gegeo 1988: 581). Etic analysis is usually steeped in the culture of the researcher or in the "culture of research" itself, that is, the specific research traditions or terminology that is a part of a particular research discipline. Roz helped me to see the value of emic/etic dimensions, as I was an insider as far as the local culture was concerned but an outsider in the institutional culture of the colleges where my co-researchers worked. I was also an "outsider" as a researcher drawing on specific pedagogical and linguistic paradigms.

Case study

The specific action research I engaged in can also be usefully described as "case study" research. Case study has been described as "an umbrella term for a research methods having in common the decision to focus an enquiry around an instance" (Adelman et al., in Bell 1999: 10). Furthermore, single case study often involves "… some type of intervention, that is, the researcher generally does something to the subject being investigated, and measures what happens as a result" (Nunan 1992: 82). In addition, case study provides "a three dimensional picture that – illustrate[s] relationships, micro-political issues and patterns of influence in a particular context" (Mansoor 2005: 138). Not only can a case study involve any number of data-gathering methods, but it can also involve the use of a number of methodologies (O'Leary 2004). Case study usefully applies to both research projects discussed here, in my emphasis on two particular and distinct contexts of teaching and learning and the explicit goal of intervening in these.

Description of the two research projects

Research study 1

The first research project was conducted in 1994 in six different colleges of Multan. Multan is a city in the south of Punjab. It has a rich agrarian economy and is conservative in its outlook and values. The project began as action research as it was based on a problem faced by teachers in Intermediate English classes. The age of students in Intermediate classes in Pakistan is normally between 16–18 years and such classes are usually imparted in colleges as distinct from schools. Two teachers of a women's college in Multan, who wanted to test if Study Skills could be taught using the existing curriculum of the Intermediate students without involving any extra time, initiated it. They had attended a UGC[1] workshop about Study Skills at the Bahauddin Zakaria University in Multan and were inspired by the idea of *skimming/scanning* to facilitate the reading skills of their students. They wanted to facilitate the reading/writing comprehension of their students by teaching them different strategies within the prescribed syllabus. The curriculum board in each province has a prescribed syllabus for the Intermediate classes. The teachers have no control over the contents. The challenge was then how to graft these strategies onto the existing syllabus.

As I had been the workshop coordinator and key resource person for this workshop, they discussed the idea with me and asked for help both in terms of the selection of materials and teaching strategies. An *innovation* was created to find out if Study Skills could be integrated into the existing curriculum for Intermediate Pre-medical students following a communicative/interactive methodology in the classroom. The innovation comprised of three modules about reading and writing techniques. The idea was discussed among other teachers and four other teachers joined us. All of them were women (between 30–42 years) who had been teaching Intermediate Pre-medical English classes in single-sex women colleges for at least six years (between 6–28 years). One of them had a Diploma

---

1. This was the University Grants Commission at the time and is now the Higher Education Commission (HEC).

in Teaching of English as an International Language UGC. Two had attended the workshop mentioned above. But the other three had Masters in English Literature and had no formal expertise about language teaching or study skills. They had acquired their knowledge and understanding through discussions with their colleagues and co-researchers. There was therefore clearly substantial diversity in the teachers' experience.

We started collaborative research with six co-researchers and me. The conception of the research tools and the process of research was a collaborative effort as was the ownership of the raw data generated from the research (Qadir 1995). The teachers decided the method of assessing the performance of the students and talked about the maintenance of records and comparative performance of learners in the different institutions. A questionnaire was to be given to the students at the end of the innovation. The time frame was six weeks of teaching consisting of 36 contact hours with the students. It began as action research with the collaborative participation of teachers trying to graft new strategies onto the existing curriculum to facilitate the reading and writing skills of their learners. During the six weeks of teaching, the teachers met twice only, quietly jubilant about the success of their hidden agenda; the students were acquiring the requisite reading and writing strategies facilitated by the co-researchers without any substantial deviation from (or threat to) the prescribed syllabus. The teachers felt empowered by the fact that without disturbing the curricular status quo they could be innovative about the teaching methodology for facilitating language comprehension in their students. They were testing out teaching strategies but also researching at the same time whether it was possible to do so without deviating from the prescribed curriculum.

After the six weeks they met once to compare their success stories. Each of them had tape recorded one teaching session, invited me to attend two of their classes and maintained progress charts of their students. They had concluded the action research. However, when I broached the subject of writing down their experiences backed by their findings, they were extremely reluctant. We had one final meeting where they handed over the copies of their progress charts and tapes to me. They had not maintained any reflective journals.

They had unanimously decided to let me handle the process of writing up the research on my own and to represent their voices. The co-researchers were conscious of the fact that they had hardly any critical awareness of the standardised conventions of academic writing; they were overwhelmed by the prestige associated with the "impersonal," "objective" academic style that was required for academic writing. We talked about the ownership of the research. They wanted to own the procedure and the data generated through it but academic writing was beyond their ken, experience and interest (Qadir 2003).

Research study 2

Two teachers, who had completed their Masters from my university in Rawalpindi, conducted the second research in two schools of Chakwal, a small town in upper Punjab, in 2004. As students they had experienced great difficulty in the use of definite and indefinite articles and had put in a lot of effort to get past this problem. I had given them specially structured Cloze exercises to practice the correct usage of articles. They had learned the correct usage to some extent and enjoyed the process of learning. Now they wanted to use Cloze tests to teach the correct usage of articles to their students in class IX (age between 13–15) in their respective schools. They did not want to alter the fundamental ways in which teachers operated but to bring about some changes that would improve the efficiency and effectiveness of what is currently done, "without disturbing the basic organisational features, without substantially altering the way that children and adults perform their role" (Cuban 1988b: 342). They reiterated Standwell's (1997) experience that ESL/EFL students tend to choose articles they "feel" are appropriate to the situation without any sound rationale operating behind their choice. They came to me for assistance. They wanted to use the prescribed texts of class IX for cloze tests so that the students and school administration had no apprehension about the teacher's going beyond the curricular requirements. We discussed the strategy of conducting the research, chose the passages from the prescribed texts and decided the time frame. Six weeks were allocated for this purpose. Twenty cloze tests were prepared, three tests for each week including the pre-test and post-test to understand the progress of the students. Each test had 25 blank spaces of articles specifically that the students had to fill. The students were given prompt feedback about their performance. The teachers conducted the research on their own but they needed my intervention to talk to the principal[2] of one school about the legitimacy of their work as other sections of class IX were getting restive about the extra work being done in this class. They kept records of their students' performance, discussed the strategy of the cloze procedure with them and maintained a reflective journal about what they were doing. The idea of the reflective journal emerged during our discussions. Reflections, whether in writing or in conversation, can be used to:

- change what is not working
- think through actions
- relieve frustrations
- connect theories of learning with the practice of instruction
- examine teaching expertise.   (Frank 1999)

---

2. The principal also had been my student at one time.

After the six weeks they sat down together and compiled the results of their research. (This was during the summer vacation period). They brought it to me, triumphant about its success. They discussed the idea of applying a statistical test called the Z Test to check the effectiveness of their research. They did so sitting in my office. I suggested that they write up the account of their research. Both researchers had, in fact, written a ten thousand-word research thesis as a part of their master's program at the university and they were thus quite familiar with the process of writing up research. We discussed the sources for literature review. They were quite enthusiastic. We decided to meet after a fortnight to look at their work. However, when we met up, both of them reluctantly told me that they were not interested in the writing up as it was "boring, tedious and time-consuming". They had brought their research findings to hand over to me along with their reflective journals. They insisted that they would be happy to have an "honourable mention" in my paper and I was free to use the research data as I wished.

There are some key differences between the two research studies:

- The research studies took place with a gap of 10 years between them;
- The location of the research sites was quite different;
- The academic level of the students was not the same;
- The teachers in the second study had written research theses as a part of their Master's program, whereas none of the teachers in the first study had ever done research or written a thesis;
- Reflective journals were maintained by the co-researchers in the Research Study 2.

However, there are also commonalities across both research projects.

- Ideas were initiated by practitioners in the classroom;
- Consultation took place between the teachers about the process of research;
- External guidance and support for designing the research material was sought out;
- Designing, creating and selecting materials were carried out together with the external consultant;
- The research procedure was followed in the classrooms;
- Collating and managing the data generated was carried out as agreed;
- There was initial agreement to document the research and then the reluctance to do so.

My role in the two research studies

These two studies bring to light certain factors that need to be considered about collaborative research. Both research studies germinated as action research. Collaboration is a part of action research; the collaboration referred to here extended beyond the walls of one institution into three institutions, spreading in a radius of 50 kilometres in case of Research Study 1, and two institutions separated by five kilometres in the case of Research Study 2. Apart from helping the teachers in selecting and organising the research material, I was also involved in facilitating their understanding of the micro politics of their institutions. In case of Research Study 1, I had to assume a lot of managerial and administrative responsibilities of a logistical nature. I became the "post office" for receiving and relaying messages and gradually I started coordinating the meetings. I tried not to be directive but at times I would put forth suggestions that they did not reject, maybe because of my status and position. I was a senior academic and most of those involved had been my students. I was an outsider in terms of the location of research of the co-researchers but I had been a product of the same environment. This made me something of an insider and, with my research experience and insight into the micro politics of staff rooms, I could bolster the confidence of the co-researchers to get on with what they had set out to do. Also I had been invited by all of them to sit through two of their classes. This had made their research location a living reality for me. I interacted with their colleagues and students and also met the principals of their respective institutions. It changed my status from an expert resource to a "valued colleague and confidante" (Zajano and Edelsberg 1993: 143) mirroring changes documented by Ivanič and with her co-researchers (Ivanič 1998).

In case of Research Study 2, I remained an outsider most of the time though I did spend a lot of time talking with the co-researchers about their institutional culture to understand the micro politics of their institutions. However, I never visited their research locations or interacted with their colleagues or students. These were visible to me only through their eyes. My status remained that of a knowledgeable and sympathetic outsider.

Reflections on co-researchers' reluctance to write

In both the research studies the researchers lacked the desire to document their research findings for dissemination and left it to me to do it if I wanted. In the case of Research Study 1, when I decided to do the write-up, it made me ponder on how to do it. Finally I decided to follow the traditions of ethnography for writing up the research in aiming to include both etic and emic perspectives. The co-researchers had done all the research: the major input for the reading and writing skills came from them. The implementation of the strategies in the classroom was their exclusive responsibility. Exploration of their views, about integrating these strategies in their teaching agendas, and which had taken place in our meetings before, during and after the completion of the innovation, provided me with insights to their situations, as perceived and interpreted by them. Moreover, the recordings of their own classes (approximately two recorded class sessions of all co-researchers) were an additional source that helped me in reconstructing their situation and classroom reality. My own observation of their classes made me something of an insider and privy to the reality of their classroom culture and interaction. I was not a stranger in the situation. I was thus able to draw on emic understandings, including the views expressed by the teachers, their colleagues in these research sites and the learners themselves. In contrast, the etic analysis followed when I extrapolated from this study to construct a view of teacher education essential for integrating specific strategies into the teaching agendas of the teachers or when I discussed how this research had furthered our understanding about cultural and institutional factors that affect the implementation of innovations. Each college in Research Study I had its own distinct institutional culture. Within this overall institutional culture, the departments of English in all colleges had their own cultural ethos – almost a sub-culture – always different and sometimes contrary to the institutional culture of the college. The reason for this sub-culture in part resides in the status and role given to English and, by transference, to the teachers of English in the colleges, on a micro level and, in society, on a macro level.

Throughout my writing about these research studies, I tried to look at each interpretation and explanation of the data from a holistic point of view by locating it within its own cultural ethos. These interpretations would make sense only if placed within the perspective of the socio-cultural context. Discrete institutional cultures and the micro politics existing within these cultures made the running of a pedagogic innovation a distinctive experience in each institution. An ethnographic approach also meant that I was interested in describing the process of conducting the research itself. Negotiations about access to, and entry into, the research sites intertwined with the appropriateness of timing (both for the researcher and the participants) are as much a part of the research process as the information yielded by these sites. Similarly the collegial relationships that reflect the interplay of wider social perceptions of status and position also need to be examined. Issues around access and roles usually merit a very peripheral reference in many research papers but are clearly the backbone of the research process itself. A reflexive ethnographic approach gave me the liberty to dwell on these issues.

However, given the teachers' unwillingness to be involved in "writing up", it made me wonder if by writing about them I changed the status of these co-researchers to that of my "subjects". The research was their idea; they prepared the innovations, conducted the research, and generated the data. In order to encourage their involvement in the writing up, I gave them the manuscripts I prepared about the research, for their corrections, revisions or any changes that they wanted to make but the response was quite lukewarm. Due to what seemed like their own lack of interest, therefore, my co-researchers had little effective control over how they were (re)presented in my papers. Though I was resolved to let their voices be audible when representing them, I wondered if I had in fact done them justice. Like Janks and Ivanič (1992) I tried to avoid the disempowerment of the co-researchers by being responsible about the way I wrote about them. Although, as I have indicated, I gave them the manuscripts for correction, revision or any changes no suggestions came forth. Why would this be? I offer the following reflections in response to this question.

We are an oral culture in Pakistan, where most information about traditions, music, and arts and crafts is transmitted through word of mouth. Formal writing is still considered an esoteric occupation despite the Internet invasion. The literacy rate for Pakistan is 54% according to *Pakistan Social and Living Standards Measurement Survey* (PSLM) 2005–2006, and 49.9% according to the *World Fact Book* 2005. The female literacy rate is quoted as 42% and 36% respectively by these sources. The total population of Pakistan is estimated at 160 million and if 50% of these millions cannot read or even sign their name, the particular status and importance attached to the written word is understandable. Students and teachers alike find writing intimidating, so that documentation becomes a formidable task. The practice of research and publishing is an alien convention for school and college teachers. Their professional advancement is not dependent upon research or publications. Length of service is the criterion for promotions and career advancement in these echelons. Moreover, there is very little mobility in these service structures. It is a rarity for school or college teachers to join a university as a professional academic. Therefore in Research Study I, the co-researchers did not understand the need for the documentation and dissemination of the research findings. In fact, two teachers did voice the opinion that in their view "research is the fieldwork". I had also noticed that a lot of the co-researchers in this Study had never seen an ELT research journal or read a research article. They had been educated through the very conventional system of education that does not challenge the established academic norms. Their perceptions of research did not extend beyond the doing of the research. The very fact that they wanted to do it, had designed tools and had implemented the innovations was an iconoclastic move on their part. They had no experience of the conventions of the writing up process;

more importantly they had no motivation for it, as they could not perceive the need for it.

Writing is not taught as a process in the state-owned schools or colleges (Qadir 1996). The Grammar Translation Method still prevails and pervades the academic scenario. Teachers themselves have little knowledge or awareness of the process of writing therefore they have few skills to transfer to their students. The situation is as discussed by Clark and Ivanič, "Not many school systems in the world teach anything about the writing process; the focus is usually on the product and often in fairly prescriptive terms" (1991: 184). It is very rare for teachers and learners to collaborate on any learning project as, until very recently, the curriculum was externally prepared and imposed at all levels and all assessment was also external. Now, with the introduction of the semester system at both the undergraduate and the graduate level, teachers have more leeway in designing materials, determining methodologies and devising assessment. Maybe now writing will be looked at as a process where "… it is not wrong to move backwards and forwards from one bit of text to another, or to start planning all over again when you are halfway through the draft: the writing process is of its nature recursive" (Clark and Ivanič 1991: 172).

We are now at the stage where the work of Ivanič will be of tremendous importance for "consciousness-raising about the writing process". Earlier we thought that as her theory and the evidence on which her writing is based is "drawn almost entirely from research and practice on writing pedagogy in Anglophone countries, its relevance is limited to similar contexts" (Ivanič 2004: 224). However, in a changing academic scenario I expect that her work will act as a "catalyst … to refine, revise or develop" (Ivanič 2004: 224) the process and framework of writing to suit the needs of the learners. The teachers at my institution are beginning to accept that "learning to write encompasses both the cognitive and practical processes: the cognitive might be learned implicitly, while the practical ones are amenable to explicit teaching" (Ivanič 2004: 231). The work of Ivanič is gaining recognition in my academic milieu.

The two teachers in Research Study 2 who had the experience of research, had been educated through the semester system that required quite rigorous academic skills. They were fluent in the use of computers and skilled Internet users. However, as they did not need to publish for professional advancement they had no incentive to do so. Moreover, their basic purpose was to understand that a strategy would work. They were not interested in investigating why it worked. Unlike Ivanič, whose writings exemplify the position of an engaged writer/researcher, they did not see writing as central to their research interests. Furthermore, academic writing would have involved them writing in English as a foreign language – making the prospect of such writing even more daunting.

However the context in which teacher/researchers are working is beginning to change in Pakistan. With the Higher Education Sector Reforms (2004) and the drive for creating a research culture in the country, maybe this apathy towards writing will cease. Furthermore the improvement in the teaching and learning of writing will also make writing a more accessible skill for learners and researchers alike.

References

Bell, J. 1999. *Doing Your Research Project*. Clevedon: Multilingual Matters.
Clark, R. & Ivanič, R. 1991. Consciousness-raising about the writing in process. In *Language Awareness in the Classroom*, C. James & P. Garett (eds). London: Longman
Cohen, L. & Manion, L. 1985. *Research Methods in Education*. Bedeenham: Croom Helm.
Cuban, L. 1988. *The Managerial Imperative and the Practice of Leadership in Schools*. Albany NY: State University of New York Press.
Fetterman. D. 1998. *Ethnography: Step-by-step*. Thousand Oaks CA: Sage.
Finnan, C. 1992. *Becoming an Accelerated Middle School: Initiating school culture change*. Palo Alto CA: The Accelerated Schools Project, Stanford University.
Firestone, W. & Pennell, J. 1993. Teacher Commitment, Working Conditions, and Differential Incentive Policies. *Review of Educational Research* 63: 489–525.
Frank, C. 1999. *Ethnographic Eyes: A teacher's guide to classroom observations*. Portsmouth ME: Heinemann.
Gordon, T., Holland, J., Lahelma, E. & Tolonen, T. 2005. Gazing with intent: Ethnographic practice in the classroom. *Qualitative Research* 5(1): 113–131.
Green, J. & Dixon, C. 1993. Talking knowledge into being: Discursive and social practices in the classrooms. *Linguistics and Education* 5(3/4): 231–239.
Hammerley, M. & Atkinson, P. 1983. *Ethnography Principles and Practice*. London: Routledge.
Henson, R. K. 2001. The effects of participation in teacher research on teacher efficacy. *Teaching and Teacher Education* 17: 819–836.
Ivanič, R. 1993. A question of attribution. The discoursal construction of identity in the academic writing of eight mature students. PhD dissertation, University of Lancaster.
Ivanič, R. 1998. *Writing and Identity: The discoursal construction of identity in academic writing*. Amsterdam: John Benjamins.
Ivanič, R. 2004. Discourses of writing and learning to write. *Language and Education* 18(3): 220–245.
Janks, H. & Ivanič, R. 1992. Critical language awareness and emancipatory discourse. In *Critical Language Awareness*, N. Fairclough (ed.), 305–331. London: Longman.
Johnson, A. P. 2005. *A Short Guide to Action Research*. Boston MA: Pearson Education.
Johnston, M. 1990. Experience and reflection on collaborative research. *International Journal of Qualitative Studies in Education* 3(2): 172–183.
Kemmis, S. & McTaggart, R. (eds) 1988. *The Action Research Planner,* 3rd edn. Geelong: Deakin University Press.
Lieberman, A. 1986. Collaborative research: Working with, not Working on. *Educational Leadership* 43(5): 28–32.

McCarthy, J. & Riner, P. 1996. The accelerated schools inquiry process: Teacher empowerment through action research. *Education* 117(2): 223–230.

Mansoor, S. 2005. *Language Planning in Higher Education*. Karachi: OUP.

Nunan, D. 1992. *Research Methods in Language Learning*. Cambridge: CUP.

Oja, S. N. & Pine, G. J. 1989. Collaborative action research. Teachers' stages of development and school contexts. *Peabody Journal of Education* 64(2): 96–115.

O'Leary, Z. 2004. *The Essential Guide to Doing Research*. New Delhi: Vistaar Publications.

Qadir, S. A. 1995. Implementation of a reading innovation in the classrooms of Multan. *Journal of Research (Humanities)* 29(2): 1–2. Lahore: University of the Punjab.

Qadir, S. A. 1996. Introducing study skills in Pakistan at the intermediate level. PhD dissertation, University of Lancaster.

Qadir, S. A. 2003. How collaborative was collaborative research? Analysis in a Pakistani setting. In *Language Policy, Planning, and Practice. A South Asian perspective*, S. Mansoor, S. Meraj & A. Tahir (eds). Karachi: OUP.

Smith V. 2001. Ethnographies of work and work of ethnographers. In *Handbook of Ethnography*, P. Atkinson, A. Coffey, S. Delamont, J. Lofland & L. Loflan (eds). London: Sage.

Standwell, G. J. 1997. The English articles: A worldwide exception? *International Review of Applied Linguistics* 35(4): 269–276.

Watson-Gegeo, K. 1988. Ethnography in ESL: Defining the essentials. *TESOL Quarterly* 22(4).

World Fact Book. 2005. USA: Central Intelligence Agency.

Zajano, N. C. & Edelsberg, C. M. 1993. Living and writing the researcher- researched relationship. *Qualitative Studies in Education* 6(4): 143–157.

REFLECTION 9

Roz Ivanič: An appreciation

Brian Street
King's College, London University

Roz has been a great inspiration in the field of literacy and learning in general and of academic literacies in particular. I will signal just some of the ways in which I feel she has made a major contribution – to myself, colleagues and students – both for her ideas and for her participatory and supportive approach.

Whenever students express concern about how they should present themselves when writing academic essays – should they use first person "I" or maintain the impersonal or passive forms that many tutors have traditionally preferred, I always refer them to Roz's 1998 book *Writing and Identity* (incidentally, one of the best selling volumes in the Benjamins Written Language and Literacy series that I co-edited for many years). Roz's Introduction to this book helps set the record straight in literacy terms – the value and validity of first person narratives – but also, in typical fashion, expresses the complex and profound academic points in accessible and friendly language. The Introduction begins:

> "Me and You"
> Who am I as I write this book? I am not a neutral, objective scribe conveying the objective results of my research impersonally in my writing. I am bringing to it a variety of commitments based on my own interests, values, beliefs which are built up from my own history as a white English woman aged 51 from a middle class family, as an adult educator in multi ethnic, central London in the 1970s and 1980s, as a wife and mother, As someone who only seriously engaged with the academic community in my late thirties, now a lecturer in a department of linguistics, teaching and researching in the field of language, literacy and education. I am a writer with a multiple social identity, tracing a path between competing ideologies and their associated discourses. I have an idea of the sort of person I want to appear in the pages of this book; responsible, imaginative, insightful, rigorous, committed to making my research relevant to adults who return to study. At any rate that is the sort of person I think I want to be as a member of the academic discourse community. I would want to appear responsible, imaginative, insightful, rigorous and committed in most of my social roles, but not all. For example, I'm not sure how important it is to me in my role as a mother to

> be rigorous. There are also parts of my identity as a mother which I don't think I portray in my academic writing, such as being loving. (Ivanič 1998: 1)

Wow, I dare any traditional tutor in the academy to now say that their students should avoid "I" because it is too individualistic, lacks rigour, fails to address the academic underpinnings of what they want to say. On the contrary, Roz shows in this exemplary "page 1" of a book, that the opposite is true – in order to be rigorous academically, to draw upon the academic underpinnings that teaching and researching, in this case in the field of language, literacy and education in a department of linguistics requires, you need to know where you have come from, to be able to reflect critically on the sources of your ideas and beliefs and recognise how this history affects what you say and how you say it. The first person here is not "trivial" and simply individualistic, as many traditional tutors might believe, but rather "imaginative", profound and socially and intellectually aware. The rest of the book backs this up as Roz works with "adults who return to study" at the university, engaging with their fears and their challenges, supporting their adjustment to the requirements of the academy without simply forcing them to capitulate to what are often narrow and unselfconscious demands of writing in the academy. If her students say "it isn't me" when required to write in ostensibly "objective" style, she listens and discuss with them what alternatives there are, how to make the case for linking writing and identity.

Roz began work in central London with the Inner London Education Authority units that addressed writing for the whole population and was able to keep that vision of the broader, democratic uses of literacy as she moved into the academy with its sometimes arcane and elitist ways. More recently she has looked outwards again, researching adults' learning and literacies in an ESRC funded project, "Literacies for Learning in Further Education" as part of the government's Teaching and Learning Research Programme (TLRP). The project has looked at literacies in students' everyday lives and on their courses – mostly vocational courses – in an attempt to find ways of helping students to bring resources from their everyday lives into their learning. Her findings feed back into Higher Education and also across into schools and offer a vision of Literacy learning and use that deeply challenges the dominant government agenda of narrow technical skills and regulatory audit. At a recent presentation on the project at a conference in Santa Barbara, where we shared a Colloquium: "New directions in academic literacies research in the UK". She offered an exciting presentation, including power point slides and video extracts, drawn from the Literacies for Learning in Further Education project, illustrating her engagement with multi modality and new technologies of presentation both in her own work and in that of her students. All this along with the very attention to identity, engagement, understanding that has run through her work from the outset.

We went afterwards to sit on the pier in Santa Barbara harbour (see photo over) with her husband Milan, and over lunch, looking down at the so blue sea, the wind surfers and the albatrosses, we discussed her future as she retires from desk work at the university and perhaps devotes herself even more to such engagement, purposefulness, and helping people identify *who they are and who they want to become*. She revealed here the multiple social identity about which she writes and which she so respects in others. And she revealed also perhaps, contra the comments in the Introduction above, that "parts of her identity" "such as being loving" may indeed be evident too in her academic work and writing. This is the inspiration that so many of her students and colleagues have taken from our encounters with her across a multi path career. I look forward to many more years of such inspiration from Roz.

Reference

Ivanič, R. 1998. *Writing and Identity.* Amsterdam: John Benjamins.

Roz Ivanič at Santa Barbara (Photo: Brian Street)
(To see the colour version of this photo please go to
http://dx.doi.org/10.1075/swll.12.figures)

Works by Roz Ivanič referred to in this book

Ivanič, R. 1988. *Linguistics and the logic of non-standard punctuation.* Lancaster Papers in Education, No. 51. Department of Linguistics and Modern English Language, Lancaster University.

Ivanič, R. 1994. 'I is for Interpersonal: Discoursal construction of writer identities and the teaching of writing.' *Linguistics and Education* 6(1): 3–15.

Ivanič, R. 1996. Linguistics and the logic of non-standard punctuation. In *Learning About Punctuation,* N. Hall & A. Robinson (eds.), 148–169. Clevedon: Multilingual Matters.

Ivanič, R. 1998. *Writing and Identity: The Discoursal Construction of Identity in Academic Writing.* Amsterdam: John Benjamins.

Ivanič, R. 2004. Discourses of Writing and Learning to Write. *Language and Education* 18(3): 220–245.

Ivanič, R. 2004. Intertextual Practices in the Construction of Multimodal Texts in Inquiry-based Learning. In *Uses of Intertextuality in Classroom and Educational Research,* N. Shuart-Faris & D. Bloome (eds.). Connecticut: Information Age Publishing.

Ivanič, R. 2006. Language, learning and identification. In *Language, Culture and Identity in Applied Linguistics,* R. Kiely, P. Rea-Dickens, H. Woodfield & G. Clibbon (eds.), 7–29. London: Equinox.

Ivanič, R. Aitchison, M. & Weldon, S. 1996. Bringing ourselves into our writing. *Research and Practice in Adult Literacy* 28/29: 2–8.

Ivanič, R. & Camps, D. 2001. I am how I sound: Voice as self-representation in L2 writing. *Journal of Second Language Writing* 10: 3–33.

Ivanič, R., Edwards, R., Satchwell, C. & Smith, J. 2007. Possibilities for pedagogy in further education: Harnessing the abundance of literacy. *British Educational Research Journal* 33(5): 703–721.

Ivanič, R., Edwards, R., Barton, D., Fowler, Z., Hughes, B., Mannion, G., Martin-Jones, M., Miller, K., Satchwell, C. & Smith, J. 2008. *Improving Learning in College: Rethinking literacies across the curriculum.* London: Routledge.

Ivanič, R. & Lea, M. R. 2006. New Contexts, New Challenges: The Teaching of Writing in UK Higher Education. In *Teaching Academic Writing in UK Higher Education,* L. Ganobcsik-Williams (ed.). Hampshire Uk/New York: Palgrave MacMillan.

Ivanič, R. & Moss, W. 1991. Bringing community writing practices into education. In *Writing in the Community,* D. Barton & R. Ivanič (eds.), 193–223. Newbury Park.

Ivanič, R. & Roach, D. 1990. Academic Writing, Power and Disguise in Language and Power. In *Selected Proceedings of the BAAL Annual Meeting Sept 1989,* R. Clark, N. Fairclough, R. Ivanič, R. McLeod, J. Thomas & P. Meara (eds.), London: Centre for Information on Language Teaching and Research.

Ivanič, R. & Satchwell, C. 2007. Boundary crossings: Networking and transforming literacies in research processes and college courses. *The Journal of Applied Linguistics* 4(1): 101–124.

Ivanič, R. & Simpson, J. 1988. Clearing Away the Debris: Learning and Researching academic writing. *Research and Practice in Adult Literacy*, Issue 6.

Ivanič, R. & Simpson, J. 1992. 'Who's who in academic writing?' In *Critical language awareness*, N. Fairclough. (ed.). London: Longman.

Ivanič, R. & Weldon, S. 1999. Researching the writer-reader relationship. In *Writing: Texts, Processes and Practices*, C. Candlin & K. Hyland (eds.), 168–192. London: Addison Wesley Longman (Applied Linguistics and Language Study Series).

Barton, D., Hamilton, M. & Ivanič, R. (eds.). 2000. *Situated Literacies. Reading and Writing in Context*. London and New York: Routledge.

Clark, R. & Ivanič, R. 1997. *The politics of writing*. London: Routledge.

Clark, R. & Ivanič, R. 1991. 'Consciousness-raising about the writing process'. In *Language Awareness in the Classroom,* C. James & P. Garrett (eds.). London: Longman.

Clark, R., Fairclough, N., Ivanič, R. & Martin-Jones, M. 1991. Critical language awareness Part 1: A critical review of three current approaches to language awareness. *Language and Education* 4(4): 249–260.

Clark, R., Fairclough, N., Ivanič, R. & Martin-Jones, M. 1992. Critical language awareness Part 2: towards critical alternatives. *Language and Education* 5(1): 41–54.

Fairclough, N. & Ivanič, R. 1989. Language education or language training? A critique of the Kingman model of the English language. In *Kingman and the Linguists*, J. Bourne (ed.), CLIE Working Paper.

Hamilton, M., Barton, D. & Ivanič, R. (eds.). 1994. *Worlds of Literacy*. Clevedon: Multilingual Matters.

Janks, H. & Ivanič, R. 1992. 'Critical Language Awareness and emancipatory discourse'. In *Critical Language Awareness*, N. Fairclough (ed.), 305–331. London: Longman.

Mannion, G. and Ivanič, R. 2007. Mapping Literacy Practices: Theory, Methodology, Methods. *International Journal of Qualitative Studies in Education* 20(1): 15–30.

Ormerod, F. & Ivanič, R. 2000. Texts in Practices: Interpreting the Physical Characteristics of Children's Project Work. In *Situated Literacies: Reading and Writing in Context*, D. Barton, M. Hamilton & R. Ivanič (eds.), 91–107. London: Routledge.

Ormerod, F. & Ivanič, R. 2002. Materiality in children's meaning-making practices. *Visual Communication* 1(1): 65–91.

Tusting, K., Ivanič, R. & Wilson, A. 2000. New Literacy Studies at the Interchange. In *Situated Literacies: Reading and writing in Context*, D. Barton, M. Hamilton & R. Ivanič (eds.), 210–218. London: Routledge.

Index

A

Academic literacies (see Reflection 9) 8–10, 151–153, 167–168, 245–247
Academy 9, 15, 24, 61, 62, 65, 70, 72, 73, 74, 170, 167, 170, 185, 246
Access(ible) (ibility) (see Reflection 7) 8, 9, 34, 70, 154–155, 159, 177–178, 180, 240, 243
Accommodation 113, 119, 121, 124
Affordances (of technology) 15–16
Apprenticeship 33, 62, 105, 108
Argument (ation) (ative) 8–9, 11, 28, 29, 33–34, 69, 116, 124, 151, 155, 157–158, 184, 224
Audience 4, 72–74
Author(s) (ing) 4, 8, 47, 48, 67, 68, 130, 154, 216
-ship 67, 68, 159, 213, 228
-ial 3, 21, 159–160, 222
Authority(ative) (see also Ownership) 8–10, 13, 15–24, 66, 68–72, 158–160, 227

B

Bakhtin, M. 65, 68, 70, 154, 156
Bartholomae, D. 227
Barton, D. 30, 63, 85, 112, 113, 114, 131, 151, 163, 169
Bazerman, C. 10, 69, 152, 178
Belief(s) (underlying literacy practices) 31, 86, 90, 92, 107–109, 115, 124, 152, 184, 190, 219, 227

C

Case study(ies) (see Methodology)
Child(ren) (see Voices) (see Pupils) 30, 31, 75, 85–87, 89–109, 189–202, 217, 237
Clark, R. 62, 66, 97, 98, 113, 129, 130–133, 144–146, 151, 152, 163, 167, 169, 173, 179, 205, 242
Class(room) 11, 16, 35, 75, 81, 87, 93, 105–107, 112–114, 120–122, 133, 159, 192, 194, 232–240
Community(ies)
  academic/school 31, 62, 66, 233, 245
  discourse 28–29, 30–31, 33, 36, 179, 245
  research 50–54, 56, 57, 58
  of practice 105
Context(s) (ual) (see also Recontextualisation)
  academic/research 8–9, 10–11, 16, 31, 49, 50, 55, 66, 72, 174–175, 176, 234–235
  EFL/L2 (see Chapters 6 and 7) 159
  learning/teaching 112, 122, 124, 175, 192, 193, 201
  digital (see Chapters 1 and 3) 58
  socio-cultural 70, 82, 86, 108, 113, 119–121, 130–131, 132, 240, 242
  socio-political 65, 90, 112, 173–174, 182
Creative(ity) Part I (see Reflection 4)
  thinking 28, 46, 115, 124
  process 63–65

and writing (see Chapter 4) 87, 94, 95, 97, 98, 100–103, 119–120, 121, 154, 218
Critical Discourse Analysis (CDA) (see Reflection 6) 167, 170, 173, 182–183, 184, 219
Critical Language Awareness (CLA) (see Reflection 6) 152, 167, 168, 169, 172–173, 179, 180
Critical
  thinking 11, 53, 106, 108, 122, 124, 236
  linguistics 9, 163, 167, 220
  literacy 124
  pedagogy 169, 172–173, 233
Conflict(ing) 72, 90, 92, 105, 107–109, 155, 159, 210
Curriculum (see also Writing) 29, 32, 106, 123, 232, 235, 236, 242

D

Dialogue(ic) 11, 12, 48, 49, 63, 65–67, 72, 73, 175, 183
Discoursal construction(s) of identity(ies) (see Chapter 1 and Reflections 1, 7 and 9) 7–24, 28, 61–62, 67–68, 81–82, 100–109, 123, 160–161, 183–184, 210, 229
Discourse(s) (al)
  choices 132
  conflicting/contradictory 45–46, 57, 92, 108–109, 113, 245
  disciplinary 151, 153, 227
  dominant 66, 67, 70, 71, 105, 106–107

of education and the academy 104, 106–107, 154, 157, 171, 182, 217
institutional 152–153, 167, 219
nature of 50, 66, 92, 108, 180
primary 227
public 171
as representation 210, 218–220
of research 48, 51
of writing & learning to write (see Chapter 6) 112
Discourse based interview (see Methodology)
Diversity 69, 70, 71, 73, 159, 236
Domain 10, 19, 69, 106, 119, 131, 172
Dyslexia(ic) x, 89–110, 211, 216–218, 224

E
English as a Foreign Language (EFL) (see Chapters 6, 7, 11 and 12)
Emic 175, 179, 180, 181, 182–183, 234, 240
Epistemic modality 10
Ethics(al) 12, 191, 194–195
Ethnographer/y
see Methodology
Errors 64, 95, 103, 104, 131–132, 135, 138, 141, 144–147, 158, 190
Education(al) Part II (see Reflection 8)
adult 68, 167, 172, 175, 190
distant (see Chapter 1) 48
formal 172, 173, 179
further 171, 180–181, 206, 207, 246
higher 8, 9, 11, 70, 75, 111, 156, 159, 167, 168, 171, 177, 179, 205, 207, 243, 210
nature of 207
primary (see Chapters 5 and 10 and Reflection 4)
secondary and tertiary (see Chapter 2) 235–238
special educational needs 89, 93

of teachers (see Chapter 11) 240, 235, 238, 242

F
Fairclough, N. (see Reflection 6) 10, 63, 66, 69, 70, 152, 173, 180, 184
Field structure 219
Freire, P. 67, 169, 173
Foucault, M. 31, 48, 51

G
Genre (see Chapter 4)
academic 66, 68, 70, 73–74, 76, 167
awareness 8, 31, 75, 106, 119, 121, 179, 184, 213, 217, 218
conventions 69, 72, 183
nature of 63, 68, 70, 71, 72, 75–76, 98, 114
story writing 98, 100
requirements 28–29, 31, 228
Grammar(tical) 32, 115, 148, 171, 178, 181, 199, 201, 214, 218, 220, 225, 242
'correct/incorrect' 104, 111, 123, 131, 132, 135, 138, 141, 145, 152, 154, 193, 199

H
Halliday, M. 28, 32, 35, 39, 219–221
Hamilton, M. 30, 63, 64, 85, 112, 151, 169, 183
Hayes, J. and Flower, L. 130
Hegemony(ies) (ic) 104, 106–107
Heteroglossia(ic) (see Chapter 8)
Heuristic 92, 93, 105, 107, 174
Holistic 27, 30, 223, 231, 234, 240
Hyland 10, 97, 98, 152, 183, 229
Hyper-real(ity) 48, 54–55, 56

I
Identity(ies) (Part I) (see also Discoursal construction of identity)
beliefs underlying 109

conflicting/contradictory 57, 107–109
construction of (see Reflection 2) 47, 51, 123, 127, 180–181
reader identity 8
researcher identity (see Chapters 3 and 12) 176–177
social possibilities for 51, 105, 108, 152, 179, 221, 245–247
and power 8, 63, 70, 71, 167, 180
and 'wrighting' 32, 34, 41
and writing (see Reflection 1) 30–32, 61, 62, 69, 70, 71, 76, 131
Identify (ies) (ication) (see Reflection 2) 4, 28, 33, 48, 57, 76, 82, 92, 105, 181, 247
Ideology(ical) 107, 113, 114, 153, 171, 172, 179, 180, 219, 245
model of literacy 174
Image(s) (see Chapter 2) (see also Multimodality) 27–43, 54–55, 74–75, 206
Intertextual(ity) 9, 10, 12–15, 19, 24, 49, 53, 55, 57–58, 66

K
Kress, G. 28, 29, 32, 48, 70, 75, 152
Knowledge
control over 8, 52–53, 113, 231
decontextualised 111, 114, 119, 120, 153
'expert' 185
-less 66, 242
making 10, 11, 17, 22, 47, 49, 50–51, 55–56, 65, 68–70, 71–72, 74, 76, 153, 156, 158, 167, 172, 195
propositional 21
shared 8, 30, 53, 236
and social practice 86–87, 152, 206
of spelling and punctuation 103–105, 192, 201

Index   253

implicit/tacit/emic   16, 31, 52, 177–178, 184, 213, 234
text knowledge   123–124

L
Lea, M.   7, 9, 10, 11, 75, 112, 152, 171, 174
Language
  as dialogic   65–67
  informal   71, 73, 81, 183, 191, 194, 234, 243
  as multi-layered   90, 229
  and meaning   32, 159
  as signifying system   53
  as social practice (see also Practices and Writing)   10, 62–63, 30, 70, 92
  spoken   194, 201, 261
  of art   28
  and research   51, 52–53
  of description   181–182
Learning
  beliefs about   9, 31, 48, 92, 105, 113, 115, 124, 173, 246
  digital (see Chapter 1)   48, 75
  process   33, 119, 181, 201, 205, 237
  and literacy   245, 246
  to punctuate (see Chapter 10)
  and teaching   48, 50, 112, 157, 232, 235, 237, 242, 243
  to write (see Chapter 5 and Reflection 8)   8, 111, 112, 120–122, 124, 171, 216, 242
Lillis, T.   8, 9, 64, 65–66, 67, 152, 153, 167, 171, 175, 176, 177, 181, 182
Linguistic
  analysis (see Chapter 11)   21–24, 173, 174, 178, 179, 180–181, 182, 184
  features (see Chapter 11)   21–24, 119, 121, 178–181
  knowledge   183, 185, 234
  mechanisms   27, 28, 32–42
  resources   28, 32
  text-linguistics   170, 177–185
Literacy(ies) (see also Academic Literacies)
  adult   67–68, 73, 246

autonomous model   174
development (see Chapter 5)
digital (see Chapter 1)   48, 74–75
event(s)   30–31, 90, 105–106, 152, 229
for learning   3, 7, 206–207, 245–246
new literacy studies   170, 173–174, 175
practice(s)   15, 16, 27, 28, 30, 31, 57, 86, 151, 152–159, 169, 174, 178, 209, 169, 229
research/studies   45, 72, 112, 151, 189, 172, 178
as social practice   9, 92, 169, 174

M
Meaning making   7–25, 112, 115, 120–122, 159, 183
Mediation   51, 55, 153
Metadiscourse   10, 20–25
Methodology(ies) Part III (see also Research)
  case study   10,152, 209–211, 234–235
  discourse based interview   177, 178–179
  ethnographer/y   72, 75, 121, 173–176, 233–234, 239–240
  interview   39–40, 65, 66, 111–112, 130, 134–135, 138, 141–147, 178, 192–195, 211–215, 227–228
  questionnaire   93, 224, 236
  talk around text (see Chapter 9)
Modes   27–42, 61, 75, 220
Multilingual   177, 182
Multimodal(ity), multi-modal(ity) (see Chapter 2 and Reflection 4)   74–75, 179

O
Ownership (see also Authority) (see Chapter 1)   74, 200, 236

P
Plagiarism(ising)   16, 47–58

Pleasure (see Reflection 8)
Power
  and meaning making (see Reflections 4 and 7)   8, 11, 63–76
  and institutions   42
  and knowledge   51, 53, 119
  relationships   31, 124, 152, 174, 176–177, 192, 223, 228
  and research community   51, 53, 57
Practice(s)
  digital literacy (see Chapter 1)   48
  literacy   7, 15, 16, 27–31, 57, 174, 178
  pedagogic (see also Education)   90–109, 111
  research (see also Methodology)   47–58, 72
  social (see also Writing and Language)   10, 57, 70, 76, 105
Post modern   70, 72
Positioning
  researcher   169–170, 174–175
  subject (see also Subject(ivity)   50, 108, 159–160, 173,179, 180–181
  writer   229

R
Recontextualise(ation) (see Chapter 11)   111, 114, 124
Reflective
  dialogue   63
  journals   236–238
Reflection   17, 21, 49–55, 131, 184, 195, 213, 214, 232, 236, 238
Representation
  of gender   76
  of ideas   190
  of modes   60, 75, 104
  of reality   47–48, 50, 54–56, 72
  of self   184
  of social action and social actor (see Chapter 11)
  visual   36, 73
Research (see also Methodology)
  action   231–240

collaborative (see Chapter 12 and Reflections 3 and 5) 172, 185
practices (see Chapter 3)
Researcher
 participant 173
 practitioner(s) 52, 72–74, 89–109, 174
 stance of 89, 92, 106
Rhetoric(al)
 effects 153
 governmental 23
 patterns and conventions 124, 153, 178, 220

S
Scaffolding 100–102
School(ing) (see Chapter 5) (see also Classroom and Education) 28–29, 75, 115, 120, 122, 136, 181, 192–202
Self hood 11, 14, 109
Semiotic
 actions 221, 222, 227–228
 practices 75, 180
 resources 152
Social practice(s) see Practice
Street, B. (see Reflection 9) 8, 112, 152, 174
Subject(ivity) (see also Position) 34, 46, 71–72, 108, 113, 153, 173, 180, 181, 182, 229

T
Technolog(ies)
 range of 179

new/information 12–25, 47–58, 74–75, 122, 128, 133, 143
Textuality 51, 52–54, 56, 57

V
Value(s) 31, 33, 55, 56, 90, 111, 124, 151, 153, 168, 173, 174–175, 184, 219, 235
van Leeuwen (see Chapter 11) 27, 29, 32
Visual (see also Chapter 2) 16, 18, 63, 65, 73, 154, 156, 158
Voice(s)
 writers' meaning making (see Chapters 4, 8 and 11) 7, 24
 writers' in research processes (see Chapter 9)
 children's (see Chapter 10)

W
Wrighter(ing) (see Chapter 2)
Writer(s)
 academic 8, 61, 62, 64, 66–68, 72–75, 175
 apprentice 33, 62, 65, 66, 105
 children as (see Chapters 2, 5 and 10)
 novice 28, 65, 209, 220
 professional 65, 177, 209
 stance of 22, 214

student 9, 65, 66, 73, 114, 129, 131, 132, 233, 148, 152, 154, 159, 175, 177, 184, 210, 213, 214
Write(ing)
 academic 8, 9, 10, 21, 24
 across the curriculum (WAC) (see Reflection 8)
 argumentation 29, 33, 41
 beliefs about 90, 92, 104, 107–109, 190
 cognitive approach to 90, 97, 130, 132–133, 227, 228, 242
 collaborative (see Reflection 5) 63
 joy of (see Reflection 8)
 learning to (see Chapters 5 and 6) 242
 online (see Chapter 1)
 pedagogy, Part II 42, 48, 98, 55, 242
 personal opinion (see Chapter 6 and Reflection 9)
 practices 9, 13, 63, 67, 93, 105, 106, 111, 114, 120, 124
 process (see Chapter 7) 61–65, 94, 97, 175, 211, 216, 228, 242
 recursive(ity) 97–99, 129–131, 145–147, 220, 242
 report 131
 thesis (see Chapter 11) 65, 156

In the series *Studies in Written Language and Literacy* the following titles have been published thus far or are scheduled for publication:

12. **CARTER, Awena, Theresa LILLIS and Sue PARKIN (eds.):** Why Writing Matters. Issues of access and identity in writing research and pedagogy. 2009. xxxii, 254 pp.
11. **VERHOEVEN, Ludo, Carsten ELBRO and Pieter REITSMA (eds.):** Precursors of Functional Literacy. 2002. viii, 360 pp.
10. **MARTIN-JONES, Marilyn and Kathryn E. JONES (eds.):** Multilingual Literacies. Reading and writing different worlds. 2001. xxvi, 396 pp.
9. **BARTON, David and Nigel HALL (eds.):** Letter Writing as a Social Practice. 2000. vi, 262 pp.
8. **JONES, Carys, Joan TURNER and Brian STREET (eds.):** Students Writing in the University. Cultural and epistemological issues. 2000. xxiv, 232 pp.
7. **AIKMAN, Sheila:** Intercultural Education and Literacy. An ethnographic study of indigenous knowledge and learning in the Peruvian Amazon. 1999. xx, 232 pp.
6. **PONTECORVO, Clotilde (ed.):** Writing Development. An interdisciplinary view. 1997. xxxii, 338 pp.
5. **IVANIČ, Roz:** Writing and Identity. The discoursal construction of identity in academic writing. 1998. xiii, 373 pp.
4. **PRINSLOO, Mastin and Mignonne BREIER (eds.):** The Social Uses of Literacy. Theory and Practice in Contemporary South Africa. With a Preface by Brian Street. 1996. viii, 279 pp.
3. **TAYLOR, Insup and Martin M. TAYLOR:** Writing and Literacy in Chinese, Korean and Japanese. 1995. xiii, 412 pp.
2. **KAPITZKE, Cushla:** Literacy and Religion. The textual politics and practice of Seventh-day Adventism. 1995. xxi, 343 pp.
1. **VERHOEVEN, Ludo (ed.):** Functional Literacy. Theoretical issues and educational implications. 1994. viii, 493 pp.